THE ARAB LEAGUE AND PEACEKEEPING IN THE LEBANON

For my Parents

The Arab League and Peacekeeping in the Lebanon

ISTVAN POGANY,
Lecturer in Law,
University of Exeter

St. Martin's Press   New York

Scholarly and Reference Division;
St. Martin's Press, Inc.,
175 Fifth Avenue,
New York,
N.Y. 10010.

First published in the United States of America 1987
Printed in Great Britain
Typeset by Rapidset, London WC1

Library of Congress Cataloging-in-Publication Data

Pogany, Istvan S.
  The Arab League and peacekeeping in the
  Lebanon.
  Bibliography: p.
  Includes index.
  1. League of Arab States—Lebanon.
2. Lebanon—History 1975.   I. Title.
DS36.2.P.64   1987   341.5'8   87–12873

ISBN   0 312 00782 5

Contents

Preface   vi

Acknowledgements   x

Abbreviations   xiii

Maps   xviii

1   The League of Arab States: an Introduction   1

2   A History of the Lebanon from Ancient Times until
      the First World War   23

3   A History of the Lebanon, 1914–75   35

4   The Creation of the Symbolic Arab Security Force   67

5   The Functions and Powers of the Arab League Force
      in the Lebanon   82

6   The Legal Basis of the Arab League Force in the Lebanon   93

7   Composition, Organization, Control and Finance of the
      Arab League Force in the Lebanon   108

8   The Performance of the Arab League Force in the Lebanon   118

9   Conclusion   159

Postscript   167

Appendix I: The Pact of the League of Arab States   179

Appendix II: Resolutions of the Arab League Council
      Regarding the War in Lebanon   186

Appendix III: Statement Issued by Six-Party Arab Summit
      Conference held in Riyadh and Related Documents   188

Appendix IV: The Cairo and Melkart Agreements   198

Index   205

Preface

The Lebanon has experienced a greater diversity of international peacekeeping activity than any other state in recent times. In June 1976, when Lebanon had been in the throes of civil war for over a year, the Council of the Arab League established a Symbolic Arab Security Force to 'maintain security and stability in Lebanon'.[1] In October of the same year, the League transformed the Force into an Arab Deterrent Force with various tasks including '[e]nsuring observance of the ceasefire and termination of hostilities', collecting heavy weapons from the militias and '[i]mplementing the Cairo Agreement and its annexes'.[2]

In March 1979, following Israel's incursion into southern Lebanon, the UN Security Council established the United Nations Interim Force in the Lebanon (UNIFIL) with a view to 'confirming the withdrawal of Israeli forces, restoring international peace and security and assisting the Government of Lebanon in ensuring the return of its effective authority in the area'.[3] In August 1982, after Israeli forces had encircled West Beirut, a Multinational Force composed of US, French and Italian troops was briefly constituted to supervise the evacuation of Palestinian guerrillas.[4] The Multinational Force was recalled in September, after the tragic Sabra and Chatila massacres, to 'facilitate the restoration of Lebanese Government sovereignty and authority over the Beirut area'.[5]

The activities of UNIFIL and of the Multinational Force have already received extensive scholarly analysis. They are also examined in considerable detail in Professor Higgins' forthcoming book on peacekeeping in the Middle East.[6] By contrast, hardly any work has been done on the Arab League Force in the Lebanon. As far as I am aware, no sustained piece of research has been published in either English or French on the Arab League Force, with the exception of a short article which appeared in the *Annuaire Français de Droit International* in 1976.[7] This lacuna in the literature on peacekeeping is regrettable. Contemporary practice suggests a growing emphasis on regional organizations as a medium for peacekeeping.[8] This reflects both the inherent limitations of the United Nations system, in which superpower antagonisms can prevent decisive action by the Security Council, and also the evident preference of many states for a regional solution to essentially local problems.[9] In view of these trends, it is all the more important to understand the limitations and potentialities of the League of Arab States as a source of international peacekeeping.

Various factors have militated against a wider appreciation of the peacekeeping activities of the League of Arab States. Foremost amongst these is the barrier of language. Official Arab League documents are available exclusively in Arabic. Nevertheless, various French and English-language publications regularly contain a selection of Arab League materials. *Le Monde* generally prints the full text of Arab Summit Conference resolutions and, occasionally, of resolutions adopted by the League Council. *Keesing's Contemporary Archives* and *Fiches du Monde Arabe* publish summaries, and sometimes quotations, of Arab League texts. *International Documents on Palestine* has been a particularly valuable source of information. Finally, UN documents regularly contain Arab League texts including Summit Conference resolutions and communications from individual Arab states to the League's Secretary-General. This occurs when, for whatever reason, an Arab state conveys such material to the UN Secretary-General with the request that it be circulated as an official document of the Security Council or of the General Assembly.

However, even for those conversant with Arabic, the consultation of official League documents can pose serious difficulties. The minutes of Arab summit conferences and of sessions of the League Council are not available to the general public as of right. Similarly, communications from member states to League organs are not automatically accessible. Permission to examine such materials may, however, be granted by the League in the exercise of its discretion.

The headquarters of the Arab League were transferred to Tunis from Cairo in 1979, following the conclusion of the Egypt–Israel Treaty of Peace. The Egyptian authorities would not permit the League's documentation and archives to be removed from Cairo.

Consequently, the bulk of League materials relating to the pre-1979 period are unavailable.

Access to the official texts of Council or Summit resolutions can also pose difficulties. Before the resolutions have been printed and distributed, permission to consult them must be granted by the League. At present, due to administrative difficulties, there is a backlog of approximately five years in the printing and distribution of resolutions. In practice, access to the official texts of resolutions which have already been printed may also be withheld. Thus, the League retains a residual discretion. Paradoxically, unofficial versions of such texts are often readily available from the secondary sources cited above.

The relative difficulty of obtaining primary, and sometimes secondary, source materials concerning the activities of the League have inevitably constrained this research. For example, while the League headquarters in Tunis furnished me with the titles, dates and reference numbers of Council and Summit resolutions relating to the Arab League Force in the Lebanon, I was denied access to the texts themselves. Fortunately, all relevant Summit resolutions, and the more important decisions of the Council, were available from secondary sources.

Nevertheless, the parameters of this book have been defined by the availability of materials. It has been possible to analyse the functions, powers, composition, finance, structure and performance of the Arab League Force in the Lebanon. Regrettably, insufficient materials have been available to warrant separate chapters on the Force's relations with the host state, with contributing states, or with other states involved. In so far as details on such questions have been available, they have been included in Chapter 8 on the performance of the Arab League Force, and in Chapter 7 on the composition, structure and finance of the Force. Despite these deficiencies, I hope that this book will contribute to a wider understanding of the Arab League Force in the Lebanon and, also, of the League of Arab States.[10]

Concerning the perennial problem of transliteration, I have eschewed consistency in favour of familiarity. Thus, Arab names are spelt in the manner in which they appear most frequently in English and American publications.

Notes

1 League Council Resolution No. 3456, 9 June 1976.
2 For details see Chapter 5.
3 SC Res. 425, 19 March 1978.

4   On MNF I, see e.g. Rikhye, *Peacekeeping*, pp.74-5.
5   For the mandate of MNF II, see e.g. N. Pelcovits, *Peacekeeping on Arab-Israeli Fronts* (1984), pp.139-68.
6   To be published by Oxford University Press.
7   G. Feuer, 'La Force Arabe de Sécurité au Liban', *AFDI*, vol. 22 (1976), p.51.
8   On peacekeeping by regional organizations, see e.g. H. Wiseman (ed.), *Peacekeeping: Appraisals and Proposals* (1983), Part IV. See also, G. Naldi, 'Peace-Keeping Attempts by the Organisation of African Unity', *ICLQ*, vol. 34 (1985), p.593.
9   The increasing emphasis on regional solutions to local problems has been evident, for example, in the recent debates within the Arab League concerning the revision of the League Pact. Iraq, Syria and Palestine went so far as to suggest that members should be required to refer local disputes to the League before referring them to the United Nations or to other extra-regional third parties. See generally S. Chaabane, 'La Réforme du Pacte de la Ligue des États Arabes', *RGDIP*, vol. 86 (1982), p.508, at pp.523-4.
10 For a recent addition to the literature see J.P. Isselé, 'The Arab Deterrent Force in Lebanon', in A. Cassesse (ed.), *Current Legal Regulation on the Use of Force* (1986), p.179. See also S. Ben Amara, 'Le Monde Arabe' in A. Pellet (ed.), *Les Forces Régionales du Maintien de la Prix* (1983), p.106, esp. at pp.136-46.

Acknowledgements

This book could not have been written without the generous support and assistance of many individuals and institutions. Amongst the latter, I should like to thank the Gilbert Murray Trust for awarding me their Senior International Award in 1983. This enabled me to visit Egypt in April 1984, where I benefited from the insights of numerous Egyptian legal scholars.

A grant from the Research Fund Committee of Exeter University allowed me to pursue my enquiries in the UN Archives in New York, and to interview UN and US officials familiar with the problems of peacekeeping in the Middle East. A research award from the British Academy enabled me to spend the Lent Term of the academic year 1985/86 in Cambridge. I am particularly indebted to Cambridge University's Research Centre for International Law, and to its Director, Mr E. Lauterpacht, QC, for appointing me a Visiting Fellow of the Centre. Chapters 1 and 6 of this book were largely written in Cambridge, where I had access to the resources of the Squire Law Library.

I should also like to express my gratitude to the League of Arab States for arranging my visit to Tunis in May 1986. During the course of several fascinating days spent at the League's headquarters, I was able to correct several misconceptions and to enrich my understanding of both the League, and of its peacekeeping operation in the Lebanon.

Certain individuals who were intimately involved in the events discussed in this book, and who generously shared their insights with me, cannot be mentioned by name. To others I readily extend my appreciation. Amongst the scholars whom I met in Egypt I should like to thank, in particular, Dr Salah El-Din Amer, Professor of Public International Law at the University of Cairo and Secretary-General of the Egyptian Society of International Law, Dr Ibrahim Al-Enani, Professor of International Law at the University of Ein Shams and Dr Nabil Hilmy, Executive Director of the Centre for International Legal and Economic Studies, Zagazig University.

Dr Adnan El Amad, Director of the League of Arab States Office in London, has helped this study in innumerable ways. I am particularly grateful to him for his instructive comments on an earlier draft of Chapter 1, and for helping to arrange my visit to Tunis. At the League's headquarters, in Tunis, I benefited from the insights of numerous officials. I should like to thank, in particular, Mr Muncef Al Mai, Assistant Secretary-General for Information, Dr Mohammad Al Fara, Assistant-Secretary-General for Palestinian Affairs, Mr Al Akhdar Ibrahimi, Assistant-Secretary-General for Special Assignments, General Abdel Rassaf Dardary, Director of the Military Department, Mr Hakam Darwaza, Director of the Arab Relations Department and Mrs Faria Al Zahawi, Director of the League's Library and Archives. While in Tunis I also met Dr Sadok Chaabane, Professor of International Law at the University of Tunis. I am indebted to Dr Chaabane for his observations concerning the proposed revisions to the League Pact. Mr Abdel Manem Seyrag Al Deen, of the League's Information Department, helped to arrange my interviews in Tunis, and gave generously of his time to ensure that my visit was a success.

A number of librarians have been of enormous assistance in identifying, locating and obtaining obscure and elusive source materials. I should like to thank, in particular, Mr Donald Ross, of the Bibliographical Services Section, British Library of Political and Economic Science, Miss Patricia Farquhar, Librarian at the UN Information Centre in London, and Mr Paul Auchterlonie, Subject Librarian for Arabic and Islamic Studies, University of Exeter. My secretary, Miss Monique Bertoni, responded with enthusiasm and efficiency to even the most daunting deadlines and has contributed in no small measure to the successful completion of this book.

The text of the Pact of the Arab League is reproduced from H.A. Hassouna, *The League of Arab States and Regional Disputes* (1975), with the permission of the publishers, Oceana Publications. The League Council's Resolution of 9 June 1976 is taken from the 1976 volume of *International Documents on Palestine*, while the texts adopted by the Riyadh and Cairo Summit Conferences were translated into English by the UN Secretariat. The Cairo Agreement and the Melkart Understanding are reproduced from Y. Lukacs (ed.), *Documents on the Israeli–Palestinian Conflict 1967–1983* (1984), with the permission of the International Centre for Peace in the Middle East. The four maps are reproduced from I. Rabinovich, *The War for Lebanon, 1970–1985* (rev. edn 1985), with the permission of Cornell University Press.

Finally, I should like to acknowledge my debt to my wife, Ruth. As for my previous books, she skilfully prepared the index and was throughout an essential source of encouragement.

Istvan Pogany
Faculty of Law
University of Exeter
August 1987

Abbreviations

A/	UN General Assembly Document
Abi-Saab, *Congo*	G. Abi-Saab, *The United Nations Operation in the Congo 1960–1964* (1978)
AFDI	*Annuaire Français de Droit International*
AJIL	*American Journal of International Law*
Anabtawi, *Arab Unity*	M.F. Anabtawi, *Arab Unity in Terms of Law* (1962)
Antonius, *Arab Awakening*	G. Antonius, *The Arab Awakening* (1938)
Boutros-Ghali, *Arab League*	B. Boutros-Ghali, 'The Arab League (1945–1970)', *REDI*, vol. 25 (1969), p.67.
Boutros-Ghali, *La Ligue des États Arabes*	B. Boutros-Ghali, 'La Ligue des États Arabes', Hague, *Recueil des Cours*, vol. 137 (1972), Part III, p.1.
Bowett, *Self-Defence*	D.W. Bowett, *Self-Defence in International Law* (1958)
Bowett, *UN Forces*	D.W. Bowett, *United Nations Forces* (1964)
Brockelmann, *Islamic Peoples*	C. Brockelmann, *History of the*

	Islamic Peoples (J. Carmichael and M. Perlmann trans., 1948)
Brownlie, *Use of Force*	I. Brownlie, *International Law and the Use of Force by States* (1963)
Bulloch, *Death of a Country*	J. Bulloch, *Death of a Country* (1977)
BYIL	*British Yearbook of International Law*
Cmd.	Command Papers
Cobban, *PLO*	H. Cobban, *The Palestine Liberation Organization* (1984)
Cobban, *Lebanon*	H. Cobban, *The Making of Modern Lebanon* (1985)
DAG	Departmental Archives Group
Dawisha, *Syria and the Lebanese Crisis*	A. Dawisha, *Syria and the Lebanese Crisis* (1980)
Foda, *Projected Arab Court of Justice*	E. Foda, *The Projected Arab Court of Justice* (1957)
GA	General Assembly
GAOR	General Assembly Official Records
GBTS	*Great Britain Treaty Series*
Gilbert, *Exile and Return*	M. Gilbert, *Exile and Return* (1978)
Gilmour, *Lebanon*	D. Gilmour, *Lebanon: the Fractured Country* (1983)
Gomaa, *League of Arab States*	A.M. Gomaa, *The Foundation of the League of Arab States* (1977)
Goodrich, Hambro, Simons, *Charter*	L.M. Goodrich, E. Hambro and A.P. Simons, *Charter of the United Nations* (3rd rev. edn 1969)
Hague, *Recueil des Cours*	*Recueil des Cours de l'Académie de Droit International de la Haye*
Hansard, HC	House of Commons Debates (*Hansard*)
Hassouna, *League of Arab States*	H.A. Hassouna, *The League of Arab States and Regional Disputes* (1975)
Hassouna, *Regionalism*	H.A. Hassouna, 'The League of Arab States and the United Nations: Relations in the Peaceful Settlement of Disputes', in B. Andemicael (ed.), *Regionalism and the United Nations* (1979),

p.299.

Higgins, *Development*	R. Higgins, *The Development of International Law Through the Political Organs of the United Nations* (1963)
Higgins, *I–IV*	R. Higgins, *United Nations Peacekeeping*, vols. I–IV (1969–81)
Hitti, *Syria*	P.K. Hitti, *History of Syria* (2nd edn 1957)
Hourani, *Syria and Lebanon*	A.H. Hourani, *Syria and Lebanon* (1946)
Hurewitz, *II*	J.C. Hurewitz (ed.), *The Middle East and North Africa in World Politics*, vol. II (2nd edn 1979)
ICJ Rep.	International Court of Justice, *Reports of Judgments, Advisory Opinions and Orders*
ICJ Rep., Pleadings	International Court of Justice, *Reports of Pleadings, Oral Arguments, Documents*
ICLQ	*International and Comparative Law Quarterly*
IDP	*International Documents on Palestine*
IJMES	*International Journal of Middle East Studies*
ILM	*International Legal Materials*
Int. Org.	*International Organization*
JPS	*Journal of Palestine Studies*
Kelsen, *United Nations*	H. Kelsen, *The Law of the United Nations* (1951)
Keesing's	*Keesing's Contemporary Archives*
Khalidi, *Conflict and Violence in Lebanon*	W. Khalidi, *Conflict and Violence in Lebanon* (1979)
Kourula, *Peacekeeping and Regional Arrangements*	E. Kourula, 'Peacekeeping and Regional Arrangements', in A. Cassese (ed.), *United Nations Peace-Keeping* (1978)
Lammens, *I, II*	H. Lammens, *La Syrie*, vols I–II (1921)
Longrigg, *Syria and Lebanon*	S. Longrigg, *Syria and Lebanon under French Mandate* (1958)
Lukacs, *Documents*	Y. Lukacs (ed.), *Documents on the Israeli–Palestinian Conflict,*

	1967–1983 (1984)
Macdonald, *League of Arab States*	R.W. Macdonald, *The League of Arab States* (1965)
McDougal and Feliciano, *World Public Order*	M.S. McDougal and F.P. Felicianos *Law and Minimum World Public Order* (1961)
Mansfield, *Ottoman Empire*	P. Mansfield, *The Ottoman Empire and its Successors* (1973)
Ma'oz, *Ottoman Reform in Syria*	M. Ma'oz, *Ottoman Reform in Syria and Palestine, 1840–1861* (1968)
MEJ	*Middle East Journal*
MES	*Middle Eastern Studies*
Monroe, *Moment in the Middle East*	E. Monroe, *Britain's Moment in the Middle East 1914–1971* (rev. edn 1981)
Moore, *III*	J.N. Moore (ed.), *The Arab–Israeli Conflict*, vol. III (1974)
Mortimer, *Faith and Power*	E. Mortimer, *Faith and Power* (1982)
Nevakivi, *Arab Middle East*	J. Nevakivi, *Britain, France and the Arab Middle East, 1914–1920* (1969)
Pogany, *Security Council*	I. Pogany, *The Security Council and the Arab–Israeli Conflict* (1984)
Proceedings ASIL	*Proceedings of the American Society of International Law*
Rabinovich, *War for Lebanon*	I. Rabinovich, *The War for Lebanon, 1970–1985* (rev. edn 1985)
Randal, *Tragedy of Lebanon*	J. Randal, *The Tragedy of Lebanon* (1983)
REDI	*Revue Egyptienne de Droit International*
RGDIP	*Revue Générale de Droit International Public*
Rikhye, *Peacekeeping*	I.J. Rikhye, *The Theory and Practice of Peacekeeping* (1984)
Ruthven, *Islam in the World*	M. Ruthven, *Islam in the World* (1984)
S/	UN Security Council Document
Sachar, *Emergence of the Middle East*	H.M. Sachar, *The Emergence of the Middle East, 1914–1924* (1969)

Salibi, *History of Lebanon*	K.S. Salibi, *The Modern History of Lebanon* (1965)
Salibi, *Crossroads*	K.S. Salibi, *Crossroads to Civil War* (1976)
SC	Security Council
Schiff and Ya'ari, *Lebanon War*	Z. Schiff and E. Ya'ari, *Israel's Lebanon War* (1985)
SCOR	Security Council Official Records
Shaw, *I, II*	S.J. Shaw and E.K. Shaw, *History of the Ottoman Empire and Modern Turkey*, vols. I–II (1976–77)
Skubiszewski, *Use of Force*	K. Skubiszewski, 'Use of Force by States etc.', in M. Sørensen (ed.), *Manual of Public International Law* (1968), p.739.
S/PV	Security Council Verbatim Records
Stone, *Legal Controls*	J. Stone, *Legal Controls of International Conflict* (2nd rev. edn 1959)
Tibawi, *History of Syria*	A.L. Tibawi, *A Modern History of Syria* (1969)
UNCIO, *Documents*	United Nations Conference on International Organisation, *Documents*
UNTS	United Nations Treaty Series
Waldock, *Regulation of the Use of Force*	H. Waldock, 'The Regulation of the Use of Force by Individual States in International Law', Hague, *Recueil des Cours*, vol. 81, 1952, Part II, p.451.
Ziadeh, *Syria and Lebanon*	N.A. Ziadeh, *Syria and Lebanon* (1957)

Maps

Map 1 Smaller and Greater Lebanon. The Autonomous Province 1861–1915 and Lebanon since 1920.

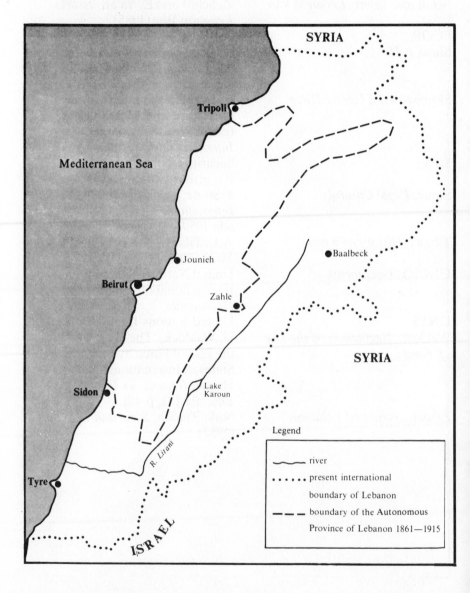

SYRIA

Tripoli

Mediterranean Sea

Baalbeck

Jounieh

Beirut

Zahle

SYRIA

Sidon

Lake
Karoun

R. Litani

Tyre

ISRAEL

Legend

— river

⋯⋯⋯ present international
boundary of Lebanon

– – – boundary of the Autonomous
Province of Lebanon 1861—1915

Source: The War for Lebanon, 1970–1985, revised edition, Cornell University Press, 1985.

Map 2. Lebanon: Approximate concentration areas of major communities.

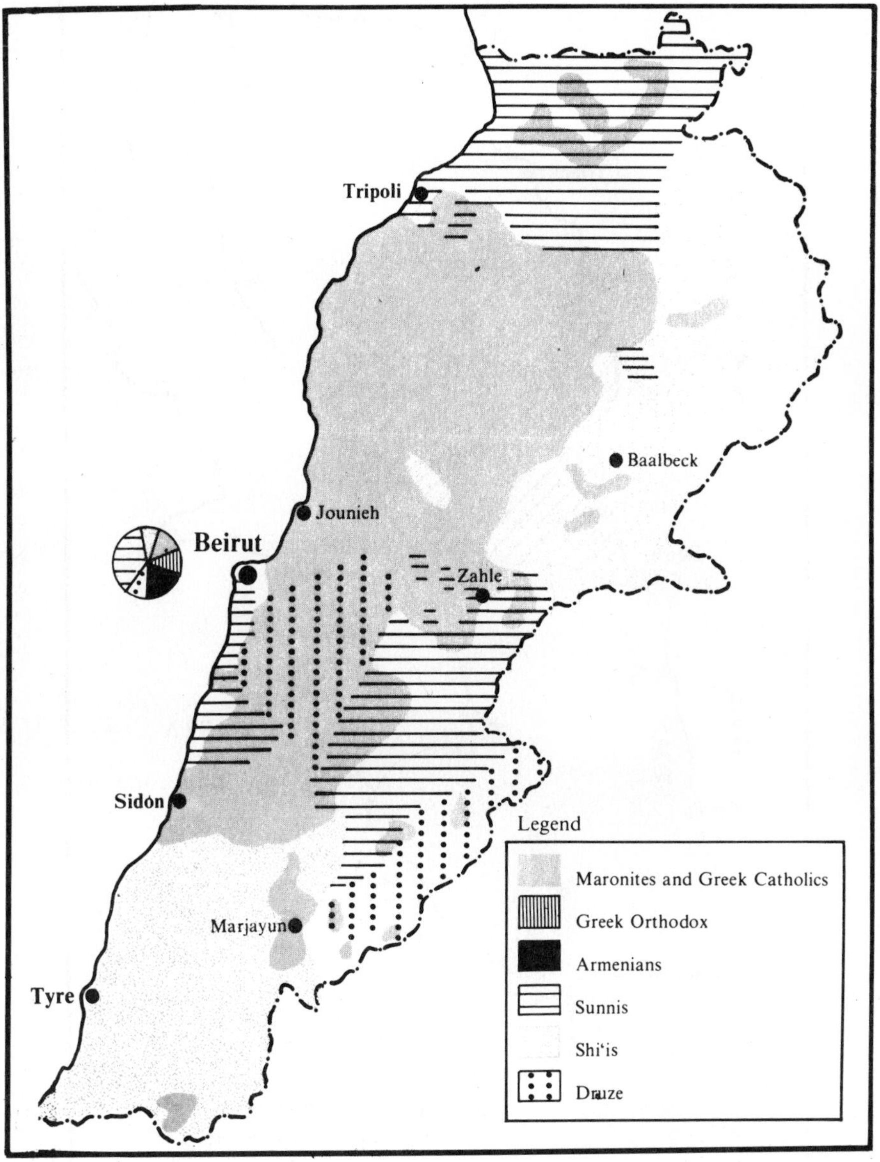
Tripoli
Baalbeck
Jounieh
Beirut
Zahle
Sidon
Marjayun
Tyre
Legend
Maronites and Greek Catholics
Greek Orthodox
Armenians
Sunnis
Shi'is
Druze

Source: Itamar Rabinovich, *The War for Lebanon, 1970–1985* revised edition, Cornell University Press 1985.

Map 3 Lebanon's virtual partition into areas of control following the 1975–76 civil war.

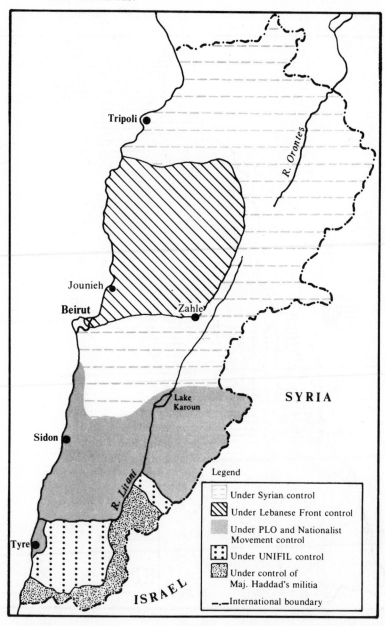

Source: Itamar Rabinovich, *The War for Lebanon, 1970–1985* revised edition, Cornell University Press 1985.

Map 4 Israel's Lebanese campaign of June 1982, major routes of advance.

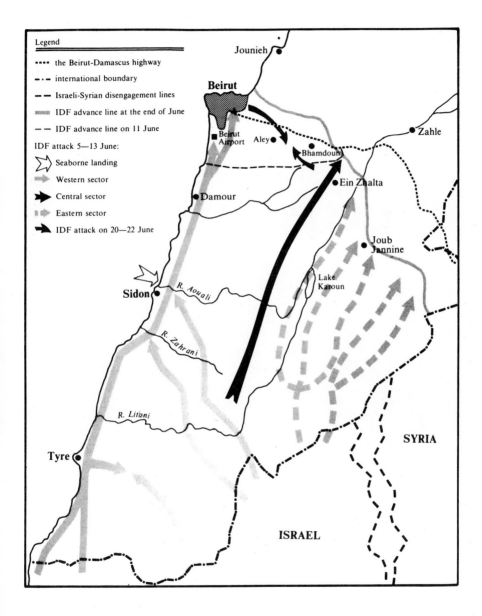

Source: Itamar Rabinovich, *The War for Lebanon, 1970–1985* revised edition, Cornell University Press 1985.

1 The League of Arab States: an Introduction

Establishment of the Arab League

The establishment of the League of Arab States must be understood in the context of Arab efforts to achieve unity and independence. The beginnings of Arab nationalist sentiment can be traced to the latter part of the nineteenth century, when much of the Middle East was controlled by the Turkish Ottoman Empire.[1] Arab hopes received a significant boost during the First World War, when Britain pledged her support for the creation of an independent Arab state encompassing the greater part of the territories then under Turkish domination.[2]

Following the defeat of the Axis powers, Arab hopes were disappointed with the incorporation of Syria, Lebanon, Palestine, Transjordan and Iraq in League of Nations mandates.[3] However, in 1941, the exigencies of war once again prompted Britain to express her support for Arab unity and independence. On 29 May, the British Foreign Secretary declared:[4]

> Some days ago I said in the House of Commons that His Majes-
> ty's Government had great sympathy with Syrian aspirations for
> independence. I should like to repeat that now. But I would go
> further. The Arab world has made great strides since the settle-
> ment reached at the end of the last War, and many Arab thinkers
> desire for the Arab peoples a greater degree of unity than they
> now enjoy. In reaching out towards this unity they hope for our

support. No such appeal from our friends should go unanswered. It seems to me both natural and right that the cultural and economic ties between the Arab countries, and the political ties too, should be strengthened. His Majesty's Government for their part will give their full support to any scheme that commands general approval.

Britain's new-found enthusiasm for the Arab cause, in the spring of 1941, was readily comprehensible. Great Britain had been alarmed by an attempted pro-Axis *coup* in Iraq, while an Allied invasion of Vichy-controlled Lebanon and Syria was imminent.[5]

Nuri al-Said, Prime Minister of Iraq, responded to the Foreign Secretary's initiative in a memorandum to the British Minister of State in Cairo. Writing in January 1943, Nuri proposed the establishment of a sovereign state comprising Syria, Lebanon, Palestine and Transjordan.[6] This amounted to the establishment of 'Greater Syria', a scheme propounded by Syrian nationalists since 1919.[7] Nuri advocated the creation of an Arab League, in which Iraq and the newly enlarged Syrian state would be founder members. Other Arab states would be eligible for membership.[8] Unlike its present-day namesake, Nuri envisaged 'a political confederation of Arab states that would eventually become a sovereign political entity'.[9] This emerges clearly from his proposal that a League Council should be formed with responsibility for '(a) defence; (b) foreign affairs; (c) currency; (d) communications; (e) customs; (f) protection of minority rights'.[10]

Britain's call for Arab unification was seized on by Emir Abdullah of Transjordan as a means of extending his own authority over the whole of geographical Syria. In April 1943, Abdullah called for a conference in Amman at which delegates from Transjordan, Palestine, Lebanon and Syria could decide on the appropriate form of government for a unified Syrian state.[11]

A third, and more cautious, response to the British initiative emerged in March 1943 when Nahas Pasha, Prime Minister of Egypt, proposed talks amongst the various Arab governments. Nahas envisaged that, in due course, an Arab Congress would be convened in Egypt to adopt a programme for Arab unification.[12]

During the next sixteen months the Egyptian Prime Minister held talks with a succession of Arab leaders.[13] As a result of these Nahas issued invitations, in June 1944, to the governments of Iraq, Syria, Lebanon, Transjordan, Saudi Arabia and the Yemen to attend a preliminary meeting in Egypt.[14]

The opening session of the Preparatory Committee of the General Arab Congress was held in Alexandria on 25 September. It was attended by the Prime Ministers of Egypt, Syria, the Lebanon, Iraq and Transjordan.[15] Following the entreaties of the delegates, Imam Yahya of the Yemen despatched an observer, while a Saudi delegate arrived in time to participate in the Committee's third session.[16] There was some uncertainty as to whether Palestine should be represented on the Preparatory Committee, in view of chronic dissension amongst Palestinian leaders and Palestine's status as a mandated territory. Nevertheless, despite the absence of a formal invitation, the Palestinian factions sent Musa Alami to represent their interests.[17]

There was little support amongst the delegates at the Preparatory Committee for the formation of a political union in which sovereign powers would be exercised by an executive body. Instead, there was general agreement on the need to establish a loose, regional organization making few concessions to supranationality.[18]

On 7 October, less than two weeks after the commencement of its deliberations, the Preparatory Committee adopted the 'Alexandria Protocol'.[19] The Protocol was approved by the Egyptian, Syrian, Lebanese, Iraqi and Transjordanian delegates. The Saudi monarch, who considered the establishment of an Arab League as premature, withheld his approval until 7 January 1945. The Imam of Yemen did not endorse the Protocol until 5 February.[20] Musa Alami, the Palestinian delegate, was not considered a full member of the Preparatory Committee, and was therefore not called upon to sign the Protocol.[21]

The Alexandria Protocol emphasized the desire of the signatories 'to strengthen and consolidate the ties which bind all Arab countries and to direct them towards the welfare of the Arab World, to improve its conditions, insure its future, and realize its hopes and aspirations'.[22] However, the 'hopes and aspirations' reflected in the Protocol were no longer those of Arab union. Instead, they had become the pragmatic goals of inter-governmental cooperation.[23] Thus, membership in the League was open to 'independent Arab states', while the objectives of the Organisation were:[24]

> to control the execution of the agreements which the above states will conclude; to hold periodic meetings which will strengthen the relations between those states; to co-ordinate their political plans so as to ensure their co-operation, and protect their independence and sovereignty against every aggression by suitable means; and to supervise in a general way the affairs and interests of the Arab countries.

The Protocol envisaged the creation of a Council in which all League members would be represented 'on an equal footing'.[25] Decisions of the Council would only bind 'those who have accepted them' – a stark reflection of the degree to which member states would retain their sovereign powers.[26]

The Protocol proscribed 'resort to force to settle a dispute between any two member states of the League',[27] and proposed a system of compulsory dispute-settlement. The text stated that 'where a disagreement arises between two member states of the League . . . the two parties shall refer their dispute to the Council for solution'.[28] The decision of the Council would be binding.[29]

There was a measure of disagreement in the Preparatory Committee as to whether both parties to a dispute need refer the question to the League Council in order for it to exercise its powers of arbitration, or whether reference by a single party was sufficient.[30] Iraq and Lebanon, anxious to preserve their sovereignty, adhered to the former view; Egypt and Syria favoured the latter.[31] In addition, the Protocol envisaged that the Council would undertake mediation: '[t]he Council will intervene in every dispute which may lead to war between a member state of the League and any other member state or power, so as to reconcile them'.[32]

In a rare concession to the ideal of Arab unity, the Protocol affirmed '[i]n no case will the adoption of a foreign policy which may be prejudicial to the policy of the League or an individual member state be allowed'.[33] However, the Lebanese President objected to this passage, thereby ensuring that it was omitted from the Pact of the League of Arab States.[34]

At the suggestion of the Iraqi Premier, who had earlier proposed a scheme of Arab unification, the Protocol alluded to the possibility of closer ties in the future between the Arab states. Thus, the text expressed the satisfaction of the Preparatory Committee at the formation of the League and declared the hope 'that Arab States will be able in the future to consolidate that step by other steps, especially if post-war world events should result in institutions which will bind various Powers more closely together'.[35]

The Alexandria Protocol included a resolution concerning 'Cooperation in Economic, Cultural, Social, and Other Matters'.[36] In accordance with the resolution, the Arab states represented on the Preliminary Committee undertook to cooperate in matters ranging from customs, currency, roads and navigation, the extradition of criminals, the execution of judgments and questions of nationality.[37]

'Special Resolutions' concerning Lebanon and Palestine were also added to the Protocol. In the former, the states represented on the Preparatory Committee emphasized 'their respect of the independence and sovereignty of Lebanon within its present frontiers, which the governments of the above States already recognized'.[38] In the latter, the Committee affirmed that 'Palestine constitutes an important part of the Arab World' and declared its support for 'the cause of the Arabs of Palestine'.[39]

In February 1945, the Egyptian government invited Arab Foreign Ministers to meet in Cairo to draft the Pact of the League of Arab States.[40] After sixteen sessions, attended by delegates from Egypt, Iraq, Lebanon, Syria, Saudi Arabia and Transjordan, agreement was reached on a draft text.[41] The Preparatory Committee was reconvened, on 17 March, to consider the draft. The Pact was finally approved, on 22 March, by the General Arab Congress.[42] The text was signed by delegates representing Egypt, Iraq, Lebanon, Syria Transjordan and Saudi Arabia.[43]

Purposes and functions of the League

Recalling the Alexandria Protocol, the Preamble of the Pact expresses the desire of the signatories to 'strengthen . . . the close relations and numerous ties which link the Arab States' and to 'direct their efforts toward the common good of all the Arab countries, the improvement of their status, the security of their future, the realization of their aspirations and hopes'. However, in a significant departure from the Protocol, the Pact emphasizes that these goals must be pursued 'upon a basis of respect for the independence and sovereignty' of member states.[44]

The purposes of the League are defined in Article 2. These encompass 'the strengthening of the relations between the member states; the co-ordination of their policies in order to achieve cooperation between them and to safeguard their independence and sovereignty; and a general concern with the affairs and interests of the Arab countries'. They include, in addition, cooperation 'with due regard to the organization and circumstances of each state' on various matters ranging from economic and financial affairs, cultural and social questions, health problems, and the extradition of criminals.[45]

Unlike the Protocol, which prohibited the 'adoption of a foreign policy which may be prejudicial to the policy of the League', the Pact does not seek to dictate the foreign policies of members.[46] Instead, as noted above, the Preamble of the Pact calls for 'respect for the independence and sovereignty' of League states. In addition, members are required to 'respect the systems of government established in the other member states and regard them as exclusive concerns of those states'.[47] Significantly, the Pact fails to reaffirm the hope, expressed in the Protocol, that Arab states will 'consolidate' their ties in the future.[48] In sum, the Pact constitutes a regression from the ideal of Arab unity enshrined in the Protocol.[49]

Membership

In accordance with Article 1, '[t]he League of Arab States is composed of the independent Arab States which have signed this Pact'. These comprise Syria, Transjordan, Iraq, Saudi Arabia, Lebanon, Egypt and Yemen.[50] In addition, any 'independent Arab State' may apply for membership of the League.[51] Decisions concerning admission are made by the Council, requiring a simple majority of League members.[52] Fifteen states have been admitted on this basis.[53] If two or more members should form a political union, they will lose their right of individual representation in the League and will be regarded, for the duration of the union, as a single state. This was the case when, in 1958, Egypt and Syria formed the United Arab Republic.[54]

An annex to the League Pact sanctioned the participation of a Palestinian delegate in the work of the Council.[55] Since December 1945, Palestine has been represented at Council meetings, and Palestinian delegates have enjoyed limited rights of participation in the Council's deliberations.[56] Following the Seventh Arab Summit Conference, held in Rabat in October 1974, the PLO has been recognized as 'the sole legitimate representative of the Palestinian people'.[57] In September 1976, the League Council unanimously admitted Palestine as the 21st member of the Organisation. It was agreed that the PLO should continue to represent Palestine within the League.[58]

The Pact provided for cooperation between the League and Arab states, other than Palestine, which had not yet attained independence and were therefore ineligible for full membership. Thus, Annex 2 notes that 'the Council has to take into account the aspirations of the Arab countries which are not members of the Council and has to work towards their realization'.[59] Similarly, Article 2 of the Pact emphasizes that the purposes of the League include 'a general concern with the affairs and interests of the Arab countries', not merely with those of member states.

Provision was made for the participation of Arab countries which had yet to secure their independence in the activities of the Organization. Thus Article 4, authorizing the establishment of various technical committees, states that delegates from non-member Arab states 'may take part in the work' of the committees.[60]

Any member may withdraw from the League, provided that it informs 'the Council of its intention one year before such withdrawal is to go into effect'.[61] As yet, no state has invoked this provision, although threats of withdrawal have been made on occasion.[62] Members may also withdraw from the League if they do not accept an amendment to the Pact which has been approved by the necessary two thirds majority of League members.[63] The Council can, in addition, expel a member state 'which fails to fulfill its obligations' under the Pact. Such a decision must be taken by an affirmative vote of all League members, excluding the state under consideration.[64]

Following the conclusion of a Treaty of Peace between Egypt and Israel in March 1979, Egypt's membership of the League was suspended.[65] In addition, the headquarters of the Organisation were transferred from Cairo to Tunis.[66]

Institutional structure

The Pact provided for the establishment of a Council, a permanent Secretariat, and various technical committees. In addition, it envisaged the creation of an Arab Tribunal of Arbitration.[67] However, the Tribunal has not been established.[68]

The Council

All member states have a seat on the Council, which is the supreme political organ of the League.[69] Each state, irrespective of size or economic importance, has a single vote.[70] States are frequently represented at Council meetings by their Foreign Ministers or, on occasion, by ambassadors accredited to the League.[71]

The functions of the Council include 'the realization of the objectives of the League' and the supervision of 'the execution of agreements which the member states have concluded'.[72] In particular, the Council is entrusted with significant responsibilities for dispute-settlement.[73] The Council is, in addition, the central element in the League's system of collective security.[74]

The Council is convened in ordinary session twice a year, in March and September.[75] In addition, the Council may 'convene in extraordinary session upon the request of two member states . . . whenever the need arises'.[76] An extraordinary session may be held at the request of a single member state, if it has been 'attacked or threatened with aggression'.[77]

In general, unanimous decisions of the Council are binding on all members of the League, while majority decisions are binding 'only upon those states which have accepted them'.[78] However, majority decisions may create binding obligations in certain circumstances. A 'majority vote of the Council shall be sufficient to make enforceable decisions' on procedural and technical matters such as the adoption of the League's budget, personnel questions, and decisions to adjourn sessions of the Council.[79] In addition, decisions concerning the appointment of a Secretary-General may be made 'by a majority of two-thirds' of League members,[80] while decisions concerning the expulsion of a member state require the concurrence of all League members with the exception of the state under consideration.[81]

The voting procedures of the League Council, together with other aspects of the Organisation, have been under review for some years. Meeting in extraordinary session in Tunis, in June 1979, the Council called for the reform of the working methods of the League, the amendment of the Charter, and of its rules of procedure.[82] The Tenth Summit Conference, held in Tunis in November 1979, underlined the necessity of accelerating the amendment of the Charter, and of restructuring the Organisation.[83]

A revised Pact, comprising 49 Articles, was completed in November 1982. Amongst a number of important innovations, the new text permits the Council to take binding decisions on certain issues by majority vote.[84] However, the amendments have not been formally adopted, and it appears increasingly unlikely that they will ever command sufficient support.[85]

Summit conferences

The Pact of the League of Arab States does not provide for 'Summit Conferences'. Nevertheless, such conferences have been a feature of the League since January 1964 when, at the instigation of President Nasser, Arab Heads of State met in Cairo to discuss a number of regional problems.[86] It was envisaged that Summit Conferences would be held on an annual basis. However, political differences between League members have prevented this from being realized.[87]

Constitutionally, there has been some doubt as to whether Summit Conferences represent a separate League organ, sometimes referred to as the 'Conference of Kings and Heads of State'.[88] However, the preponderant view is that Summit Conferences should be regarded as sessions of the League Council.[89]

The permanent secretariat

The Pact authorized the establishment of a 'permanent Secretariat-General' consisting of 'a Secretary-General, Assistant Secretaries, and an appropriate number of officials'.[90] The Secretary-General is appointed by the Council, voting by a two-thirds majority.[91] The Secretary-General may, with 'the approval of the Council', appoint the Assistant Secretaries and the principal officials of the League.[92]

The Secretary-General is responsible for preparing the draft budget of the League, which must be submitted to the Council for its approval 'before the beginning of each fiscal year'.[93] He is also charged with convening meetings of the Council.[94] In addition, the Secretariat serves as a depositary for treaties concluded by member states.[95] Beyond these largely technical functions, the Pact does not elaborate the responsibilities of either the Secretary-General or the Secretariat. Further details concerning their work and activities are specified in various internal regulations.[96]

The first three Secretary-Generals – Abdel Rahman Azzam, Abdel Khalek Hassouna and Mahmoud Riad – were Egyptian nationals. However, in March 1979, Secretary-General Riad resigned from office when it became clear that, as a result of the imminent conclusion of a peace treaty between Egypt and Israel, Egypt's membership of the League would be suspended, and the League's headquarters transferred from Cairo to Tunis.[97] In June 1979, an extraordinary meeting of the Council of the League appointed Chedli Klibi, formerly Tunisian Minister of Information, as Secretary-General.[98]

The functions and activities associated with the office of Secretary-General far exceed the administrative duties specified in the Pact. Secretary-Generals have often undertaken mediation between League members who are involved in disputes. They have also been entrusted with significant responsibilities by the League Council.[99] Inevitably, the personality of each Secretary-General has influenced the way in which he has exercised the responsibilities of his office.[100]

The political role of the Secretary-General is based, in part, on internal regulations. The internal regulations of the Council authorize the Secretary-General to 'draw the attention of the Council or the Member States to any question which may prejudice the existing relations between the Arab States or between them and other States'.[101] The regulations also permit the Secretary-General to 'submit to the Council, at any time, reports or statements on any question being considered by the Council' provided that the approval of the President of the Council has been secured.[102]

The permanent committees

The Pact sanctioned the establishment of a number of 'special committees' concerned with social, economic and cultural matters.[103] These include the Cultural Committee, the Information Committee, the Health Committee and the Communications Committee.[104]

In November 1946, the Council established the Political Committee.[105] This frequently meets at Foreign Minister level, and is charged with coordinating the foreign policies of member states. Meetings are held during sessions of the League Council, as well as at other times, and decisions are taken by a simple majority.[106] The Political

Committee has become increasingly important as a forum for decision-making within the League. To some degree this has been at the expense of the Council, with which its work overlaps.[107]

Joint Defence and Economic Cooperation Treaty

The conclusion of the Joint Defence and Economic Cooperation Treaty, in 1950, resulted in the creation of a number of additional organs.[108] The Treaty, which was designed to strengthen the League's system of collective security, provided for the establishment of a Joint Defence Council, a Permanent Military Commission, a Consultative Military Council and an Economic Council.[109]

Specialized agencies

Member states have established a number of specialized agencies which are affiliated to the League.[110] These include the Arab Postal Union, the Arab Labour Organization, the Arab League Educational, Cultural and Scientific Organization, and the Arab Organization for Agricultural Development.[111]

The Arab League and the United Nations

The Pact of the League of Arab States entered into force on 10 May 1945, more than a month before the signing of the UN Charter.[112] Nevertheless, the League's powers must be understood in terms of the legal and institutional framework established by the UN Charter.

Recognition of the right of regional organizations, such as the Arab League, to operate systems of collective security may be found in Article 51 of the Charter.[113] This provides '[n]othing in the present Charter shall impair the inherent right of individual or *collective* self-defence if an armed attack occurs against a member of the United Nations'.[114] This provision was inserted in the Charter largely to accommodate Latin American states, who wished to ensure that regional security mechanisms could function without Security Council authorization.[115]

Recognition of the right of regional organizations to operate procedures for the peaceful settlement of disputes and, by implication, to engage in peacekeeping, can be found in Chapter VIII of the Charter. Thus, Article 52(1) provides:

> Nothing in the present Charter precludes the existence of regional arrangements or agencies for dealing with such matters relating

to the maintenance of international peace and security as are appropriate for regional action, provided that such arrangements or agencies and their activities are consistent with the Purposes and Principles of the United Nations.

Some encouragement of the use of regional mechanisms, in the maintenance of international peace and security, can be found in Articles 52(2) and 52(3). Article 52(2) states that UN members 'entering into such arrangements or constituting such agencies shall make every effort to achieve pacific settlement of local disputes through such regional arrangements or by such regional agencies before referring them to the Security Council'. Article 52(3) provides '[t]he Security Council shall encourage the development of pacific settlement of local disputes through such regional arrangements or by such regional agencies'. However, regional organizations do not enjoy exclusive, or even primary, jurisdiction over regional disputes. Thus, Article 52(4) affirms '[t]his Article in no way impairs the application of Articles 34 and 35'.[116]

A further limitation on the competence of regional organizations is contained in Article 53(1). This provides that '[t]he Security Council shall, where appropriate, utilize such regional arrangements or agencies for enforcement action under its authority'. Crucially, 'no enforcement action shall be taken under regional arrangements or by regional agencies without the authorization of the Security Council'.[117]

The meaning of 'enforcement action' has given rise to understandable difficulties of interpretation.[118] However, this limitation on the competence of regional organizations serves to emphasize the 'primary responsibility' of the Security Council for the maintenance of international peace and security.[119]

The Arab League and the peaceful settlement of disputes

The League Pact proscribes '[a]ny resort to force in order to resolve disputes arising between two or more member states of the League'.[120] Unlike the UN Charter, the Pact does not prohibit the mere 'threat' of force. Nor does it impose an obligation on members to pursue a peaceful settlement.[121] However, the Joint Defence and Economic Cooperation Treaty goes some way to rectifying these deficiencies. Article 1 expresses the desire of the parties 'to settle their international disputes by peaceful means'.[122]

The techniques of dispute settlement available to member states are set out in Article 5 of the Pact. These comprise 'arbitration' or 'mediation' by the League Council.[123] Arbitration is only available where the parties to a dispute are League members.[124] In such cases, the states involved 'shall not participate in the deliberations and decisions of the Council'.[125] Significantly, arbitral decisions are taken by majority vote, and are 'enforceable and obligatory'.[126]

The jurisdiction of the Council in cases of arbitration is limited to disputes which do not 'concern a state's independence, sovereignty, or territorial integrity'.[127] There is a measure of disagreement amongst commentators as to whether the Council, or individual member states, are competent to determine whether a particular dispute falls into this category.[128] However, the matter is of less than compelling interest as no dispute can be referred to the Council for arbitration without the prior consent of the parties.[129]

Arbitration is normally associated with decisions taken in accordance with law, by persons who are themselves expert lawyers.[130] However, arbitration before a political organ such as the League Council may result in decisions being taken in accordance with principles of justice or fairness, rather than of law, and by diplomats or politicians, rather than by lawyers.[131]

There has been no instance of arbitration by the League Council in accordance with Article 5, although Syria and the Lebanon referred a minor territorial dispute to arbitration in 1949.[132] However, it is significant that Syria and Lebanon did not submit their dispute to the League Council. Instead, resort to arbitration was suggested by Egypt and Saudi Arabia, who were also responsible for appointing the arbitrators.[133]

The reluctance of League members to resort to arbitration has been ascribed to various factors, of which the most fundamental is their preference for diplomatic negotiations.[134] During discussions in the Political Subsidiary Committee, which was charged with drafting the League Pact, both Egypt and Saudi Arabia advocated schemes of *compulsory* arbitration for disputes between League members. However, the Egyptian and Saudi proposals were omitted from the Pact because of the opposition of Lebanon and Iraq, who feared such far-reaching encroachments on their sovereignty.[135]

As noted above, the Council can only undertake arbitration if the parties choose to refer a dispute to it, and if they are League members. However the Council may, on its own initiative, 'mediate in all differences which threaten to lead to war between two member states, or a member state and a third state, with a view to bringing about their reconciliation'.[136] The Council can attempt mediation even though a dispute affects a state's 'independence, sovereignty, or territorial integrity', provided that the dispute is one which 'threaten[s] to lead to war'.[137] Such decisions are not, however, binding on the parties to a dispute.[138]

Whereas the Council can only arbitrate in disputes between League members, it may mediate in disputes in which non-members are also involved.[139] As with arbitration, decisions concerning mediation are taken by majority vote.[140]

An excessively legalistic analysis of the Pact's provisions concerning dispute-settlement would, however, be inappropriate. Frequently, the Council has exercised informal techniques of conciliation, in disregard of Article 5 of the Pact.[141]

The Arab League and collective security

The Pact of the Arab League instituted a system of collective security, complementing the mechanisms for dispute settlement outlined above. Thus, in 'case of aggression or threat of aggression by one state against a member state, the state which has been attacked or threatened with aggression' may demand the immediate convocation of the Council'.[142] The Council is empowered to 'determine the measures necessary to repulse the aggression', by a unanimous decision if the aggressor is a non-member, or by a decision of all member states other than the aggressor, if the latter is a member of the League.[143]

Where, as a result of the attack, the government of the attacked state 'finds itself unable to communicate with the Council', the state's representative in the Council 'shall have the right to request the convocation of the Council'.[144] If the representative is unable to communicate with the Council 'any member state of the League shall have the right to request the convocation of the Council'.[145]

The unsatisfactory character of these provisions was exposed by the League's failure to respond effectively to the establishment of Israel in 1948.[146] This, combined with the desire of Arab states to secure recognition of the League as a regional organization, within the meaning of Chapter VIII of the UN Charter, led to the conclusion of the Joint Defence and Economic Cooperation Treaty.[147] In theory, if not in practice, the Treaty established a more credible system of collective security. Contracting states are bound to consider:[148]

> any [act of] armed aggression made against any one or more of them or their armed forces, to be directed against them all. Therefore, in accordance with the right of self-defence, individually and collectively, they undertake to go without delay to the aid of the State or States against which such an act of aggression is made, and immediately to take, individually and collectively, all steps available, including the use of armed force, to repel the aggression and restore the security and peace.

The Treaty provides that, at the invitation of any one of the signatories:[149]

> the Contracting States shall hold consultations whenever there are reasonable grounds for the belief that the territorial integrity, independence, or security of any one of the parties is threatened. In the event of the threat of war or the existence of an international emergency, the Contracting States shall immediately proceed to unify their plans and defensive measures, as the situation may demand.

As noted previously, the Joint Defence and Economic Cooperation Treaty created a number of organs in order to co-ordinate the military policies of contracting states. These include the Permanent Military Commission, and the Joint Defence Council.[150]

The Joint Defence and Economic Cooperation Treaty has not, in practice, established an effective system of collective security. In consequence, many League members have concluded additional treaties of mutual defence.[151]

The Arab League and peacekeeping

The Pact of the Arab League does not provide for peacekeeping *per se*. However, the League has established two military forces during its 40-year existence of which the second, chronologically, is the Arab League Force in the Lebanon. The first, constituted in 1961, was sent to Kuwait, to deter an attack by Iraq.[152]

Whether either, or both, of these constituted 'peacekeeping' forces depends, at least in part, on the theoretical assumptions of the observer. As Professor Higgins has noted '[t]he concept of "peacekeeping" is open to a variety of definitions'.[153]

The requirements of 'peacekeeping', as understood by international law, are analysed in some detail, in Chapter 6. It will be suggested that the Arab League Force in the Lebanon was conceived as a genuine peacekeeping operation. By contrast the Arab League Force in Kuwait, in the opinion of the present writer, was an example of collective self-defence or of collective security rather than of international peacekeeping.[154] Nevertheless, as the first military force constituted by the Arab League, it merits detailed consideration.

The Arab League Force in Kuwait

The Arab League Force in Kuwait was established in 1961, in response to Iraqi threats to annex the newly-independent territory of Kuwait.[155]

Kuwait achieved independence on 19 June 1961, applying immediately for membership of the League of Arab States.[156] The Baghdad government of General Kassem contested Kuwait's application on the grounds that, historically, Kuwait was an integral part of Iraq.[157] At the request of Kuwait's ruler, British troops were despatched to Kuwait.[158]

The Arab League, while alarmed by the prospect of Iraqi aggression against Kuwait, was equally concerned at the reintroduction of British troops in the area. Following meetings of the League Council and of the Political Committee, a partial compromise was achieved. On 20 July 1961, the Council adopted a resolution admitting Kuwait as a member of the League.[159] In addition, the resolution envisaged the withdrawal of British troops from Kuwait, while pledging 'effective assistance for the preservation of Kuwait's independence'. The League Secretary-General was entrusted with responsibility for taking 'the necessary measures for the urgent implementation of this resolution'.[160]

On 12 August, an agreement concerning the status of the Arab League Force was signed by the League Secretary-General and by the ruler of Kuwait.[161] On the same day, the Kuwaiti ruler requested the withdrawal of British troops from his territory, while two days later Kuwait acceded to the Joint Defence and Economic Cooperation Treaty.[162]

Following the adoption of the Council resolution of 20 July, the Secretary-General issued invitations to League members to participate in the proposed Arab League Force. Libya and the Lebanon declined to contribute contingents. However, units were eventually drawn from the United Arab Republic, Saudi Arabia, Sudan, Jordan and Tunisia.[163] In all, the Force comprised some 3300 troops, of which the largest contingents (1200 men apiece) were sent by the United Arab Republic and by Saudi Arabia.[164] A Saudi officer, Major-General Abdullah Al-Isa, was appointed Commander of the Force.[165]

Units of the Arab League Force began to arrive in Kuwait in mid-September, reaching their full strength by 3 October.[166] As the Arab Force deployed along the border with Iraq, the British troops were progressively withdrawn. On 11 October, the ruler of Kuwait announced that the British evacuation had been completed.[167] Within days of the British departure from Kuwait, the United Arab Republic declared that its troops would be withdrawn from the Arab League Force.[168] This was achieved in two stages, during December 1961. To compensate, additional forces were despatched by Jordan and Saudi Arabia.[169]

The size of the Arab League Force was reduced substantially, following a request by the Kuwaiti government, in December 1962.[170] A coup in Iraq, in February 1963, toppled the government of the unpredictable General Kassem, installing a regime of more moderate views.[171] In a conciliatory gesture, the ruler of Kuwait requested the withdrawal of the remaining contingents of the Arab League Force. The last units of the Force were withdrawn during February 1963.[172]

The Arab League Force in Kuwait has been widely characterized, especially by Arab commentators, as a 'peacekeeping' operation.[173] Attention has been drawn, in particular, to the fact that the Arab troops were not 'directed against' any state. To the present writer, such arguments appear somewhat artificial. The purpose of the Force, as expressed in the Council resolution of 20 July 1961, was to ensure 'effective assistance for the preservation of Kuwait's independence'.[174] As such, the operation was an example of collective self-defence, or of collective security, rather than of peacekeeping.[175] If the Arab Force was not 'directed against' any state that was largely because Iraq held back from invading Kuwait. Had an attack materialized the Arab League Force would, presumably, have attempted to repel the aggressor. That is scarcely compatible with conventional notions of 'peacekeeping'.

Notes

1   For an influential discussion of the development of Arab nationalism, see e.g. Antonius, *Arab Awakening*.
2   The pledges were made by Sir Henry McMahon, the British High Commissioner in Egypt, in his celebrated correspondence with Sherif Hussein of Mecca. The correspondence is reproduced in Hurewitz, *II*, pp.46-56.
3   See, generally, Mansfield, *Ottoman Empire*, Chapter 5. See, also, A. Williams, *Britain and France in the Middle East and North Africa* (1968), Chapter 2.
4   See e.g. *The Times*, 30 May 1941, p.2.
5   See e.g. G. Kirk, *The Middle East in the War* (1952), p.334.
6   The text is partially reproduced, in English, in M.H. Khalil, *The Arab States and the Arab League* (1962), vol. II, pp.9-12.
7   See e.g. Ziadeh, *Syria and Lebanon*, pp.48-9.
8   Gomaa, *League of Arab States*, p.69.
9   Macdonald, *League of Arab States*, p.35. See, also, C.A. Hourani, 'The Arab League in Perspective', *MEJ*, vol. I (1947), p.125, at pp.128-9.
10 Quoted in Gomaa, *League of Arab States*, p.69.
11 See e.g., Kirk, op. cit., note 5, p.336. See also Y. Porath, 'Abdallah's Greater Syria Programme', *MES*, vol. 20 (1984), p.172, at p.183.
12 See e.g. Kirk, op. cit., note 5, p.336. See, also, Gomaa, *League of Arab States*, p.161.
13 Kirk, op. cit., note 5, pp.336-9. See, also, Gomaa, *League of Arab States*. p.161 et seq.
14 See e.g. Gomaa, *League of Arab States*, p.202.
15 Ibid., p.217.
16 Ibid., pp.217-18. Imam Yahya authorized his representative to participate fully in the final meeting of the Preparatory Committee.

17 Gomaa, *League of Arab States*, pp.211-13.
18 Ibid., p.219. See, also, Foda, *Projected Arab Court of Justice*, pp.6-11.
19 The text is reproduced, in English, in Gomaa, *League of Arab States*, p.272.
20 Ibid., pp.224-5, 232-4.
21 Ibid., p.223, note 2.
22 Preamble, Alexandria Protocol.
23 See e.g. Gomaa, *League of Arab States*, pp.226-7. See also Foda, *Projected Arab Court of Justice*, pp.6-11.
24 Resolution 1, Alexandria Protocol.
25 Ibid.
26 Ibid.
27 Ibid.
28 Ibid.
29 Ibid.
30 The term 'arbitration' is used in Article 5 of the Pact to denote the power of the League Council to adopt binding decisions in disputes arising between member states. For a more detailed analysis of Article 5, see below.
31 Foda, *Projected Arab Court of Justice*, pp.8-11.
32 Resolution 1, Alexandria Protocol.
33 Ibid.
34 Gomaa, *League of Arab States*, p.228, note 1.
35 Resolution 3, Alexandria Protocol.
36 Resolution 2, Alexandria Protocol.
37 Ibid.
38 Resolution 4, Alexandria Protocol. Lebanon did not achieve formal independence till 1943. See e.g. Salibi, *History of Lebanon*, pp.187-90.
39 Resolution 5, Alexandria Protocol.
40 The invitations were extended in accordance with the Alexandria Protocol which had envisaged the establishment of a committee 'formed of the members of the Preparatory Committee' to prepare the text of the Pact. See Resolution 1, Alexandria Protocol.
41 The Yemen did not participate in the meetings of what came to be known as the Political Subsidiary Committee. However, a Palestinian delegate was present as an observer. See e.g. Gomaa, *League of Arab States*, pp.239-40. On the discussions in the Political Subsidiary Committee, see e.g. Foda, *Projected Arab Court of Justice*, pp.11-17.
42 See e.g. Gomaa, *League of Arab States*, p.239. The text of the Pact is reproduced in Hassouna, *League of Arab States*, p.403; Macdonald, *League of Arab States*, p.319.
43 Yemen failed to send a delegate to the General Arab Congress. Nevertheless, on 10 May 1945, the Imam signed a copy of the Pact which had been sent to him, transforming the Yemen into one of the founder members of the League. See Gomaa, *League of Arab States*, p.239, n.2.
44 Preamble, League Pact. This significant provision was included at the instigation of Iraq and the Lebanon, with the support of Saudi Arabia. See Gomaa, *League of Arab States*, p.241.
45 The reference to the particular circumstances of each member state reflected Saudi concern that she should not be compelled to adopt legislation contrary to Islamic tenets. See Gomaa, *League of Arab States*, p.241.
46 See, generally, Macdonald, *League of Arab States*, p.43. See also Hourani, op. cit., note 9, at pp.132-3.
47 Art. 8, League Pact.
48 Resolution 3, Alexandria Protocol.

49   See e.g. Anabtawi, *Arab Unity*, pp.66, 71.

50   In fact, not all of these states were fully independent when they signed the Pact. See, generally, Gomaa, *League of Arab States*, p.242. Since March 1979, Egypt's membership of the Arab League has been suspended.

51   Art. 1, League Pact. On the separate Islamic Conference Organization, in which membership is not confined to 'Arab' states, see e.g. M. Flory, 'Les Conférénces Islamiques', *AFDI*, vol. XVI (1970), p.233.

52   Initially, it was thought that the admission of a new state required the unanimous approval of League members. However, this principle has been gradually relaxed. In 1961, Iraq did not participate in the vote to admit Kuwait, while in 1967 Saudi Arabia abstained in the vote to admit South Yemen. In 1971, two member states, Saudi Arabia and the Yemen, opposed the admission of Oman, and the Democratic Republic of Yemen opposed the admission of the United Arab Emirates. Saudi Arabia abstained in the vote on the admission of the UAE. Nevertheless, all of these states secured admission to the Arab League. See generally Boutros-Ghali, *La Ligue des Etats Arabes*, pp.31-3.

53   These comprise Algeria (1962), Bahrain (1961), Djibouti (1977), Kuwait (1961), Libya (1953), Mauritania (1973), Morocco (1958), Oman (1971), Palestine (1976), Qatar (1971), Somalia (1974), Sudan (1956), Tunisia (1958), United Arab Emirates (1971), Democratic Republic of Yemen (1968). It is generally believed that all states eligible for membership of the League are already members. See e.g. Hassouna, *Regionalism*, p.300.

54   Boutros-Ghali, *La Ligue des Etats Arabes*, p.30.

55   Annex 1, League Pact.

56   See generally Hassouna, *League of Arab States*, pp.264-9. See also Boutros-Ghali, *La Ligue des Etats Arabes*, pp.34-6.

57   For the text of the communiqué adopted at the Seventh Arab Summit Conference, see e.g. Lukacs, *Documents*, p.223.

58   League Council Resolution No. 3462, 9 September 1976. See generally *Keesing's* (1976), p.27955.

59   Annex 2, League Pact.

60   On the application of these provisions, see e.g. Boutros-Ghali, *La Ligue des Etats Arabes*, pp.36-7.

61   Art. 18, League Pact.

62   Boutros-Ghali, *La Ligue des Etats Arabes*, p.37.

63   Art. 19, League Pact. No state has invoked this provision in order to withdraw from the League. See e.g. Boutros-Ghali, *La Ligue des Etats Arabes*, p.37.

64   Art. 18, League Pact.

65   For the text of the Treaty of Peace and related documents, see e.g. *ILM*, vol. XVIII (1979), p.362.

66   An Arab Summit Conference convened in Baghdad in November 1978, after the Camp David Agreements, decided that if Egypt concluded a peace treaty with Israel the headquarters of the Arab League would be removed from Cairo, and that Egypt's membership of the Organization would be suspended. See *Keesing's* (1979), pp.29659-60. A meeting of Arab Foreign and Finance Ministers, convened in late March 1979 after the conclusion of the Egypt–Israel Treaty of Peace, reaffirmed the substance of the decisions adopted by the Baghdad Summit Conference. See e.g. *Le Monde*, 3 April 1979, p.6.

67   Art. 19, League Pact.

68   See generally Foda, *Projected Arab Court of Justice*.

69   Art. 3, League Pact.

70   Ibid.

71   Boutros-Ghali, *La Ligue des Etats Arabes*, p.39.

72 Art. 3, League Pact.
73 Art. 5, League Pact. This will be examined in greater detail below.
74 Art. 6, League Pact.
75 Art. 11, League Pact.
76 Ibid.
77 Art. 6, League Pact.
78 Art. 7, League Pact.
79 Art. 16, League Pact.
80 Art. 12, League Pact.
81 Art. 18, League Pact.
82 League Council Res. No. 3842, 28 June 1979. See generally S. Chaabane, 'La Réforme du Pacte de la Ligue des Etats Arabes', *RGDIP*, vol. 86 (1982), pp.508-42.
83 Chaabane, op. cit., note 82, at pp.510-11.
84 In accordance with the revised Pact, an absolute majority of League members will be sufficient to take binding decisions concerning the approval of the budget, amending the internal regulations of League organs, etc. Decisions on other matters, such as the appointment of the Secretary-General, shall be taken by a two-thirds majority of League members. Chaabane, op. cit., note 82, pp.531-3. With respect to substantive issues, such as the peaceful settlement of disputes etc., only unanimous decisions will bind all members of the League. However, a state will be deemed to have consented to a decision unless it signifies its dissent.
85 In accordance with Article 19, the Pact may be amended 'with the consent of two-thirds of the states belonging to the League'. However, '[n]o decisions shall be taken on an amendment except in the session following that in which it was proposed'. Ibid.
86 On the first Arab Summit Conference, see e.g. Hassouna, *League of Arab States*, pp.186-7.
87 The last Arab Summit Conference was held in Fez (Morocco) in 1982. However, an Extraordinary Arab Summit Conference was convened in Casablanca, in August 1985. See e.g. *The Times*, 10 August 1985, p.4.
88 Boutros-Ghali, for example, classified summit conferences separately from sessions of the League Council, in an article published in 1969. See Boutros-Ghali, *Arab League*, p.77.
89 See e.g. Hassouna, *League of Arab States*, p.389; Macdonald, *League of Arab States*, p.69. By 1971, Boutros-Ghali had also adopted this position. See Boutros-Ghali, *La Ligue des Etats Arabes*, pp.43-4.
90 Art. 12, League Pact.
91 Ibid.
92 Ibid.
93 Art. 13, League Pact.
94 Art. 15, League Pact.
95 Art. 17, League Pact.
96 *Internal Regulations of the Council of the League of Arab States*, adopted on 13 October 1951, and revised on 24 July 1973; *Internal Regulations of the Secretariat-General of the League of Arab States*, adopted 10 May 1953, and revised on 24 July 1973. These are available, in English, in Hassouna, *League of Arab States*, pp.417, 433.
97 See, generally, *Keesing's* (1979), pp.29951-3.
98 Ibid., p.29953.
99 See, generally, Macdonald, *League of Arab States*, Chapter 7. See also Hassouna, *Regionalism*, pp.314-16. The Internal Regulations of the Secretari-

at-General, referred to above, state that the Secretary-General 'shall perform the functions entrusted to him, follow up the implementation of the resolutions adopted by the Council and other bodies of the League, and report on the impediments in their implementation and the means to overcome them.' See Internal Regulations of the Secretariat-General, op. cit. note 96, Art. II(2).

100 See e.g. Boutros-Ghali, *Arab League*, p.74.
101 Internal Regulations of the Council, op. cit., note 96, Art. XII(2).
102 Ibid., Art. XII(1).
103 Arts. 2, 4, League Pact.
104 At present there are some sixteen Permanent Committees. For details see *The Middle East and North Africa 1984–85* (31st edn, 1984), p.198.
105 See e.g. A. Y. El-Kurai, 'The Arab League and Arab International Affairs', *Arab Affairs*, vol. I (1983), p.5, at p.7.
106 Ibid., pp.7-8.
107 See, generally, ibid., pp.7-8. See also Macdonald, *League of Arab States*, pp.63-5; Boutros-Ghali, *Arab League*, pp.74-5; A. R. Radwan, *The Political Committee of the League of Arab States and its Role in Joint Political Action*, 1973 (in Arabic). In 1956, the Secretary-General suggested that the Political Committee should replace the Council as the principal organ of the League. See Anabtawi, *Arab Unity*, p.161.
108 The text of the treaty is reproduced in Hassouna, *League of Arab States*, p.411. See also Macdonald, *League of Arab States*, p.327. All of the members of the League are parties to the Treaty, with the exception of Djibouti, Mauritania and Oman.
109 See, generally, on the Joint Defence and Economic Cooperation Treaty Macdonald, *League of Arab States*, pp.48-50; Hassouna, *League of Arab States*, pp.13-15; Boutros-Ghali, *Arab League*, pp.75-6.
110 See, in particular, Boutros-Ghali, *La Ligue des Etats Arabes*, pp.44-6. See also Hassouna, *League of Arab States*, p.11; Macdonald, *League of Arab States*, p.126.
111 For a comprehensive citation of the Specialized Agencies, see *The Middle East and North Africa*, op. cit., note 104, p.199.
112 The UN Charter entered into force on 24 October 1945.
113 The Charter does not define the terms 'regional arrangement' or 'regional organization'. Nevertheless, it is broadly accepted that the Arab League qualifies for the purposes of Chapter VIII. For details see below, Chapter 6.
114 My emphasis.
115 See e.g. Goodrich, Hambro, Simons, *Charter*, pp.342-4. See also, R.B. Russell, *A History of the United Nations Charter*, 1958, Chapter XXVII.
116 Article 34 empowers the Security Council to investigate 'any dispute, or any situation which might lead to international friction or give rise to a dispute . . .' Article 35 permits Members and non-Members to refer disputes to the Security Council or the General Assembly.
117 Art. 53(1).
118 For details see below, Chapter 6.
119 Article 24(1) of the Charter provides: 'In order to ensure prompt and effective action by the United Nations, its Members confer on the Security Council primary responsibility for the maintenance of international peace and security . . .'
120 Art. 5, League Pact.
121 On these lacunae in the Pact, see e.g. S.J. Al-Kadhem, 'The Role of the League of Arab States in Settling Inter-Arab Disputes', *REDI*, vol. 32 (1976), p.1, at pp.18-19. The UN Charter, by contrast, proscribes 'the threat or use

of force' (Art. 2 (4)), while the parties to a dispute 'the continuance of which is likely to endanger the maintenance of international peace and security' are required, prior to submitting it to the Security Council, to 'seek a solution by negotiation, enquiry, mediation, conciliation, arbitration, judicial settlement, resort to regional agencies or arrangements, or other peaceful means of their own choice' (Art. 33(1)). If the parties are unable to settle their dispute by the means indicated in Article 33 'they shall refer it to the Security Council' (Art. 37(1)).

122   As noted above, the majority of League members are parties to the Joint Defence Treaty. Nevertheless, the term 'desire' is less peremptory than the injunction in Art. 2(3) of the UN Charter enjoining Members to 'settle their international disputes by peaceful means'.

123   Art. 5, League Pact.

124   Ibid.

125   Ibid.

126   Ibid.

127   Ibid. This drastic restriction on the jurisdiction of the League Council was introduced, very largely, at the insistence of the Lebanese delegate to the Political Subsidiary Committee, which was charged with drafting the League Pact. See e.g. Foda, *Projected Arab Court of Justice*, p.25, note 2.

128   See ibid., pp.29-30.

129   Al-Kadhem, op. cit., note 121, p.19.

130   See e.g. J.L. Brierly, *The Law of Nations* (6th edn, 1963), pp.347-8.

131   Foda, *Projected Arab Court of Justice*, pp.38-47.

132   See e.g. Boutros-Ghali, *La Ligue des Etats Arabes*, pp.47-8.

133   Ibid.

134   See e.g. Al-Kadhem, op. cit., note 121, p.22. See also Boutros-Ghali, *Arab League*, pp.82-3.

135   On the wrangles in the Political Subsidiary Committee see e.g. Gomaa, *League of Arab States*, pp.251-5. See also Foda, *Projected Arab Court of Justice*, pp.11-15.

136   Art. 5, League Pact.

137   Ibid. See generally Foda, *Projected Arab Court of Justice*, pp.56, 58.

138   See e.g. Al-Kadhem, op. cit., note 121, p.23. See also, Foda, *Projected Arab Court of Justice*, pp.56, 58.

139   Art. 5, League Pact.

140   Ibid.

141   See e.g. Hassouna, *Regionalism*, p.310.

142   Art. 6, League Pact.

143   Ibid.

144   Ibid.

145   Ibid.

146   On the establishment of Israel, and the first Arab–Israeli War, see e.g. J. and D. Kimche, *Both Sides of the Hill* (1960). See also R. Ovendale, *The Origins of the Arab-Israeli Wars* (1984), Chapter 7.

147   See, generally, Macdonald, *League of Arab States*, pp.221-9. See also Hassouna, *League of Arab States*, pp.13-15.

148   Art. 2.

149   Art. 3.

150   For further details see above.

151   See generally Boutros-Ghali, *La Ligue des Etats Arabes*, pp.58-63. See also Macdonald, *League of Arab States*, pp.221-40; Hassouna, *League of Arab States*, 13-15. The Gulf Cooperation Council, comprising Bahrain, Kuwait,

Oman, Qatar, Saudi Arabia and the United Arab Emirates, is currently considering the adoption of a treaty of mutual defence. See e.g. *The Times*, 29 October 1985, p.8. See generally on the Gulf Cooperation Council, I Bouachba, 'Le Conseil de Coopération des Etats Arabes du Golfe', *RGDIP*, vol. 89 (1985), p.29. On the issue of regional security, see ibid., pp.61-4.

152 See generally Hassouna, *League of Arab States*, pp.114-30.

153 Higgins, *I*, p.ix.

154 The overriding purpose of the Arab League Force in Kuwait was 'to provide effective assistance for the preservation of Kuwait's independence' in the face of a possible attack by Iraq. See League Council Resolution No. 1777, 20 July 1961. The substantive parts of the resolution are reproduced in Hassouna, *League of Arab States*, p.101. It is difficult to reconcile this function with conventional notions of peacekeeping.

155 See generally, on the Arab League operation in Kuwait, Hassouna, *League of Arab States*, pp.91-130. See also Macdonald, *League of Arab States*, pp.235-7; Rikhye, *Peacekeeping*, pp.133-4; Ben Amara, op. cit., p.ix, note 10, pp.129-36.

156 Hassouna, *Peacekeeping*, p.98.

157 Ibid.

158 Mansfield, *Ottoman Empire*, p.143.

·159 League Council Resolution No. 1777, 20 July 1961. The operative part of the resolution is reproduced, in English, in Hassouna, *League of Arab States*, p.101. Iraq was absent when the vote was taken.

160 Ibid.

161 The text of the Agreement is reproduced as Appendix G in Hassouna, *League of Arab States*, p.447.

162 Ibid., pp.99-101.

163 Rikhye, *Peacekeeping*, p.133.

164 Macdonald, *League of Arab States*, p.237.

165 Ibid.

166 Hassouna, *League of Arab States*, p.105.

167 Ibid.

168 Ibid., pp.105-6.

169 Ibid., p.106.

170 Ibid.

171 Ibid.

172 Ibid., p.107.

173 Ibid., pp.125-6. See also, Boutros-Ghali, *La Ligue des Etats Arabes*, p.53; Rikhye, *Peacekeeping*, p.133.

174 See note 159.

175 For contrasting analyses of the concept of collective self-defence see e.g. Bowett, *Self-Defence*, Chapter 10; Brownlie, *Use of Force*, pp.328-31. On the distinction between collective self-defence and collective security, see e.g. Kelsen, 'Collective Security and Collective Self-defence under the Charter of the United Nations', *AJIL*, vol. 42 (1948), p.783.

2 A History of the Lebanon from Ancient Times until the First World War

Definitional problems

Any discussion of the history of the Lebanon is complicated by the fact that its territorial extent and politico-legal status has undergone a succession of changes. Throughout the latter part of the nineteenth century the 'Lebanon', or 'Mount Lebanon', designated a largely mountainous area inhabited chiefly by Maronite and Druze villagers, and administered as an autonomous *sanjaq* of the Ottoman Empire. In 1920, France established the State of 'Grand Liban' or 'Greater Lebanon', adding Beirut, Tripoli, Sidon, Tyre, their hinterlands, and the Bekaa to the original *sanjaq* of Mount Lebanon. In November 1941, France proclaimed the independence of the Lebanon, although genuine independence was not granted immediately and French forces were not withdrawn completely until August 1946.[1]

Further complications arise from the fact that Arab and other sources frequently treat 'Syria', or 'geographical Syria', as representing a single cultural and geographical unit, encompassing the Lebanon, Palestine and Transjordan which was, in this view, arbitrarily dismembered in the political settlement following the First World War.[2] Thus, Professor Hitti refers to Palestine as 'the southern part of Syria "amputated" and mandated to Great Britain', and to Transjordan as having been 'amputated' from Palestine.[3]

Evidence of this viewpoint can also be found in the resolutions adopted by the General Syrian Congress in 1920. A plenary session of the Congress, meeting on 7 March, adopted a resolution proclaiming the independence of Syria, in an area including the Lebanon, Palestine and Transjordan, in addition to modern-day Syria.[4] Previously, on 2 July 1919, the Congress had adopted a resolution seeking independence for a unitary Syrian State within the following boundaries: 'The Taurus System on the North; Rafah and a line running from Al Jauf to the south of the Syrian and the Hejazian line to Akaba on the south; the Euphrates and Khabur Rivers and a line extending east of Abu Kamal to the east of Al Jauf on the east; and the Mediterranean on the west'.[5]

Throughout this chapter, dealing with the history of the Lebanon until the First World War, references to 'Syria', or to 'geographical Syria', should be regarded as extending to the Lebanon, Palestine and to Transjordan, unless specific indications are given to the contrary.

The ancient and early medieval period

Situated on the eastern fringes of the Mediterranean, geographical Syria occupies a strategic position between the continents of Europe, Asia and Africa. Since ancient times, it has fallen to a succession of conquerors. These have included the Egyptians, the Assyrians, the Persians, the Macedonians under Alexander the Great, the Seleucids and Rome.[6] At the end of the fourth century AD, with the division of the Roman Empire, Syria became part of the Byzantine (or Eastern Roman) Empire.[7] However, control over Syria was wrested from Byzantium by the Arabs in the seventh century AD.

The Arab conquest

For over 200 years, the empires of Persia and Byzantium dominated the affairs of the Near East. However, by the middle of the seventh century AD, both empires were in decline. The collapse of the ancient empires of the Near East coincided with the rise of the Arabs as a political and military power. United through Islam by the Prophet Muhammad, the Arabs became an increasingly formidable military power.[8]

In 634, Arab forces were despatched to Syria, defeating Byzantine armies in Palestine and Transjordan, and occupying Damascus in the following year.[9] An attempt by a fresh Byzantine army to check the Arab advances in Syria ended ignominiously at the Battle of Yarmouk.[10] The Arabs completed their conquest of Syria in 640.[11]

In 661, following the proclamation of the Governor of Syria, Mu'awiya, as Caliph, Syria became the centre of the Umayyad

Caliphate.[12] However, in the eighth century the Umayyad was replaced by the Abbasid Caliphate, with its capital in Baghdad. In consequence, Syria lost its place at the centre of the Islamic Empire.[13]

The conquest of geographical Syria by Muslim Arab armies did not have an immediate impact on the religious freedoms of its peoples, who were largely Christian.[14] The Arab conquests were predominantly economic in inspiration, and the new Muslim rulers were initially content to grant freedom of worship to both Christians and to Jews, who were treated as *dhimmi*, or subject peoples, whose privileges were contingent on the payment of a special tax.[15] However, in the ninth century, discrimination against Christians and Jews became more widespread. Inevitably, the rate of conversion to Islam rose in Syria.[16] However, the Maronite Christian community, which had settled in northern Lebanon at the beginning of the eighth century, remained loyal to their faith.[17] The Maronites had moved to the Lebanon from the Orontes valley in northern Syria, as a result of persecution by Christians outraged by their heretical beliefs.[18]

(The term 'Maronite' has been variously ascribed to John Maroun, a late seventh-century cleric, and the first Maronite patriarch, and to St Maron, a fourth-century Syrian monk.[19] Since the eighteenth century, the Maronites have been in union with Rome.[20])

The Muslims, who had swept into Syria in the seventh century, rapidly lost their united religious and political character. In particular, a schism had emerged between the majority, adherents of the Sunni sect, and a minority, the Shia. These divisions can be traced to the contest for the succession following the death of the Prophet in 632. Ali, a cousin and son-in-law of Muhammad, emerged as the fourth Caliph (following Abu Bakr and Uthman) and was succeeded briefly by his elder son, Hassan.[21] However, Hassan was forced to abdicate by Mu'awiya, the head of the Umayyad clan, who assumed the Caliphate.[22] Hussein, the younger son of Ali, refused to take an oath of allegiance to Mu'awiya's son and successor, Yazid.[223] Hussein's defiance led to the battle of Karbala at which Hussein, and a small band of followers, were killed.[24]

The Shia, or followers of Ali, are distinguished in part by their belief that, after the death of the Prophet, the succession passed to Ali and thereafter down through a line of hereditary Imams. Since the disappearance of the twelfth Imam, in the tenth century, the Shia have accepted the guidance of the *ulama*, or religious scholars. By contrast the Sunni, who comprise more than 80 per cent of Muslims, recognize the authority of successive caliphs.[25]

During the ninth century the Abbasid Caliphate began an inexorable decline. The period was characterized by an increase in religious heterodoxy. Muhammad ibn-Nusair, who died in the latter part of the ninth century, is generally credited with having founded the Nusairi or Alawite sect.[26] Their religious tenets, which are shrouded in secrecy, are alleged to include a belief in Ali as an incarnation of the deity.[27] Alawis constitute a significant element in the officer corps of the present-day Syrian army, and include President Hafez Assad and other prominent members of the Syrian Ba'ath Party.[28]

During the latter part of the tenth century the Fatimid Caliphate, with its capital in Cairo, established control over Syria.[29] The Fatimids adhered to the Isma'ili sect, which is derived from the Shia, and which is distinguished in part by the belief that religious truth can only be revealed to an elite following a period of instruction.[30]

The third Fatimid Caliph, al-Hakim, is revered by the Druze sect, an offshoot of the Isma'ilis.[31] The Druze are named after al-Darazi, an eleventh-century Turkish missionary who preached the new faith amongst the people of southern Lebanon.[32] By the time of the Crusades, the Druze community was also well-established in the Chouf mountains.[33]

The Crusades

The First Crusade was launched at the end of the eleventh century, following the call of Pope Urban II for the recovery of the Holy Land.[34] The Crusaders besieged Antioch, in the north-west of geographical Syria, occupying the city on 3 June 1098.[35] Moving southwards along the coast towards Acre, the Crusaders befriended the Maronite community.[36] On 15 July, the Crusaders entered Jerusalem, after a siege lasting one month, and established the Kingdom of Jerusalem.[37] During the following years, the Kingdom of Jerusalem gradually extended its control over the coastal towns of Jaffa, Caesarea, Haifa, Acre, Sidon and Beirut, and inland along a line roughly equivalent to the River Jordan.[38] To the south, it stretched as far as Aqaba.[39] In the north, three principalities were established centred on Tripoli, Antioch and Edessa, owing nominal allegiance to Jerusalem.[40]

However, the power of the Crusader kingdom began to wane towards the middle of the twelfth century. At the end of the thirteenth century, under repeated onslaughts from Mamluk armies, the Crusaders lost their last foothold in Syria.[41]

The Mamluks

Syria was governed by the Mamluk dynasty until conquest by the Ottoman Turks in the sixteenth century.[42] However, the region was beset by internal and external problems. At the end of the thirteenth century, the Druze, Shia and Nusairi communities rebelled briefly against the Mamluks in northern Lebanon.[43]

In the latter part of the fifteenth century, the Mamluks confronted the growing power of the Ottoman Turks, centred on Anatolia and Constantinople.[44] Fighting had erupted between the Mamluks and the Ottomans in 1486 over Adana, Tarsus and neighbouring towns.[45] However, hostilities between the two empires assumed more serious proportions in the first quarter of the sixteenth century. In August 1516, a Mamluk army was defeated by an Ottoman force north of Aleppo.[46] Aleppo and Damascus were occupied by the Ottomans in the same year, while Ottoman control was gradually extended over the whole of Syria.[47]

The Ottoman period

Following the Turkish conquest in 1516, Syria remained within the Ottoman Empire for over 400 years. Initially, the effects of Ottoman rule were limited. For administrative purposes, Syria was divided into two large *eyalets* centred on Damascus and Beirut.[48] Towards the end of the sixteenth century, a third *eyalet* was established with its centre in Tripoli; while in 1616, a fourth *eyalet* was constituted with its capital in Sidon.[49] However, the practicalities of day-to-day administration were often entrusted to local chieftains, through whom the Ottomans were content to rule, provided that they undertook the collection of taxes and the levying of troops, and that they swore an oath of allegiance.[50] This was notably the case in Mount Lebanon.[51] The principle of self-rule was further extended by reliance on the *millet* system.[52] The doctrine permitted religious communities, such as the Jews, the Maronites and the Druze, to be largely autonomous in civil and religious matters.[53]

The eighteenth century witnessed bitter conflicts in the Lebanon between rival Druze chieftains, prompting many Druze to emigrate to Jebel Druze in present-day Syria.[54] By contrast, the Christian population in central and southern Lebanon was gradually augmented.[55]

In 1788, Bashir Shihabi became Emir of the Lebanon. Despite intermittent opposition from Ahmad al-Jazzar, Governor of the *eyalets* of Sidon and Damascus, Bashir achieved considerable success in expanding the frontiers of the Lebanon and in extending its autonomy.[56]

As the eighteenth century drew to a close, the Ottoman Empire became increasingly enfeebled. Russia and Austria annexed Ottoman territory in Europe and central Asia, while the *Porte* faced mounting difficulties from its Christian subjects.[57] As Ottoman power continued its inexorable decline, intervention in Syria became more frequent. In 1798, a French army under Napoleon was despatched to Egypt, defeating the forces of the local Mamluk princes.[58] In the following year, the French extended their campaign along the Mediterranean coast, reaching Acre in March.[59] However, with the aid of a British fleet, Acre withstood the French siege, compelling Napoleon to order a retreat from Syria.[60] French forces were finally withdrawn from Egypt in 1801.[61]

The middle years of the nineteenth century were to prove critical in the history of the Lebanon. Smouldering tensions between Druze and Maronite communities, fuelled by a cynical Ottoman administration intent on extending its own power, resulted in clashes of mounting severity in 1841, 1845 and 1860.[62]

In 1860, fighting of unprecedented ferocity broke out, as Druze bands massacred Christians in Mount Lebanon.[63] The disturbances in the Lebanon precipitated a second wave of killing in Damascus, where a largely Muslim mob slaughtered thousands of Christians.[64] The carnage in Damascus was due, only in part, to events in the Lebanon. In large measure, it had its roots in Muslim resentment at the emancipation of the Christian subjects of the Ottoman Empire.[65]

In 1839, Sultan Abdul-Majid had issued the Gulhane Decree, in which he pledged to reform the system of taxation, and to safeguard the life, honour and property of his subjects.[66] Controversially, these commitments had been extended to all Ottoman subjects, irrespective of religion.[67] In 1856, after the Crimean War and under pressure from his European allies, the Sultan had issued the Reform Decree. This provided for Christian entry into the civil service and the army, and for improved Christian representation in provincial and local councils.[68] The Decree failed to inspire universal enthusiasm amongst the Empire's Christian subjects, while engendering considerable hostility amongst the Muslims.[69]

The disturbances in Syria provoked a twofold reaction. The Sultan, fearful of European anger, despatched Fuad Pasha, the Ottoman Foreign Minister, to Syria, together with a military force.[70] Fuad Pasha proceeded to Damascus, and then to Beirut, where he supervised the restitution of property to Christians, and the punishment of Muslims and Druzes who had been implicated in the disturbances.[71]

In Europe, the plight of the Lebanese Christians had evoked widespread indignation and had prompted the European Powers to agree, in August, to send a military force to assist in the restoration of order.[72] Six thousand French troops were duly despatched to the Lebanon, although as the disturbances had already been pacified, they occupied themselves with largely humanitarian tasks among the

Christian community.[73] The French troops were withdrawn in June 1861, under pressure from Britain and the Ottoman Sultan.[74]

European outrage had also led to the formation of an International Commission with the function of supervising the punishment of the instigators of the disturbances, ensuring adequate reparation for its victims, and proposing a new administrative system for the Lebanon.[75] Meeting in Beirut, and later in Constantinople, the Commission, comprising delegates from France, Great Britain, Russia, Prussia and Austria, submitted various proposals which formed the basis of the Beyoglu Protocol, signed by the Sultan and the European Powers in June, 1861. Significantly, and contrary to the wishes of a majority of the Commission, the territorial boundaries of the new Lebanese entity were severely curtailed. The fertile Bekaa valley, the district of Sidon and the city of Beirut were shorn from the Lebanon.[76]

Under the terms of the Beyoglu Protocol a new Lebanese Organic Statute was promulgated. This provided that Mount Lebanon should be administered by a Christian Governor *(mutasarrif)* who would be appointed by the *Porte* after consultations with the Signatory Powers. The Governor would be responsible directly to the *Porte*, and would be assisted by an administrative council composed of representatives from the various religious communities. Lebanon would have its own system of courts and locally recruited militia, while Ottoman forces would not be permitted to enter the territory.[77] The administrative reforms of 1861 were not altered until the First World War.

Two significant, and related, developments were to transform Syria during the remainder of the century. These were a steady increase in Western influence, particularly in the towns and amongst the Christian communities, and the gradual stirrings of Arab political consciousness.

Western influence in Syria can be traced back to the Capitulations granted to France, England and to various other powers by the *Porte* in the sixteenth century. In the wake of the Capitulations, French Catholic missionaries had established themselves in Syria, forging close links with the Maronite and other Uniate Christian communities. In time, France came to regard herself as the protector of Catholic interests in Syria and the 'Holy Land'.[78] For its part, Russia assumed a comparable position in relation to the Greek Orthodox subjects of the Ottoman Empire.[79] As a counterweight to French influence amongst the Maronites, Great Britain cultivated increasingly close links with the Druze community.[80]

European interest in Syria, and in the Ottoman Empire generally, was only partially spiritual. In addition to purely religious factors, France's involvement in Syria was bound up with commercial considerations, and with the imponderables of national prestige.[81] Russian interest was stimulated in large measure by the desire to secure warm-water ports in the eastern Mediterranean;[82] while Britain, mindful of her Indian possessions, was anxious to thwart Russia's strategic objectives.[83]

Commercial and trading links between Syria and various European states became increasingly pronounced during the nineteenth century. In particular, French and German firms played a leading part in the construction of roads and railways.[84]

Emigration, particularly of Lebanese Christians, also stimulated a larger awareness of the West,[85] while European and North American influence grew in the sphere of education. The origins of the latter can be traced to the seventeenth century with the establishment of schools by Catholic missionaries. However, the scale of Western involvement increased significantly in the nineteenth century. Various Catholic orders took an active part in the establishment of schools and colleges, while American Protestant foundations also exerted a major influence.[86] As the culmination of these activities, the Jesuits established the Université Saint-Joseph in Beirut in 1874, while American Protestants had some years previously founded a college which subsequently became the American University of Beirut.[87] Both Protestants and Catholics also contributed to the educational and social development of Syria through the establishment of printing presses.[88]

Western influence brought in its train secular concepts such as nationalism and democracy.[89] Arab political consciousness was also stimulated by a reawakening of interest in Arab literature, history and culture.[90] Muslim discontent with Ottoman rule in Syria, which had manifested itself as early as the 1850s, also fuelled interest in the ideology of Arab nationalism.[91]

Nevertheless, demands for Arab autonomy, and finally for independence, did not become widespread until the first decade of the twentieth century. In part, this may be explained by the underlying contradiction between nationalism, 'a time-bound set of principles related to the qualities and needs of a particular group of human beings', and Islam, 'an eternal, universalist message, drawing no distinction between its adherents except on the criterion of their piety'.[92] Thus, in the final decades of the nineteenth century, Sultan Abdul-Hamid II was able to retard the spread of Arab political consciousness by appealing for Islamic unity in the face of European expansionism.[93] As Professor Tibawi notes: '[t]here is no question that in the 1880's this Islamic movement had a stronger appeal to the majority of Syrians than any regional, racial or national movement that may then have been in the making'.[94]

In 1908, a mutiny amongst Ottoman army officers led, ultimately, to the deposition of Abdul-Hamid and to rule by the Committee of Union and Progress (CUP), imbued with a reformist and progressive ideology.[95] While many Arabs initially sympathized with the aims of the revolt, they were rapidly alienated by the increasingly nationalist and centralist character of the CUP's ideology.[96] Secret societies were formed calling for greater autonomy, or even for total independence, for the Arab peoples.[97] An Arab National Congress, held in Paris in June 1913, demanded greater autonomy for the Arabs of the Empire, and broader participation by the Arabs in its administration.[98]

However, Arab hopes of self-determination, particularly in Syria, were doomed to clash with increasingly forceful Jewish claims for a national existence in Palestine.[99] At the beginning of the nineteenth century, there were some 5000–6000 Jews living in Palestine. By the eve of the First World War, the Jewish community had grown to 85 000, largely as a result of emigration from Europe.[100]

Notes

1 See below, Chapter 3.
2 See e.g. Hourani, *Syria and Lebanon*, pp.4-5; Longrigg, *Syria and Lebanon*, p.1; Hitti, *Syria*, p.3; Ziadeh, *Syria and Lebanon*, p.13; Tibawi, *History of Syria*, p.19; Antonius, *Arab Awakening*, p.284. The term 'Palestine' is used here to designate present-day Israel, Gaza and the West Bank.
3 Hitti, *Syria*, p.703.
4 Longrigg, *Syria and Lebanon*, p.98.
5 See para. 1, Resolution of the General Syrian Congress at Damascus, 2 July 1919, reproduced in Hurewitz, *II*, p.180, at pp.180-1.
6 See, generally, Hitti, *Syria*, Chapters XI–XXVII.
7 For a description of Syria during the Byzantine period, see e.g. Hitti, *Syria*, Chapters XXVII–XXVIII.
8 See generally, Brockelmann, *Islamic Peoples*, pp.12-45.
9 J.B. Glubb, *The Great Arab Conquests*, (1980), pp.131-46, 149-60.
10 Ibid., pp.174-9.
11 Ibid., pp.180-4.
12 See generally Hitti, *Syria*, Chapters XXXIII–XL.
13 On the Abbasid Caliphate, see generally Brockelmann, *Islamic Peoples*, pp.107-31.
14 Christianity, which had its roots in geographical Syria, achieved accelerated recognition following the conversion of the Emperor Constantine and the adoption of Christianity as the official religion. See generally Hitti, *Syria*, pp.349-51. On the diverse Christian sects in Syria, see ibid., Chapter XXXIX.
15 Ibid., pp.419-20, 485-6.
16 Ibid., p.545.
17 See e.g. Randal, *Tragedy of Lebanon*, p.35.
18 Hitti, *Syria*, p.521.
19 See generally Hitti, *Syria*, pp.521-2.
20 Ibid., p.522.
21 See generally Brockelmann, *Islamic Peoples*, pp.45-71.
22 Ibid., pp.68-71.
23 Ibid., p.75.

24   Ibid., pp.75-6.
25   See generally on the theological tenets of the Sunni and the Shia, Mortimer, *Faith and Power*, pp.39-46. See also Ruthven, *Islam in the World*, Chapter 5. The term 'Sunni' means followers of 'Sunna', i.e. of tradition.
26   See e.g. Ruthven, *Islam in the World*, pp.218-19.
27   Ibid., pp.209-11.
28   See generally M.A. Faksh, 'The Alawi Community of Syria: A New Dominant Political Force', *MES*, vol. 20 (1984), p.133.
29 ' Brockelmann, *Islamic Peoples*, pp.160-2.
30   See generally Mortimer, *Faith and Power*, pp.47-8.
31   Ruthven, *Islam in the World*, pp.213-14.
32   Ibid., p.214.
33   See generally Hitti, *Syria*, pp.585-6.
34   Ibid., p.590.
35   Brockelmann, *Islamic Peoples*, p.221.
36   Hitti, *Syria*, p.594.
37   Ibid., p.595.
38   Ibid., pp.595-7.
39   Ibid., p.596.
40   Brockelmann, *Islamic Peoples*, pp.221-2.
41   P.K. Hitti, *History of the Arabs*, (10th edn 1970), pp.657-8.
42   See generally ibid., Chapters XLVII–XLIX.
43   See e.g. Hourani. *Syria and Lebanon*, pp.23-4.
44   On the origins, and history, of the Ottoman Turks see e.g. Shaw, *I*, Chapters 2–4. The Ottomans had occupied Constantinople in 1453 AD. See ibid., pp.56-7.
45   Ibid., p.73.
46   Ibid., p.84.
47   Brockelmann, *Islamic Peoples*, p.289.
48   See e.g. Lammens, *II*, p.55. Most authorities refer to Ottoman provinces, in the period before the Vilayet Law of 1864, as *Pasaliks* or as *eyalets*. Thereafter, they were known as *vilayets*. See e.g. R.C.H. Davison, *Reform in the Ottoman Empire 1856-1876*, 1973, p.146. See, also, Ma'oz, *Ottoman Reform in Syria*, pp.31-2.
49   Lammens, *II*, p.60.
50   Ibid., pp.65-6.
51   See e.g. Hitti, *Syria*, pp.665-6.
52   The term is based on the Arabic 'milla' meaning religion, or nationality.
53   See e.g. Shaw, *I*, pp.151-3.
54   Cobban, *Lebanon*, pp.39-40.
55   Lammens, *II*, pp.78, 93.
56   Salibi, *History of Lebanon*, Chapter II.
57   See generally Shaw, *I*, pp.257-60, 266-7.
58   Ibid., p.268.
59   Ibid.
60   Tibawi, *History of Syria*, pp.37-8.
61   Shaw, *I*, p.269.
62   The majority of sources attribute some responsibility to the Ottoman authorities for inciting the sectarian strife. See e.g. Hourani, *Syria and Lebanon*, p.31; Hitti, *Syria*, p.694; Brockelmann, *Islamic Peoples*, p.363; Ma'oz, *Ottoman Reform in Syria*, pp.235-8; Salibi, *History of Lebanon*, pp.45-6,50. For a contrasting view see e.g. Tibawi, *History of Syria*, pp.99-100.
63   The majority of sources suggest the active support, or at least acquiescence, of the Ottoman authorities in the massacres perpetrated by the Druze and Muslims

in 1860. See e.g. Brockelmann, *Islamic Peoples*, p.368; Hourani, *Syria and Lebanon*, p.32; Lammens, *II*, pp.181-3; Salibi, *History of Lebanon*, pp.98-105; Ma'oz, *Ottoman Reform in Syria*, pp.235-8. However, Tibawi argues that it was a lack of military resources, rather than of political will, that prevented the Ottoman administration from ending the massacres. Tibawi, *History of Syria*, pp.125-7.

64 See generally Shaw, *II*, p.143.
65 See e.g. Ma'oz, *Ottoman Reform in Syria*, p.231.
66 See generally Shaw, *II*, pp.59-61.
67 Ibid., p.61.
68 Ibid., pp.87, 100.
69 Tibawi, *History of Syria*, pp.118-20.
70 See e.g. Shaw, *II*, p.143.
71 See, generally, Tibawi, *History of Syria*, pp.130-1.
72 Shaw, *II*, p.143. See also Lammens, *II*, pp.183-4.
73 See generally, Lammens, *II*, pp.184-7. See also Salibi, *History of Lebanon*, pp.107-9. The French intervention has frequently been cited as an example, sometimes as the *only* example, of 'humanitarian intervention'. As understood by publicists, in the nineteenth and early twentieth centuries, this permits 'reliance upon force for the justifiable purpose of protecting the inhabitants of another state from treatment which is so arbitrary and persistently abusive as to exceed the limits of that authority within which the sovereign is presumed to act'. E.C. Stowell, *Intervention in International Law* (1921), p.53. However, history furnishes remarkably few instances of humanitarian intervention. States have generally invoked the doctrine when intervening, at bottom, because of commercial or strategic considerations. See e.g. Brownlie, *Use of Force*, pp.338-40. See also T.M. Franck and N. Rodley, 'After Bangladesh: the Law of Humanitarian Intervention by Military Force', *AJIL*, vol. 67 (1973), p.275, at pp.279-85. Even the French intervention in Syria is suspect. The decision to despatch a military force was taken *after* the disturbances in Syria had subsided, and in circumstances which suggest that French motives were probably ambivalent. See e.g. I. Pogany, 'Humanitarian Intervention in International Law: the French Intervention in Syria Re-examined', *ICLQ*, vol. 35 (1986), p.182, at pp.187-8. In addition, it is doubtful whether the deployment of French troops amounted to 'intervention' for the purposes of international law. See ibid., pp.188-90. Nevertheless, a large body of jurists currently accept the lawfulness of humanitarian intervention. These include the following: L. Oppenheim, *International Law* (8th edn 1955), vol. I, p.312; P. Guggenheim, *Traité de Droit International Public* (1953), vol. I, p.289; Bowett, *Self-Defence*, p.95. (However, Bowett has apparently changed his mind. See D. Bowett, 'The Interrelation of Theories of Intervention and Self-Defense', in J.N. Moore (ed.), *Law and Civil War in the Modern World* (1974), p.38, at p.45) R. Lillich, 'Intervention to Protect Human Rights', *McGill Law Journal*, vol. 15 (1969), p.205, at p.212; V. Nanda, 'The United States' Action in the 1965 Dominican Crisis: Impact on World Order – Part I', *Denver Law Journal*, vol. 43 (1966), p.439, at pp.477-8; M. Reisman and M.S. McDougal, 'Humanitarian Intervention to Protect the Ibos' in R.B. Lillich (ed.), *Humanitarian Intervention and the United Nations* (1973), p.167, at pp.171-8. However, it is noteworthy that, in the post-war period, states have consistently declined to cite humanitarian intervention as a justification for their use of armed force. See e.g. M. Akehurst, 'Humanitarian Intervention', in H. Bull (ed.), *Intervention in World Politics* (1984), p.95, at pp.96-9. Jurists rejecting the lawfulness of humanitarian intervention include the following:

Brownlie, *Use of Force*, p.342; Franck and Rodley, op. cit., pp.299-302; Akehurst, op. cit., pp.104-11.

74   Lammens, *II*, p.186. Two months after the French force arrived in the Lebanon, Britain expressed its 'insuperable objections' to a prolonged occupation, and recommended 'that the pacification of the country should be left entirely to the Turkish authorities'. C.H. Churchill, *The Druzes and the Maronites Under the Turkish Rule, from 1840 to 1860* (1862), p.251.

75   See e.g. Lammens, *II*, p.186.

76   Salibi, *History of Lebanon*, p.110.

77   Ibid., pp.110-11.

78   Lammens, *II*, pp.83-4.

79   Salibi, *History of Lebanon*, p.41.

80   Ibid., pp.57-8.

81   See generally Hitti, *Syria*, p.697.

82   See e.g. Mansfield, *Ottoman Empire*, p.10.

83   The opening of the Suez Canal, in 1869, greatly increased the strategic importance of the Mediterranean, prompting Britain to occupy Egypt. Mansfield, *Ottoman Empire*, p.10.

84   Hourani, *Syria and Lebanon*, pp.35-8. See also Tibawi, *History of Syria*, pp.135-6. For details of French commercial and trading links with the Ottoman Empire on the eve of the First World War, see W.I. Shorrock, 'The Origin of the French Mandate in Syria and Lebanon: The Railroad Question, 1901–1914', *IJMES*, vol. I (1970), p.133, at p.134. Shorrock notes that, by 1902, French companies were operating five railroad systems in Asia Minor, including lines between Jaffa and Jerusalem, and between Beirut and Damascus. Ibid., p.135. In addition, a French company had built the port of Beirut. Lammens, *II*, p.199. German financiers obtained a concession to construct a railway connecting Berlin and Baghdad. Shorrock, op. cit., p.135.

85   Hourani, *Syria and Lebanon*, pp.34-5.

86   Salibi, *History of Lebanon*, pp.130-40.

87   Hitti, *Syria*, p.701.

88   Ibid.

89   Hourani, *Syria and Lebanon*, p.39.

90   Antonius, *Arab Awakening*, pp.39-55.

91   Tibawi, *History of Syria*, pp.158-67.

92   H. Enayet, *Modern Islamic Political Thought* (1982), p.112. See also ibid., p.115.

93   Antonius, *Arab Awakening*, pp.68-71.

94   Tibawi, *History of Syria*, p.171.

95   Shaw, *II*, pp.273-9.

96   Antonius, *Arab Awakening*, pp.102-7.

97   Ibid., pp.108-12.

98   Ibid., pp.114-16.

99   The Programme adopted by the first World Zionist Congress in Basle, in 1897, stated that '[t]he aim of Zionism is to create for the Jewish people a home in Palestine secured by public law'. The Programme is reproduced in Moore, *III*, p.3.

100   See e.g. H.M. Sachar, *A History of Israel* (1977), pp.86, 88.

3 A History of the Lebanon, 1914–75

The First World War and the post-war settlement

The decision of the Ottoman Empire to ally itself with Germany in the First World War was to prove of decisive importance for the Lebanon. In a protracted correspondence with Sherif Hussein of Mecca, Sir Henry McMahon, the British High Commissioner in Egypt, pledged Britain's support for Arab independence after the war, thereby inciting the Arabs of the Near East to rebel against the Turks.[1] However, Sir Henry excluded present-day Lebanon, and the coastal strip of modern Syria, from the area intended for Arab independence. In a letter dated 24 October 1915, the British High Commissioner stated: '[t]he two districts of Mersina and Alexandretta and portions of Syria lying to the west of the districts of Damascus, Homs, Hama, and Aleppo cannot be said to be purely Arab and should be excluded from the limits demanded'.[2]

Sir Henry's circumspection was understandable. Following the outbreak of war, Great Britain and France had begun talks with a view to harmonizing their respective designs on the Arab provinces of the Ottoman Empire.[3] The French representative at these discussions, Georges-Picot, had already asserted France's claim to the whole of Syria.[4]

An agreement was initialled by the principal negotiators on 3 January 1916. It was endorsed by the British and French governments in the following month.[5] The Russian government, which was notified of the Anglo-French understanding, gave its approval in return for British and French pledges to support Russian claims in north-eastern Anatolia.[6]

The Sykes–Picot agreement provided that the coastal region of north-ern Syria, together with much of the hinterland including the Bekaa valley, would become a French sphere of influence in which France could institute 'such direct or indirect administration or control' as it wished.[7] For its part, the United Kingdom was 'accorded' the ports of Haifa and Acre, and an exclusive British sphere of influence around Baghdad, over which it could establish such control as it chose.[8] Jerusalem and the Holy Places were entrusted to 'an international administration', the form of which was to be decided upon 'after con-sultation with Russia, and subsequently in consultation with the other Allies, and the representatives of the Shereef of Mecca'.[9] Outside these areas, the Sykes–Picot agreement contemplated a form of qualified independence for the Arabs, in which Anglo-French interests would be safeguarded.[10]

Clearly, the terms of the Sykes–Picot agreement cannot be easily reconciled with the pledges made to Sherif Hussein by Sir Henry McMahon. Much of Palestine was removed entirely from the proposed area of Arab independence, together with the whole of the Lebanon.[11] In addition, the *degree* of sovereignty conceded to the Arabs in other areas was severely limited.

The uncertain course of the war during the winter of 1917 prompted the British government to issue the celebrated 'Balfour Declaration'. On 2 November 1917, the British Foreign Secretary, Lord Balfour, wrote to Lord Walter Lionel Rothschild, a convinced Zionist and a prominent member of the Jewish community of Great Britain, in the following terms:[12]

> His Majesty's Government view with favour the establishment in Palestine of a national home for the Jewish people, and will use their best endeavours to facilitate the achievement of this object, it being clearly understood that nothing shall be done which may prejudice the civil and religious rights of existing non-Jewish communities in Palestine, or the rights and political status enjoyed by Jews in any other country.

The Balfour Declaration was prompted by the desire to consolidate the support of the sizeable Jewish communities in Russia and the United States, which were believed to be overwhelmingly sympathetic to Zionism, for the Allied war effort.[13] The assistance of Russian Jewry was sought in order to counteract the flagging morale of the Russian armies, following the revolution in March. The support of

American Jews was seen as a means of precipitating the involvement of the United States in the war.[14] The Balfour Declaration, which favoured the establishment of 'a national home for the Jewish people' in Palestine, could be reconciled neither with the pledges made to Sherif Hussein, nor with the terms of the Sykes–Picot agreement.[15] Sir Henry McMahon had, arguably, included Palestine within the area intended for Arab independence, while the Sykes–Picot agreement envisaged an 'international administration' for the greater part of Palestine.

Arab troops were the first to enter Damascus, on 30 September 1918, after the withdrawal of Ottoman forces.[16] Feisal, the third son of Sherif Hussein, established his headquarters in Damascus and rapidly extended his authority over the inland areas of Syria and Transjordan.[17] However, the prospects for Arab independence, already weakened by the Sykes–Picot agreement and the Balfour Declaration, were eroded further by the decision of the Peace Conference, on 30 January 1919, to place the Arab provinces of the Ottoman Empire under the tutelage of the League of Nations, as mandated territories.[18]

On 6 February, Feisal appeared before the Peace Conference to demand independence for the Arabs. Acknowledging the interests of the Great Powers in Lebanon and Palestine, he indicated his willingness to accept some alternative arrangement for these territories.[19]

At the suggestion of President Wilson, the Supreme Council of the Peace Conference appointed an international commission to determine Arab wishes. Eventually known as the King–Crane Commission, after its two American members Henry C. King and Charles B. Crane, it confined its enquiries to Syria, submitting a report in August 1920.[20] The King–Crane Commission recommended that Syria should remain undivided and that it should become a League of Nations mandate, with Feisal as its constitutional monarch.[21] In the view of the Commissioners, there was a clear preference amongst the local population that, if Syria should be designated a mandate, the United States should become the mandatory power.[22] There was little support for France.[23]

While the King–Crane Commission was pursuing its enquiries, a General Syrian Congress was convened in Damascus, in June 1919. The delegates included representatives from the Lebanon and Palestine.[24] On 2 July, the Congress adopted a resolution in which it rejected attempts to delay Syrian independence calling, instead, for 'absolutely complete political independence for Syria' within boundaries encompassing present-day Lebanon, Syria, Jordan and Israel.[25] The resolution urged the establishment of a unitary state in Syria, with Feisal as its constitutional monarch.[26] The Congress was emphatic in its rejection of partition:[27]

We ask that there should be no separation of the southern part of Syria, known as Palestine, nor of the littoral western zone, which includes Lebanon, from the Syrian country. We desire that the unity of the country should be guaranteed against partition under whatever circumstances.

The General Syrian Congress was reconvened in Damascus at the beginning of March 1920.[28] On 7 March, the Congress adopted a resolution declaring the independence of Syria, including both Lebanon and Palestine, although the Lebanon was promised a measure of autonomy. Feisal was proclaimed King of the new Syrian state.[29]

The United Kingdom and France, incensed by the demands of the General Syrian Congress, jointly protested at the 'illegal' character of the resolutions.[30] The Supreme Allied Council was hastily called into session at San Remo, on 19 April, in order to achieve a final settlement of the Syrian question. The Conference resolved that Syria should become a French mandate, while Mesopotamia and Palestine should become British mandates.[31] A treaty incorporating these provisions was signed by a reluctant Ottoman government at Sèvres in August 1920, although it was never ratified.[32] The cession of the Arab provinces of the Ottoman Empire was ultimately achieved in July 1923, in accordance with the Treaty of Lausanne, negotiated with the newly-established Turkish nationalist government of Mustafa Kemal.[33]

News of the deliberations at San Remo led to attacks by Arab irregulars, operating under the nominal control of Feisal, against the French zone of occupation in Lebanon.[34] On 14 July 1920, General Gouraud, the French High Commissioner for Syria and the Lebanon, sent an ultimatum to Feisal, in which he demanded, *inter alia*, recognition of the French mandate, and punishment of the Arab irregulars who had attacked French forces. Although Feisal accepted the ultimatum, General Gouraud seized on a pretext to order the occupation of Damascus.[35] French forces secured Damascus on 25 July, and Feisal was sent into exile.[36]

With the occupation of Damascus, geographical Syria was effectively divided between France and Great Britain. The process of fragmentation was continued within the separate British and French spheres of influence. In August 1920, General Gouraud issued a decree creating the State of Greater Lebanon.[37] This was made up of the Ottoman *sanjaq* of Lebanon, together with the coastal cities of Beirut, Sidon, Tyre and Tripoli, the Bekaa, and the districts of Rashaya and Hasbaya.[38]

The effect of the French decree was to outrage the Arab nationalists who had proclaimed a united and independent Syria, and to create a demographic time-bomb.[39] General Gouraud's decree fatally weakened the relative homogeneity of the Lebanon. In the Ottoman *sanjaq* of Mount Lebanon there had been a substantial Christian majority, and a sizeable Druze minority.[40] Within the boundaries of Greater Lebanon, the Christians barely constituted a majority, while the Maronites comprised scarcely 30 per cent of the total population.[41] In addition to the Druzes, the other sizeable communities now included in the Lebanon were the Shia, who were established in the Bekaa valley and in southern Lebanon, and the large Sunni communities in Tripoli, Beirut and Sidon.[42]

Lebanon under the French mandate

France's mandate for Syria and Lebanon was governed by Article 22 of the League Covenant. This stated that the mandates system would apply to 'peoples not yet able to stand by themselves under the strenuous conditions of the modern world', whose well-being and development formed 'a sacred trust of civilisation'. In accordance with Article 22, responsibility for such peoples would be entrusted to 'advanced nations who, by reason of their resources, their experience, or their geographical position, can best undertake this responsibility, and who are willing to accept it'. In recognition of the relatively advanced character of some of the peoples who would be subject to a mandate, particularly in the Near East, Article 22 (4) stated: '[t]he wishes of these communities must be a principal consideration in the selection of the Mandatory'.

Certain ironies will already be apparent. While the mandates system was intended to apply to peoples 'not yet able to stand by themselves under the strenuous conditions of the modern world', the more backward regions of the Arab sub-continent were readily conceded full independence, while the most advanced were relegated to the status of mandates. Thus, in January 1917, Britain and France recognized Sherif Hussein as king of the Hejaz, while much of the remainder of the Arabian peninsula was left under the control of Ibn Saud.[43] In January 1926, after a successful military campaign against Hussein, Ibn Saud was proclaimed King of the Hejaz. In 1932, he was recognized as King of Saudi Arabia.[44]

A further irony lay in the Covenant's stipulation that the wishes of the people living in the mandated territories 'must be a principal consideration in the selection of the Mandatory'.[45] As noted previously, the King–Crane Commission found in Syria and the Lebanon that 'more than 60 per cent of all the petitions, presented to the Commission, directly and strongly protested against any French Mandate'.[46]

Nevertheless, the French mandate made some concessions to Syrian aspirations for independence. France was required, within three years, to frame 'an organic law for Syria and the Lebanon . . . in agreement with the native authorities' and taking account of the 'wishes of all the population inhabiting the said territory'.[47] In addition, the Mandatory was required to 'enact measures to facilitate the progressive development of Syria and the Lebanon as independent states' and to encourage local autonomy 'as far as circumstances permit'.[48]

France was subject to regular scrutiny in the discharge of its mandate. Thus, Article 17 stated: '[t]he Mandatory shall make to the Council of the League of Nations an annual report to the satisfaction of the Council as to the measures taken during the year to carry out the provisions of this mandate'.[49] This was consistent with Article 22 (7) of the League Covenant which provided '[i]n every case of Mandate, the Mandatory shall render to the Council an annual report in reference to the territory committed to its charge'. Examination of the reports was the responsibility of a specially constituted body, the Permanent Mandates Commission.[50]

The mandate for Syria and the Lebanon was formally approved by the Council of the League of Nations in July 1922, and entered into force in the following year.[51] However, anticipating the final form of the mandate, France had already initiated the process of 'local autonomy' within geographical Syria. As noted above, the French High Commissioner in Syria and the Lebanon had issued a decree, in August 1920, creating Greater Lebanon, a state encompassing the Ottoman *sanjaq* of Lebanon, together with the major coastal cities, the Bekaa, and the district of Wadi al-Taym.[52]

In May 1926, after a constitution had been drafted, Greater Lebanon became the Lebanese Republic.[53] The constitution provided for a bicameral Parliament, a President and a Prime Minister. However, it did little to impinge on the reality of French control over the Lebanon.[54]

The principle of 'local autonomy' was also applied within Syria. In September 1920, France established the states of Aleppo and Damascus, and the Territory of the Alawis.[55] In April 1922, Jebel Druze, with its predominantly Druze population, was declared independent.[56]

During the following years, the Lebanon retained its separate existence. However, the other states which had been established by France, in the period 1920–22, underwent successive changes.[57]

France's decision to divide Syria into a number of smaller units has been ascribed to various motives. In part, it was no doubt a response to Article 1 of the mandate, which called on the Mandatory to 'encourage local autonomy'.[58] In part, however, it was seen as a means of discouraging Arab nationalism, and of facilitating French control over Syria.[59]

French authoritarianism failed to quell the growing tide of nationalism in Syria and the Lebanon. In 1925, there was a serious revolt in Jebel Druze which spread to Damascus and to other parts of Syria.[60] In the early 1930s, a number of political parties were established. These included the Syrian National Party, the League of National Action and a youth movement, the Phalanges Libanaises.[61]

In 1936, following a politically motivated general strike in the major Syrian towns, the French government negotiated treaties with Syria and the Lebanon.[62] The treaties were intended to define relations between France and her mandates, once the latter had attained full independence, and were to enter into force three years after ratification.[63]

The conclusion of the Franco-Lebanese treaty provoked considerable anger amongst the Sunni population of the Lebanon, who had hoped for union with Syria. The Maronites, by contrast, viewed the treaty with satisfaction.[64] In Syria, a newly-elected Chamber of Deputies approved the treaty with France.[65] However, relations between France and Syria deteriorated rapidly as a result, in particular, of French concessions to Turkey in Alexandretta, a district in north-western Syria with a substantial Turkish minority.[66] The Syrian President resigned in July 1939, prompting the French High Commissioner to dissolve the Chamber of Deputies and to suspend the Syrian Constitution.[67] After the outbreak of war, in September 1939, the French High Commissioner suspended the Lebanese Constitution.[68]

On 8 June 1941, a combined British and Free French force invaded Syria and the Lebanon, ousting the Vichy administration.[69] In a proclamation issued the same day, on behalf of the Free French government, General Catroux declared 'je viens mettre fin au régime du mandat et vous proclame libres et indépendants'.[70]

In 1943 the Free French authorities decided to reactivate the Syrian and Lebanese Constitutions, which had been suspended in 1939, and to hold elections leading to the restoration of legislative institutions and to the formation of governments. In due course, Shukri al-Quwatli was elected President of the Syrian Republic, while Sa'dallah al-Jabiri became Prime Minister. In the Lebanon a Maronite Christian, Bishara Khoury, assumed the presidency and a Sunni Muslim, Riad Solh, was appointed Prime Minister.[71]

Bishara Khoury and Riad Solh had jointly negotiated the 'National Pact', an unwritten agreement laying the foundations of Muslim-Christian cooperation in post-independence Lebanon.[72] The Pact constituted an ingenious balance between Muslim and Christian aspirations in matters of domestic and foreign policy. Thus, the Pact stipulated that the Lebanon should not ally itself with any European power, nor enter into a union with an Arab state.[73] Public offices were to be distributed in accordance with the notional size of the various communities; the President was to be a Maronite Christian, the Prime Minister a Sunni Muslim, the Speaker of the Chamber of Deputies a Shia. Seats within the Chamber of Deputies were to be allocated on the basis of six Christian seats for every five Muslim places.[74]

The essence of the Pact was outlined to the Lebanese Chamber of Deputies by Prime Minister Riad Solh on 7 October 1943. The Pact, as a commentator has noted, indicated that the 'Lebanese polity was not based on the presumed existence of a Lebanese nation but on a confederation of protonational communities, each of which claimed the ultimate allegiance of its members'.[75]

French and British troops were gradually withdrawn from Syria and the Lebanon, although French dilatoriness prompted the two former mandates to bring the matter before the UN Security Council.[76] Although the Council failed to adopt a resolution on the matter, there was a clear consensus amongst the members that British and French forces should withdraw.[77] Under persistent international pressure, French troops were withdrawn from Syria by April 1946. French forces finally left the Lebanon in August of the same year.[78]

Lebanon, 1946–58

Lebanon's first years of independence were clouded by widespread corruption during the parliamentary elections in 1947, and by the amendment of the Constitution in order to allow President Khoury to serve for a second term.[79] These practices alienated many Muslims, and also a significant number of prominent Maronites, including Camille Chamoun.[80] Lebanon's stability was also threatened by the increasingly strained relations between the two architects of the National Pact, President Bishara Khoury and his Prime Minister, Riad Solh.[81]

Lebanon was also embroiled in the unfolding conflict over Palestine. On 2 April 1947 the United Kingdom, as the Mandatory power with responsibility for Palestine, had placed the Palestine question before the United Nations General Assembly.[82] The British decision was prompted by the increasingly onerous burden of maintaining order in Palestine, and by a sense of hopelessness in the face of the irreconcilable aspirations of Palestine's Arab and Jewish communities.[83]

On 29 November 1947, the General Assembly adopted a resolution in which it called for the partition of Palestine into Arab and Jewish states, linked together in an economic union. Jerusalem was to be placed under a special international regime.[84] The British Colonial

Secretary announced in the House of Commons, on 11 December 1947, '[t]he decision of the Assembly is regarded by His Majesty's Government as the decision of a court of international opinion.' He stated that Great Britain would surrender the mandate by 15 May 1948.[85]

On the afternoon of 14 May 1948, Jewish authorities in Tel Aviv proclaimed the establishment of the State of Israel.[86] On the following day, units of the Lebanese, Egyptian, Syrian, Iraqi and Transjordanian armed forces invaded Palestine with the object of crushing the nascent Jewish state.[87] The Arab armies were almost wholly unsuccessful. With the exception of Iraq, the Arab states were compelled to conclude armistice agreements with Israel.[88] The war had been disastrous for Lebanon. In addition to the trauma of defeat, Lebanon was faced with the task of absorbing some 140 000 Palestinian refugees, who had been displaced from Palestine as a result of the fighting.[89]

In September 1952, a general strike forced Bishara Khoury to resign.[90] He was replaced by Camille Chamoun, under whose *laissez-faire* economic policies the Lebanese economy prospered, bringing a general improvement in living standards.[91] Nevertheless, the underlying cleavage in Lebanese society between the Arab-oriented Muslim population, and the Western-looking Maronite community could not be bridged.[92] The cleavage was accentuated by Egypt's charismatic President, Gamal Abdel Nasser, who had a substantial following amongst Lebanon's Sunni Muslim population.[93]

The establishment of a United Arab Republic by Syria and Egypt, in February 1958, bolstered the Arab consciousness of Lebanon's Muslims, while accentuating the fears of her Christian population.[94] Divisions between Christians and Muslims were also exacerbated by the stridently pro-Western and anti-Nasser foreign policy of President Chamoun.[95] Thus, Chamoun refused to censure the Anglo-French intervention in Suez, and readily espoused the Eisenhower Doctrine, which involved the offer of United States military and financial assistance to any country in the Middle East 'requesting such aid against overt aggression from any nation controlled by international communism'.[96] Chamoun's policies led, inevitably, to increasing friction with the United Arab Republic.[97]

Passions were seriously inflamed by the President's alleged resort to fraud during the general elections of 1957.[98] Several prominent and popular politicians who had opposed Chamoun, including the Sunni Saeb Salam, the Druze Kamal Jumblatt and the Shia Ahmad Assad, failed to secure re-election.[99] However, opposition to Chamoun was not purely on confessional lines. During the course of his administration, the President antagonized a number of prominent Maronites, including the Maronite Patriarch, Paul Meouchi.[100]

The murder, on 8 May 1958, of Nasib al-Matni, the proprietor of a Beirut newspaper which had been consistently critical of the Chamoun administration, finally led to civil war.[101] The mainly Muslim United National Front declared a national strike and called for the resignation of President Chamoun.[102] In both Tripoli and Beirut, clashes occurred between demonstrators and security forces.[103] Gradually, the fighting spread throughout the whole country.[104] The army, under General Shihab, avoided extensive involvement in the disturbances.[105] Instead, the government relied on the police, the gendarmerie, the para-military Phalange, and the Syrian Social Nationalist Party.[106]

On 21 May the Lebanese government, claiming that the conflict had been instigated by the United Arab Republic, referred the matter to the Council of the Arab League.[107] On the following day, Lebanon called for an urgent meeting of the UN Security Council.[108]

The League Council was convened on 31 May, holding six sessions to consider the Lebanese complaint. However, the Council failed to adopt a resolution due to a lack of consensus.[109] On 6 June, once it had become clear that the League would be unable to take any action, the UN Security Council met to consider the Lebanese complaint.[110] On 11 June, the Security Council adopted a resolution in which it decided 'to dispatch urgently an observation group to proceed to Lebanon so as to ensure that there is no illegal infiltration of personnel or other *matériel* across the Lebanese borders'.[111] The hastily constituted observer group, known as the United Nations Observer Group in the Lebanon (UNOGIL), submitted a report on 3 July, which failed to confirm the Lebanese contention that the United Arab Republic was lending massive support to the rebels.[112]

On 14 July, army officers in Iraq overthrew the pro-Western régime of King Feisal, and proclaimed a republic.[113] Fearing the rapid erosion of American interests in the Middle East, the US government readily responded to a request for military assistance from Lebanon's President Chamoun. US marines landed in Beirut on 15 July.[114] In view of the importance of the issues raised, the legality of the American intervention will be examined in some detail.

International law and the American intervention in the Lebanon

At successive meetings of the Security Council, between 15 and 22 July, the United States argued that its action constituted collective self-defence in accordance with Article 51 of the Charter.[115] For example, on 15 July, Ambassador Lodge contended:[116]

> Now we confront here a situation involving outside involvement in an internal revolt against the authorities of the legitimate

Government of Lebanon. Under these conditions, the request from the Government of Lebanon to another Member of the United Nations to come to its assistance is entirely consistent with the provisions and purposes of the United Nations Charter. In this situation, therefore, we are proceeding in accordance with the traditional rules of international law, none of which in any way inhibits action of a character which the United States is undertaking in Lebanon.

Ambassador Azkoul of the Lebanon also claimed that the disturbances were not wholly domestic in character:[117]

[c]onvoys of armed men and arms have been reported entering Lebanon from Syria and while the world has been pacified by press reports describing the situation as one approaching calm, clandestine preparations have been under way for the launching of a great offensive designed to overthrow the Lebanese Government.

Ambassador Azkoul confirmed that the Lebanese government had requested the assistance of US troops, in accordance with Article 51 of the Charter:[118]

the Lebanese Government has decided, in view of the immediacy of the threat to Lebanon's independence and to the maintenance of international peace and security in the Middle East . . . to rely on Article 51 of the Charter, which recognizes the inherent right of individual or collective self-defence. Consequently, the Lebanese Government has asked for direct assistance from friendly countries.

The lawfulness of the American action was defended by the United Kingdom, France, Canada and China.[119] However, the American measures came under criticism from Ambassador Sobolev of the Soviet Union. The Soviet delegate rejected the view that there had been external involvement in the Lebanese crisis, and characterized the American action as 'an act of aggression against the peoples of the Arab world and a case of gross intervention in the domestic affairs of the countries of that area'.[120] Ambassador Sobolev argued: '[n]o one has attacked Lebanon and there is no threat of an armed attack against Lebanon'.[121] Similarly Ambassador Loutfi, of the UAR, contended that 'the Lebanese problem is a domestic issue concerning only the Lebanese themselves'.[122] The UAR representative stated that the American intervention was incompatible with the Charter, as 'Article

51 mentions armed attack as a condition for its application'.[123] Criticism of the American operation also came from Sweden. Ambassador Jarring stated:[124]

> [o]ne of the conditions for Article 51 of the Charter to be applicable is that an armed attack has occurred against a Member State. The Swedish Government does not consider that this condition has been fulfilled in the present case, nor does my Government consider that there is an international conflict in the terms of Article 51.

The US intervention raises questions of fact and of law. In terms of the former, it is necessary to establish whether the Lebanese conflict was of a purely 'domestic' character as claimed by the USSR and by the United Arab Republic. In terms of the latter, the US operation must be assessed in the light of the concept of collective self-defence and the rules governing intervention in civil conflicts.[125]

The nature of the conflict   As stated previously, UNOGIL's first report, dated 3 July, did not disclose that armed men, or weapons, had been infiltrated into the Lebanon from the United Arab Republic. UNOGIL noted the presence of armed men, and of quantities of weapons, at various locations in the Lebanon. However, the Observer Group stated: '[i]t has not been possible to establish where these arms were acquired. . . . Nor was it possible to establish if any of the armed men observed had infiltrated from outside.'[126]

In part, the findings in UNOGIL's first report must be read in the light of the Group's failure to deploy effectively in Lebanese territory contiguous to the border with the United Arab Republic.[127] However, an interim report, dated 15 July, noted that the Group had achieved 'full freedom of access to all sections of the Lebanese frontier'.[128] The report did not indicate that either arms or men were being infiltrated into the Lebanon from the United Arab Republic. In addition, the Group concluded, in a report dated 30 July, that the infiltration of arms 'cannot be on anything more than a limited scale' and that 'in no case have United Nations observers, who have been vigilantly patrolling the opposition-held areas and have frequently observed the armed bands there, been able to detect the presence of persons who had indubitably entered from across the border for the purpose of fighting'.[129]

However, it should be borne in mind that the measures of observation instituted by UNOGIL were condemned as unsatisfactory by the Lebanese government.[130] It is also significant that numerous commentators have concluded that, while the claims of the Lebanese government may have been exaggerated, the government was substantially correct in alleging the complicity of the UAR in the infiltration of armed men and of weapons into the Lebanon.[131]

Materials contained in the UN Archives, in New York, confirm the reservations which have been expressed concerning the efficacy of UNOGIL's operations. In particular, they disclose that a significant number of UNOGIL's military observers lacked proficiency in English, the working language of the Group, or competence in handling jeeps in rugged country, of the type encountered along Lebanon's border with Syria.[132] In addition, the Archives reveal that UNOGIL's Air Observers were instructed to observe stringent rules regarding the minimum height of aerial reconnaissance flights.[133] Such rules, while clearly conducive to the safety of the Observers, may have detracted from the reliability of their observation.

Self–defence in international law   On the assumption that the United Arab Republic was involved in infiltrating armed men and weapons into the Lebanon, it is necessary to establish whether this was sufficient to permit the United States to respond to a request for military assistance from the Lebanese government. Article 51 of the UN Charter recognizes the right of individual and collective self-defence:

> Nothing in the present Charter shall impair the inherent right of individual or collective self-defence if an armed attack occurs against a Member of the United Nations, until the Security Council has taken measures necessary to maintain international peace and security.

In order to determine whether the US measures amounted to a legitimate application of the doctrine of collective self-defence the following issues must be examined:

1 Did the infiltration of armed men and of weapons into the Lebanon amount to an 'armed attack', or otherwise entitle the Lebanon to respond in self-defence? If the circumstances did not give rise to a right of *individual* self-defence on the part of the Lebanon, the US could not rely on a right of *collective* self-defence to justify its intervention.

2 Were the measures taken by the Security Council, prior to the US intervention, such as were 'necessary to maintain international peace and security' for the purposes of Article 51? If so, neither the Lebanon nor the United States could claim a continuing right of self-defence. A further and related question is whether the Security Council alone is competent to determine whether the necessary measures have been taken, or whether the state which is exercising the right of self-defence may decide for itself.

3 Was the US intervention consistent with the doctrine of collective self-defence as understood in international law? Even though the Lebanon may have enjoyed a right of individual self-defence, it does not follow automatically that the US, or any other State, was entitled to assist the Lebanon.
4 Even if the above issues are resolved, it remains necessary to determine whether the Lebanese conflict was of such a character as to preclude foreign intervention. The UAR and the Soviet Union argued that the US measures amounted to unlawful intervention in a civil conflict. It is therefore important to establish whether the US action was compatible with the law governing intervention in civil wars.

Was the Lebanon entitled to exercise self-defence?   Any attempt to answer this question is complicated by the lack of consensus amongst jurists concerning the nature and scope of the right of self-defence. In essence, international lawyers are divided between those who believe that Article 51 of the Charter is constitutive of the right of self-defence,[134] and those who argue that the Charter reaffirms the 'inherent' right of self-defence as founded on customary norms, which continues 'except in so far as obligations inconsistent with those existing rights are assumed under the Charter'.[135]

For those adhering to the former view, it would be necessary to demonstrate that the infiltration of armed men and of weapons amounted to an 'armed attack', thereby permitting the Lebanon to respond in self-defence. The Charter itself does not indicate whether an 'armed attack' may encompass measures of support for armed bands which are infiltrated into another state. Nevertheless, there is substantial support in both state practice and in the writings of publicists for the view that the term 'armed attack' should be interpreted broadly. Thus Professor Brownlie, generally a stern critic of forcible self-help, comments 'a co-ordinated and general campaign by powerful bands of irregulars, with obvious or easily proven complicity of the government of a state from which they operate, would constitute an "armed attack".'[136]

State practice which can be furnished in support of the proposition that an 'armed attack' encompasses support for, or even acquiescence towards, armed bands which infiltrate across the borders of a state and engage in subversion, may be found in the Middle East, and elsewhere. In June 1982 at the start of Operation 'Peace for Galilee', whose declared objective was the removal of Palestinian guerrillas from southern Lebanon, Israel's Ambassador to the UN stated:[137]

Faced with intolerable provocations, repeated aggression and harassment, Israel has now been forced to exercise its right of self-defence, to arrest the never-ending cycle of attacks against Israel's northern border.

In 1947, at the height of the civil war in Greece, the Greek delegate to the General Assembly characterized the support of Albania, Bulgaria and Yugoslavia for the Greek rebels as an attack against Greece.[138] In 1958, the Lebanese and Jordanian reaction to the UAR's alleged support for rebels may also be cited.

No attempt has been made here to draw analogies between Article 51 and Article 2 (4) of the Charter, which proscribes 'the threat or use of force' by UN members. Article 2(4) has frequently been interpreted as proscribing not merely an attack by regular forces, but also support for armed bands which are infiltrated into another state.[139] However, it is important to recognize that Articles 2(4) and 51 are not coterminous. As Professor Brownlie has commented:[140]

the prohibition in Article 2, paragraph 4, is in absolute terms and the delegations at San Francisco regarded it in this light: any use of force was to be authorized by the Organization and any proviso, implied or express, as to self-defence, was understood to be an exceptional right, a privilege. The whole object of the Charter was to render unilateral use of force, even in self-defence, subject to control by the Organization. . .

On the assumption that the right of self-defence is defined by general international law, rather than by the Charter, it is unnecessary to demonstrate that the UAR's support for armed bands operating in the Lebanon amounted to an 'armed attack'. Instead, it is sufficient to show that the measures taken by the United Arab Republic amounted to a 'forcible threat' to the Lebanon's 'legal rights'.[141] These include the rights of territorial integrity and of political independence.[142] Manifestly, the UAR's support for armed bands operating in the Lebanon against the government and the security forces constituted a serious infringement of Lebanon's territorial integrity and political independence.

In addition to the existence of an 'armed attack', or of a 'forcible threat' to the Lebanon's 'legal rights', there is also a requirement of 'necessity'. Thus, a state may only resort to force in self-defence if there are no satisfactory non-forcible means by which it can assure its defence.[143] In view of the Lebanon's earlier efforts to invoke the assistance of the Arab League and of the UN Security Council, in persuading the UAR to withdraw its support for the Lebanese insurgents, the Lebanon had plainly exhausted all peaceful means at its disposal.

Had the Security Council taken the measures necessary to maintain international peace and security?   In accordance with Article 51 of the Charter, states may only exercise the right of self-defence 'until the Security Council has taken the measures necessary to maintain international peace and security'. It is therefore necessary to determine whether, when the American intervention was initiated, the Security Council had already taken the measures 'necessary to maintain international peace and security' and whether, accordingly, the right of self-defence, both individual and collective, had already lapsed.

Ambassador Azkoul of the Lebanon argued that his government enjoyed complete discretion in deciding whether the Security Council had taken the necessary measures: '[i]t is understood that it rests entirely with the Lebanese Government to decide whether or not the measures taken are adequate'.[144] However, Ambassador Sobolev of the USSR expressed the view that the Council had already taken the necessary measures and that the right of self-help had thus been extinguished:[145]

> It is true that the Charter provides for the right of individual or collective self-defence if an armed attack occurs against a Member of the United Nations until the Security Council has taken the measures necessary to maintain international peace and security. But in this case the situation is quite different. The Security Council is taking action in Lebanon. It has taken a decision which makes possible a settlement of the situation in that country.

The Russian view was supported by the representative of the United Arab Republic.[146]

The Lebanese view is scarcely tenable. Each state cannot be free to determine for itself whether the Security Council has taken the 'measures necessary to maintain international peace and security'. Such a situation would undermine the utility of the United Nations.[147] Nevertheless, the Council failed to condemn the US intervention.[148] In these circumstances, it cannot be stated with any degree of assurance that the Security Council had taken 'the measures necessary to maintain international peace and security' and that the right of individual or collective self-defence had therefore lapsed.

Was the US intervention consistent with the doctrine of collective self-defence?   Both the Lebanon and the United States argued before the Security Council that the American intervention constituted collective self-defence, in accordance with Article 51 of the Charter. While the doctrine of collective self-defence is recognized in Article 51, the parameters of the right have been the subject of controversy.

Professor Bowett argues for a restrictive interpretation: '[t]he requirements of the right of collective self-defence are two in number; firstly
that each participating state has an individual right of self-defence,
and secondly that there exists an agreement between participating
states to exercise their rights collectively.'[149] Thus, Professor Bowett
rejects the view that one state may invoke the doctrine of collective
self-defence merely to lend armed assistance to another state which
is exercising its right of self-defence:[150]

> on such a view 'collective self-defence' becomes assistance by one
> state, not itself possessing any right of self-defence, to another
> state which *may* be exercising the right of self-defence. The range
> of individual state action, permissible without prior authorization
> by a competent organ of the United Nations, becomes almost
> unlimited on this hypothesis. It cannot be a view consistent with
> the whole system of the Charter.

Nevertheless, Professor Bowett concedes that geographical, economic,
strategic or political links may be so close between two or more
states that an attack on one threatens the security of the other,
thereby legitimating a response in collective self-defence.[151] Professor
Bowett concludes: 'the important question is always, in final analysis,
whether an attack upon one state in fact threatens the security of the
other.'[152] On this view, the US intervention in the Lebanon cannot be
justified as collective self-defence. The infiltration of armed men and
of weapons into the Lebanon, by the United Arab Republic, cannot
be characterized as a serious threat to the security of the United States.

However numerous jurists, and a large body of state practice,
suggest that a broader construction of the doctrine of collective
self-defence may be appropriate. Goodrich, Hambro and Simons, in
their commentary on the UN Charter, conclude: 'it is clear from the
discussions at San Francisco and the practice of member states since
then that the right of collective self-defence is interpreted to justify
collective measures taken by some states in support of another state that
is the sole victim of an armed attack.'[153] It is also significant that the
principal reason for the inclusion of Article 51 in the Charter was to
legitimate regional collective security arrangements, such as the Treaty
of Chapultepec, which provides that an attack by a non-American state
against an American state 'shall be considered as an act of aggression
against all American States'.[154]

Collective security arrangements concluded since 1945 have also
relied expressly on the right of collective self-defence contained in
Article 51.[155] Thus, Article 5 of the North Atlantic Treaty, conclud

> The parties agree that an armed attack against one or more of them in Europe or North America shall be considered as an attack against them all; and consequently they agree that, if such an armed attack occurs, each of them, in exercise of the right of individual or collective self-defence recognized by Article 51 of the Charter of the United Nations, will assist the Party or Parties so attacked by taking forthwith, individually and in concert with the other Parties, such action as it deems necessary, including the use of armed force. . .

Similarly, Article 3(1) of the Inter-American Treaty of Reciprocal Assistance, concluded in 1947, states:[157]

> The High Contracting Parties agree that an armed attack by any State against an American State shall be considered as an attack against all the American States and, consequently, each one of the said Contracting Parties undertakes to assist in meeting the attack in the exercise of the inherent right of individual or collective self-defence recognised by Article 51 of the Charter of the United Nations.

Adopting this broader construction of the doctrine of collective self-defence, it would seem that the American intervention was lawful in so far as Lebanon was the victim of an armed attack, or was otherwise entitled to exercise the right of self-defence.

Was the US operation an unlawful intervention in a civil conflict? The legitimacy of the US action was questioned by the United Arab Republic and by the Soviet Union on the grounds, *inter alia*, that the Lebanese crisis was a purely domestic conflict. Ambassador Loutfi of the UAR commented; 'what is happening in Lebanon is a civil war and therefore a purely Lebanese problem.'[158] Ambassador Sobolev, of the Soviet Union, stated:[159]

> There is in fact a state of civil war in Lebanon . . . In these circumstances, the sending of US troops to Lebanon is an act of aggression against the peoples of the Arab world and a case of gross intervention in the domestic affairs of the countries of that area.

However, this argument is legally and factually suspect. It is far from well-established, in international law, that a government is precluded from seeking foreign aid to deal with an insurrection;[160] nor is it clear that the 1958 Lebanese crisis was a civil conflict in the ordinary sense. As noted previously, the United Arab Republic was actively involved in infiltrating armed men and weapons into the Lebanon. Thus, the Lebanese conflict cannot be characterized as a purely domestic affair.

There is substantial support in state practice, and in the academic literature, for the proposition that a government may lawfully request foreign assistance in order to counter a threat from rebels who are supported by an outside power. Thus, Professor Higgins has commented: 'if there is evidence of support of the insurgents from foreign states, the government may call for help from a foreign Power itself, even if the fighting on its territory has reached the dimensions of a civil war.'[161] This was clearly the understanding of the British government in 1958. In a statement to the House of Commons, concerning the US intervention in the Lebanon, the Prime Minister concluded:[162]

> A legitimate Government have, it seems to me, the right to ask for help in their difficulties from another friendly Government . . . I do not think that there is anything legally improper for a nation faced either with aggression from outside, or with internal disturbances supported from outside, to ask for help.

Comparing the Lebanese and Jordanian crises of that year, the Prime Minister commented:[163]

> The situations are . . . similar . . . in both cases legitimate, friendly Governments requested military assistance from their friends so as to enable them to preserve the independence and integrity of their countries. In both cases, these small countries were threatened with aggression organised from outside. . .

On balance, therefore, it would seem that the US intervention in the Lebanon constituted a legitimate application of the doctrine of collective self-defence.[164]

Lebanon, 1958–75

The Lebanese crisis gradually eased after President Chamoun indicated that he would not offer himself for re-election and after the Chamber of Deputies, meeting in July, had elected General Shihab to the presidency. A government was formed under Rashid Karami, in September.[165] American forces were withdrawn from the Lebanon by 25 October.

On 17 November, UNOGIL reported '[i]n view of the absence for some time of any reports of infiltration of personnel or smuggling of arms and of the recent marked improvement in the general security situation in Lebanon, and in relations between Lebanon and its eastern neighbour, the Group has come to the conclusion that its task . . . may now be regarded as completed.'[166] On the same day, a letter from Lebanon's Foreign Minister, to the President of the Security Council, had stated: 'cordial and close relations between Lebanon and the United Arab Republic have resumed their normal course' and requested that the Lebanese complaint be removed from the Council's agenda.[167] UNOGIL was withdrawn from the Lebanon by 9 December.[168]

Throughout his presidency, General Shihab endeavoured to reform the administrative and political infrastructure of the Lebanon, to improve public education and to introduce roads and basic amenities to the more backward areas of the country, where the Shia formed a majority.[169] Ironically, these policies had the effect, in part, of fuelling discontent amongst the rural poor, who began to migrate to Beirut in large numbers, in search of improved opportunities.[170] Nevertheless, President Shihab remained broadly popular with Lebanon's Muslims, particularly on account of his shrewdly pro-Nasser foreign policy.[171]

Charles Helou, General Shihab's successor, was elected to the presidency in 1964. He tried to continue his predecessor's policies, although he lacked President Shihab's political power-base and personal authority.[172]

The June War of 1967 seriously undermined the painstaking efforts of President Shihab, and of Charles Helou, to create a *modus vivendi* between Lebanon's disparate communities. In six days, Israeli forces inflicted a crushing defeat on the armies of Egypt, Syria and Jordan, occupying Sinai, Gaza, the Golan and the West Bank.[173]

Although Lebanon did not take part in the hostilities, she was gravely affected by its consequences. Palestinian guerrillas became increasingly active in the Lebanon, where Palestinians formed 12 per cent of the population.[174] Prior to the war, the Lebanese authorities had refused to allow the guerrillas to launch raids from Lebanese territory.[175] However, after the defeat of 1967, it became much more difficult for the Lebanon to interdict guerrilla operations against Israel. The Palestine Liberation Organisation established military bases in the Arqoub region of south-eastern Lebanon.[176] To the intense annoyance of the authorities in Beirut, the bases received regular supplies from neighbouring Syria.

Palestinian raids into Israel provoked increasingly severe reprisals against targets in the Lebanon.[177] In December 1968, an Israeli air-borne assault on Beirut airport resulted in the destruction of thirteen Arab-owned aircraft. The Israeli operation was a reprisal for an attack on an El Al plane, at Athens airport, by Palestinian guerrillas who were directed from the Lebanon.[178]

The Palestinian issue exacerbated the latent tensions in Lebanese society. For the most part, Lebanese Muslims favoured support for the Palestinians and their armed struggle against Israel. However, the Maronite community tended to regard the Palestinians as a threat to Lebanon's internal cohesion and external security.[179] After a period of mounting friction, fighting erupted between the Lebanese Army and Palestinian commandos in May 1969.[180] The fighting continued intermittently until October, when it was finally resolved following mediation in Cairo.[181] Lebanon's General Emile Bustani and PLO Chairman Yassir Arafat signed the Cairo Agreement, which expressed a new understanding between Lebanon and the guerrillas. The Agreement affirmed the right of the guerrillas to operate freely in Lebanon's Palestinian refugee camps and, implicitly, to launch operations against Israel from their bases in the Arqoub. In return, the PLO undertook to refrain from interfering in the internal affairs of the Lebanon.[182]

In August 1970, Suleiman Frangieh, a Maronite from Zghorta in northern Lebanon, was elected President. Frangieh enjoyed the support of Maronite leaders including Camille Chamoun, Raymond Eddé and Pierre Gemayel, in addition to that of the Sunni Muslim Saeb Salam and the Shia Kamal Assad.[183] Frangieh's popularity amongst the bulk of Maronites stemmed, in large measure, from his vocal opposition to encroachments by Palestinian guerrillas on Lebanon's independence.[184] However, his regime rapidly lost support because of its chronic nepotism and disinclination to effect much-needed reforms.[185]

Lebanon's precarious stability was significantly eroded by the arrival of thousands of Palestinian guerrillas from Jordan, following their rout by the Jordanian army in 1970–71.[186] The guerrillas turned southern Lebanon into their principal theatre of operations, mounting repeated raids into Israel and incurring massive reprisals.[187]

The cycle of Palestinian raids and Israeli reprisals resulted in an exodus of predominantly Shia villagers to Beirut, and in a brief confrontation between Palestinian guerrillas and Kataeb militia.[188] As the Israeli reprisals escalated in response to further Palestinian incursions, a number of villages in southern Lebanon were abandoned.[189] The mounting tension between Lebanon's Muslim and Maronite communities over the Palestinian issue was brought to a head by an incident in April 1973, when Israeli commandos assassinated three leading members of Al Fatah in their apartments in the centre of Beirut.[190] The failure of the Lebanese army even to challenge the Israeli troops prompted Prime Minister Saeb Salam to tender his resignation.[191]

In May, the simmering antagonism between the Palestinian guerrillas and the Lebanese army led to a series of clashes. During the course of the fighting, Lebanon's Air Force was used to bomb Palestinian refugee camps around Beirut.[192] Peace was restored by 18 May with the conclusion of the Melkart Understanding. The agreement provided for the establishment of a Joint High Commission, comprising Lebanese army officers and Palestinian commandos, to effect a settlement of mutual problems. In addition, the guerrillas undertook to suspend military operations across the border into Israel.[193]

However, tensions remained high between the increasingly militant Maronite community and the Palestinian guerrillas and their Lebanese allies in the National Movement.[194] Both sides purchased substantial quantities of arms.[195] In July 1974, fighting erupted between Phalangist units and Palestinian commandos,[196] while in January 1975, the veteran Phalangist leader, Pierre Gemayel, warned of the danger posed to Lebanon's independence by the Palestinian guerrillas.[197]

In addition to the Palestinian issue, there were other potent sources of inter-communal strife. The disproportionate political and economic power wielded by the Maronites became increasingly intolerable to Lebanese Muslims, emboldened by a resurgence of Islamic self-confidence throughout the Arab world.[198] In particular, the disadvantaged Shia community showed signs of growing militancy under the leadership of Musa Sadr, who had established the Movement of the Disinherited to lobby for Shia rights.[199]

On 26 February 1975, a large demonstration in Sidon, in support of local fishermen, clashed with an army unit. Marouf Saad, the popular mayor of Sidon, received fatal injuries in the incident. Further clashes, in which the army engaged Lebanese left-wing gunmen acting in concert with radical Palestinian guerrillas, prompted the army commander to order the shelling of Sidon. The events in Sidon tarnished the reputation which the army had previously enjoyed for neutrality, prompting Lebanese Muslims to demand equal representation for Muslims and Christians in the Army's officer corps.[200] In an atmosphere of mounting tension and mutual recrimination, Lebanon careered inexorably towards civil war.

Notes

1　See generally on British motives, Gilbert, *Exile and Return*, pp.86-7. See also Nevakivi, *Arab Middle East*, pp.36-7; Monroe, *Moment in the Middle East*, p.31; Sachar, *Emergence of the Middle East*, pp.122-5.
2　The text of the Hussein–McMahon correspondence is reproduced in Hurewitz, *II*, pp.46-56. For the text of the letter dated 24 October 1915, see ibid., p.50.
3　See e.g. Nevakivi, *Arab Middle East*, pp.26-7.
4　Ibid., p.31.
5　See generally Nevakivi, *Arab Middle East*, pp.26-35. See also Sachar, *Emergence of the Middle East*, pp.158-66; Monroe, *Moment in the Middle East*, pp.32-3.

6 See generally Nevakivi, *Arab Middle East*, p.35.
7 The text of the Sykes–Picot agreement is reproduced in Hurewitz, *II*, p.60. See, in particular, at p.62.
8 Ibid., p.62.
9 Ibid.
10 Ibid.
11 See generally on the discrepancies between the two texts, Monroe, *Moment in the Middle East*, pp.33-7.
12 The text of the Balfour Declaration is reproduced in Hurewitz, *II*, p.106.
13 See generally Gilbert, *Exile and Return*, Chapter 9. See also L. Stein, *The Balfour Declaration* (1961), p.550. See in addition discussions in the War Cabinet on 3 September, 4 and 31 October 1917. See, respectively, War Cabinet Minutes: Foreign Office Papers, 371/3083; War Cabinet Minutes: Cabinet Papers, 23/4; War Cabinet Minutes: Cabinet Papers, 23/4. These are reproduced in Hurewitz, *II*, pp.103-6. For additional factors motivating members of the British Cabinet in support of the Balfour Declaration see e.g. W. Laqueur, *A History of Zionism* (1972), pp.187-9.
14 Gilbert, *Exile and Return*, pp.96, 100, 105. See also Minutes of War Cabinet Meeting No. 261, Minute No. 12, 31 October 1917. The Minute is reproduced in Hurewitz, *II*, p.105.
15 See, however, a message from Commander Hogarth, of the Arab Bureau in Cairo, to King Hussein, of the Hejaz, which attempted to reconcile the Balfour Declaration with the pledges made to Sherif Hussein. The message is reproduced in Hurewitz, *II*, p.111.
16 See e.g. Nevakivi, *Arab Middle East*, p.71.
17 Ibid., pp.71-2.
18 Ibid., p.116. The object of the mandates system was to place territories formerly under the control of the defeated powers, which were 'inhabited by peoples not yet able to stand by themselves under the strenuous conditions of the modern world', under the tutelage of developed states, subject to the ultimate control of the League of Nations. See Article 22, League Covenant. The mandates idea, which was embraced by US President Wilson, has been widely ascribed to General Jan Smuts. See e.g. C. Howard-Ellis, *The Origin, Structure and Working of the League of Nations* (1928), pp.80-3. See also J.C. Smuts, *Jan Christian Smuts* (1952), pp.216, 220. For General Smuts' views on the subject of mandates see J.C. Smuts, *The League of Nations: A Practical Suggestion* (1918), esp. at pp.12-23. However, Professor Zimmern reveals that Smuts was elaborating on proposals contained in an earlier UK Foreign Office memorandum. See A. Zimmern, *The League of Nations and the Rule of Law, 1918–1935* (1936), pp.210-12. For the text of the Foreign Office memorandum see ibid., pp.196-208, esp. Part I, art. VII: 'Trusts or, to speak more precisely, charters should be drawn up for the various territories for whose future government the signatory Powers have to issue a mandate, and particular areas handed over to individual States who would be responsible to the League for the discharge of that mandate. Arrangements of this kind will require to be made for tropical Africa, for the Pacific Islands and for Western Asia.' See, generally, D.H. Miller, *The Drafting of the Covenant*, vol. I (1928), Chapter IX.
19 Longrigg, *Syria and Lebanon*, p.87.
20 The recommendations of the King–Crane Commission are reproduced in Hurewitz, *II*, p.191.
21 Recommendation nos. 2, 4.
22 Recommendation nos. 1, 3, 6(3), 6(6).

23   Recommendation no. 6(6).
24   For details concerning the delegates see e.g. Longrigg, *Syria and Lebanon*, p.90.
25   See paras. 1, 3, Resolution of the General Syrian Congress at Damascus, 2 July 1919. The text is reproduced in Hurewitz, *II*, p.180.
26   Ibid., paras. 2, 8.
27   Ibid., para. 8.
28   Nevakivi, *Arab Middle East*, pp.206-8.
29   Ibid., p.216.
30   Hourani, *Syria and Lebanon*, p.53.
31   See generally Nevakivi, *Arab Middle East*, pp.246-8. See also Longrigg, *Syria and Lebanon*, p.99.
32   For the text of the treaty see *GBTS*, 1920, no. 11, Cmd. 964, pp.16-32. The relevant provisions are reproduced in Hurewitz, *II*, p.219.
33   For the text of the Treaty of Lausanne see *GBTS*, 1923, no.16, Cmd. 1929. The treaty is reproduced in Hurewitz, *II*, p.325. See in particular Article 16.
34   Nevakivi, *Arab Middle East*, p.253.
35   Longrigg, *Syria and Lebanon*, pp.101-3.
36   Hourani, *Syria and Lebanon*, p.54.
37   Longrigg, *Syria and Lebanon*, p.123.
38   Ibid.
39   See e.g. Rabinovich, *War for Lebanon*, p.21. See also Longrigg, *Syria and Lebanon*, p.123.
40   See e.g. Hourani, *Syria and Lebanon*, pp.129, 180.
41   Ibid., pp.180-1.
42   Ibid., p.181.
43   See e.g. Mansfield, *Ottoman Empire*, pp.43, 58.
44   Ibid., pp.58-9.
45   Article 22(4).
46   See Recommendation no. 6(6), King–Crane Commission, op. cit., note 20.
47   Article 1. For the text of the French mandate for Syria and Lebanon see *League of Nations Official Journal* (August 1922), pp.1013-17. The mandate is reproduced as Appendix D in Longrigg, *Syria and Lebanon*, p.376, and as Appendix A, No.1 in Hourani, *Syria and Lebanon*, p.308.
48   Article 1.
49   France submitted annual reports to the Council of the League of Nations from 1924 until 1938. See Ministère des Affaires Etrangères, *Rapport sur la Situation de la Syrie et du Liban* (1924) – Ministère des Affaires Etrangères, *Rapport à la Societé des Nations sur la Situation de la Syrie et du Liban* (1938).
50   See Article 22(9), League Covenant. For the reports of the Permanent Mandates Commission on the French mandate over Syria and Lebanon see Permanent Mandates Commission, *Report on the Work of the Fifth (Extraordinary) Session of the Commission* (1924), pp.2-3 – Permanent Mandates Commission, *Report to the Council on the Work of the 36th Session of the Permanent Mandates Commission* (1939), p.273, at pp.277-9.
51   For the text of the mandate see note 47 above.
52   See note 37 above, and the accompanying text.
53   Hourani, *Syria and Lebanon*, p.180.
54   Ibid.
55   See generally Longrigg, *Syria and Lebanon*, pp.125-6.
56   Ibid., pp.126-7.
57   Ibid., pp.123-32.
58   In fact, the process of granting local autonomy was initiated prior to the conclusion of the mandate. See note 37 above, and the accompanying text.

59 See e.g. Hourani, *Syria and Lebanon*, p.167. See also Ziadeh, *Syria and Lebanon*, p.50; Tibawi, *History of Syria*, p.340; Mansfield, *Ottoman Empire*, p.73. France claimed that she was simply implementing the mandate, and that the administrative divisions permitted the French authorities to adapt themselves efficiently 'aux tendances particularistes marquées qui caractérisent des minorités importantes dans les pays confiés au Mandat français'. See Ministère des Affaires Etrangères, *Rapport sur la Situation de la Syrie et du Liban* (1924), p.11.

60 On the background to the revolt, see e.g. J.L. Miller, 'The Syrian Revolt of 1925', *IJMES*, vol. 8 (1977), p.545, at pp.552-3. See in addition Permanent Mandates Commission, *Report to the Council of the League on the Work of the Eighth (Extraordinary) Session of the Commission* (1926), pp.1-12. One of the causes of the revolt, identified by the Commission, was the frustration of many Syrians at having been denied genuine independence: 'It must in fairness be admitted that the proclamation of the right of peoples to determine their own destiny and the declarations regarding the future of Syria made during the war by the British and French Governments may have led the Syrians to believe that their country would be accorded complete independence without further delay.' Ibid., p.6. France ascribed the spread of the revolt to a variety of factors, including the lure of pillage, antipathy to the mandate and latent hostility towards non-Muslims. See Ministère des Affaires Etrangères, *Rapport à la Société des Nations sur la Situation de la Syrie et du Liban* (1925), pp.26-30.

61 See generally Hourani, *Syria and Lebanon*, pp.197-8.

62 Ziadeh, *Syria and Lebanon*, pp.53-5.

63 For the text of the Treaty of Friendship and Alliance between France and Syria (1936), and of certain associated documents, see e.g. Ministère des Affaires Etrangères, *Rapport à la Societé des Nations sur la Situation de la Syrie et du Liban* (1936), p.201. For the text of the Treaty of Friendship and Alliance between France and Lebanon (1936), and of certain associated documents, see ibid., p.229.

64 Ziadeh, *Syria and Lebanon*, p.56.

65 See e.g. Hourani, *Syria and Lebanon*, p.205.

66 Ziadeh, *Syria and Lebanon*, pp.56-8.

67 Hourani, *Syria and Lebanon*, pp.227-8.

68 Ibid., p.230.

69 Mansfield, *Ottoman Empire*, p.93.

70 For the text of the proclamation, see e.g. Hourani, *Syria and Lebanon*, Appendix A, No.11, p.371.

71 Ziadeh, *Syria and Lebanon*, pp.70-2.

72 See generally on the origins of the agreement Salibi, *Modern History of Lebanon*, p.187.

73 See generally on the Pact, F.I. Qubain, *Crisis in Lebanon* (1961), pp.17-18. See also M. Hudson, *The Precarious Republic* (1968), pp.44-5; Khalidi, *Conflict and Violence in Lebanon*, p.36; Salibi, *Modern History of Lebanon*, pp.187-8.

74 Hudson, op. cit., note 73, p.44.

75 Rabinovich, *War for Lebanon*, p.24.

76 S/5, 4 February 1946.

77 See generally SCOR 20th mtg., 15 February 1946, pp.282-95; SCOR 21st mtg., 15 February 1946, pp.295-317; SCOR 22nd mtg., 1 February 1946, pp.317-36; SCOR 23rd mtg., 1 February 1946, pp.336-68. Although a number of draft resolutions were submitted, they failed to secure adoption. See SCOR 23rd mtg., 16 February 1946, pp.356-7.

78   See e.g. Ziadeh, *Syria and Lebanon*, p.92.
79   Ibid., pp.93-4.
80   Salibi, *Modern History of Lebanon*, p.193.
81   Ziadeh, *Syria and Lebanon*, pp.110-1.
82   A/286, 2 April 1947.
83   See discussions in the Cabinet Defence Committee on 1 January 1947. See Cabinet Defence Committee: Cabinet Papers, 129/16. See also discussions in the Cabinet on 22 January and 14 February 1947. See, respectively, Cabinet Minutes: Cabinet Papers, 128/11, 128/9. See also Gilbert, *Exile and Return*, pp.297-300; Monroe, *Moment in the Middle East*, pp.164-6.
84   GA Res. 181 (II), 29 November 1947. For a fuller discussion of the UN's handling of the Palestine question in 1947, see e.g. Pogany, *Security Council*, pp.21-3.
85   *Hansard*, H.C., vol. 445, col. 1212.
86   For the text of the declaration see e.g. Moore, *III*, pp.34-51. For analyses of the legal issues arising from Israel's declaration of independence, and of the subsequent intervention by the Arab states, see e.g. H. Cattan, *Palestine and International Law* (2nd edn 1976), esp. Chapters IV–VI; Colloque des Juristes Arabes sur la Palestine, *La Question Palestinienne* (1968), esp. pp.104-16; N. Feinberg, 'The Arab–Israel Conflict in International Law, A Critical Analysis of the Colloquium of Arab Jurists in Algiers', in N. Feinberg, *Studies in International Law* (1979), p.433, esp. at pp.460-85; N. Feinberg, 'On an Arab Jurist's Approach to Zionism and the State of Israel', in Feinberg, op. cit., p.515, esp. at pp.528-35; J. Stone, *Israel and Palestine*, 1981, esp. Chapters 1–4; Pogany, *Security Council*, esp. at pp.35-41.
87   For details of the first Arab-Israeli war, see e.g. C. Herzog, *The Arab–Israeli Wars* (1982), Book I.
88   The texts of the armistice agreements are reproduced in Moore, *III*, pp.380-414. For the text of the Israel–Lebanon General Armistice Agreement see ibid., p.390. See generally on the legal aspects of the agreements, S. Rosenne, *Israel's Armistice Agreements with the Arab States* (1951).
89   See e.g. Gilmour, *Lebanon*, pp.86-8.
90   Ziadeh, *Syria and Lebanon*, pp.116-22.
91   Salibi, *Modern History of Lebanon*, p.197.
92   The extent of the divisions should not, however, be exaggerated. As noted above, Maronites as well as Muslims were alienated by President Khoury's political manoeuvrings in 1947 while, in 1952, a number of Maronites cooperated with Muslims in forcing Khoury to resign. In the general election of 1957, prominent Maronites joined Muslim and Druze leaders in forming the United National Front to oppose President Chamoun and his supporters.
93   Qubain, op. cit., note 73, pp.49-51.
94   Salibi, *Modern History of Lebanon*, p.201.
95   Ibid., pp.199-200.
96   Quoted in Mansfield, *Ottoman Empire*, p.123.
97   See generally Qubain, op. cit., note 73, pp.35-8.
98   Ibid., pp.53-8.
99   Ibid., p.57.
100   Salibi, *Modern History of Lebanon*, pp.197-8.
101   Al-Matni was, in fact, a Maronite. See generally Qubain, op. cit., note 73, pp.68-9.
102   Ibid., pp.69-71. The United National Front included the Sunni Muslims Saeb Salam and Rashid Karami, and the Druze Kamal Jumblatt. The Front had been formed, prior to the general election of 1957, by opponents of President

Chamoun, and included a number of prominent Maronites. See generally Salibi, *Modern History of Lebanon*, p.200.

103 Ibid., p.201.
104 Ibid., pp.201-4.
105 Qubain, op. cit., note 73, pp.81-3.
106 Ibid., pp.83-5.
107 See Memorandum of 21 May 1958 from the Lebanese Embassy in Cairo to the League Secretariat-General, Cairo. The Lebanese request for a meeting of the League Council was made under Article 6 of the Pact of the Arab League. This provides: 'In case of aggression or threat of aggression by one state against a member state, the state which has been attacked or threatened with aggression may demand the immediate convocation of the Council.' For further details concerning Article 6 and the League's system of collective security, see Chapter 1.
108 S/4007, 22 May 1958.
109 See generally on the League's handling of the Lebanese complaint, Hassouna, *League of Arab States*, pp.62-5. See also Qubain, op. cit., note 73, pp.89-91. Unanimity is required for the adoption of a decision under Article 6 of the Pact of the Arab League: 'The Council shall by unanimous decision determine the measures necessary to repulse aggression. If the aggressor is a member state, his vote shall not be counted in determining unanimity.' Lebanon refused to endorse a draft resolution submitted jointly by Libya, Saudi Arabia, Iraq, Jordan and Yemen, even though the text had received the support of other members of the Council. See e.g. Hassouna, *League of Arab States*, pp.64-5.
110 At a meeting on 27 May, the Security Council had adopted the Lebanese complaint on to its agenda. However, in accordance with an Iraqi proposal, it had decided to postpone consideration of the item until 3 June. See SCOR 818th mtg., 27 May 1958, p.8. The Council complied with a subsequent Lebanese request to defer its meeting for an additional period in order to enable the League to pursue a settlement. See S/4018, 2 June 1958. The readiness of the Security Council to allow the Arab League a reasonable opportunity to achieve a peaceful settlement is consistent with the UN Charter which envisages that other means, including resort to regional organizations, shall be attempted *prior* to a reference to the Security Council. Thus, Article 33(1) provides: 'The parties to any dispute, the continuance of which is likely to endanger the maintenance of international peace and security, shall, first of all, seek a solution by negotiation enquiry, mediation, conciliation, arbitration, judicial settlement, resort to regional agencies or arrangements. . .' Similarly, Article 52(2) states: 'The Members of the United Nations . . . shall make every effort to achieve pacific settlement of local disputes through . . . regional arrangements or by . . . regional agencies before referring them to the Security Council.' However, it must be emphasized that the Security Council was not bound to defer to the Arab League. Thus, Article 52(4) emphasizes that Article 52 'in no way impairs the application of Articles 34 and 35'. Article 35(1) states '[a]ny Member of the United Nations may bring any dispute, or any situation of the nature referred to in Article 34, to the attention of the Security Council.'
111 See SC Res. 128, 11 June 1958.
112 First Report of UNOGIL, S/4040 and Add. 1, 3 and 5 July 1958, esp. paras. 18–27.
113 Mansfield, *Ottoman Empire*, p.128.
114 Ibid. On 17 July, British troops were airlifted to Jordan at the request of the Jordanian government, which had accused the UAR of interfering in its domestic affairs.

115   See, generally, SCOR 827th mtg., 15 July 1958 to SCOR 837th mtg., 22 July 1958. Article 51 provides: 'Nothing in the present Charter shall impair the inherent right of individual or collective self-defence if an armed attack occurs against a Member of the United Nations, until the Security Council has taken the measures necessary to maintain international peace and security.' For an analysis of the US legal argument, see below.

116   SCOR 827th mtg., 15 July 1958, p.8.

117   Ibid., pp.15-16.

118   Ibid., p.16.

119   See, respectively, SCOR 827th mtg., 15 July 1958, pp.16-17; SCOR 828th mtg., 15 July 1958, p.2; ibid., pp.3-4; ibid, p.5.

120   SCOR 827th mtg., 15 July 1958, p.21.

121   Ibid.

122   SCOR 828th mtg., 15 July 1958, p.5.

123   Ibid. See also the statement of Ambassador Sobolev of the Soviet Union: 'the Charter clearly states that the right of collective self-defence may be used only if there is a direct attack against a country or if a country is under threat of destruction from outside.' See SCOR 829th mtg., 16 July 1958, p.9.

124   SCOR 830th mtg., 16 July 1958, p.9.

125   See generally on the legal implications of the US intervention in the Lebanon, P.B. Potter, 'Legal Aspects of the Beirut Landing', *AJIL*, vol. 52 (1958), p.727; Q. Wright, 'United States Intervention in the Lebanon', *AJIL*, vol. 53 (1959), p.112; E. Lauterpacht, 'The Contemporary Practice of the United Kingdom in the Field of International Law', *ICLQ*, vol. 8 (1959), p.146, at p.148; R. Higgins, 'The Legal Limits to the Use of Force by Sovereign States: United Nations Practice', *BYIL*, vol. 37, 1961, p.269, esp. at pp.292-4, 304-5, 308-11; Higgins, *Development*, pp.193-4, 206, 210-11.

126   First Report of UNOGIL, op. cit., note 112, para. 21.

127   Ibid., paras. 5-8.

128   Interim Report of UNOGIL, S/4051, 15 July 1958, para. 1.

129   Second Report of UNOGIL, S/4069, 30 July 1958, paras. 62–3.

130   See e.g. S/4043, 8 July 1958; SCOR 833rd mtg., 18 July 1958, pp.2-8.

131   For a detailed analysis of this question see Qubain, op. cit., note 73, Chapter VIII. See, also, Salibi, *Modern History of Lebanon*, p.201; Dawisha, *Syria and the Lebanese Crisis*, pp.20-1.

132   See e.g. letter, dated 3 October 1958, from S. Habib Ahmed, UNOGIL's Chief Administrative Officer, to Colonel J. MacCarthy, UNOGIL's Deputy Chief of Staff:

> It has come to my attention that UNMOs [United Nations Military Observers] without adequate knowledge of English and without adequate qualifications as drivers are arriving in increasing numbers . . . the lack of these qualifications seriously limits their usefulness.

See DAG 13/3.7.0., Box No. 1, File No. 200, Part B.

133   For details of the instructions issued to the Group's Air Observers see Air Wing Order No. 2, p.2, 9 September, 1958, in DAG 13/3.7.0., Box No. 2, File No. 207:

> No flights closer than 5 kilometres of the borderline. . . . Minimum height over Opposition-held area will be 300 metres. If small arms fire is expected, the minimum height should not be less than 800 metres.

134 See e.g. Brownlie, *Use of Force*, p.273. See, also, H. Kelsen, *Recent Trends in the Law of the United Nations* (1951), p.914; J.L. Kunz, 'Individual and Collective Self-Defence in Article 51 of the Charter of the United Nations', *AJIL*, vol. 41 (1947), p.872, at p.877; Skubiszewski, *Use of Force*, pp.766-9.

135 Bowett, *Self-Defence*, pp.184-5. See also Waldock, *Regulation of the Use of Force*, pp.496-9; Stone, *Legal Controls*, pp.243-4; McDougal and Feliciano, *World Public Order*, pp.232-8.

136 Brownlie, *Use of Force*, p.279. See also ibid., pp.372-3. See also C.A. Pompe, *Aggressive War* (1953), pp.110-12; H.A.H. Al Chalabi, *La Légitime Défense en Droit International* (1952), pp.86-8; Stone, *Legal Controls*, p.244, note 8; J.E.S. Fawcett, 'Intervention in International Law', Hague, *Recueil des Cours*, vol. II (1961), p.347, at pp.387-9.

137 S/PV. 2375th mtg, 8 June 1982, p.33.

138 GAOR 86th Plen. Mtg., 1947, pp.20, 146.

139 See e.g. the Declaration on Principles of International Law etc., Annex, GA Res. 2625 (XXV), 24 October 1970 (adopted without vote). See also the 'Essentials of Peace' resolution, GA Res. 290 (IV), 1 December 1949 (adopted by 53 votes for, 5 against and no abstentions); GA Res. 193 (III), 27 November 1948 (adopted by 47 votes for, 6 against and no abstentions); the 'Peace through Deeds' resolution, GA Res. 380 (V), 17 November 1950 (adopted by 50 votes for, 5 against and 1 abstention).

140 Brownlie, *Use of Force*, p.273.

141 Waldock, 'Regulation of the Use of Force', p.496.

142 See e.g. Bowett, *Self-Defence*, p.270, and Chapters 2, 3.

143 See Chapter 8, notes 105, 261.

144 SCOR 836th mtg., 22 July 1958, p.3.

145 SCOR 827th mtg., 15 July 1958, p.21.

146 See SCOR 828th mtg., 15 July 1958, p.6.

147 See e.g. Higgins, *Development*, p.206, who argues that the UN alone is competent to make such a determination. See also Stone, *Legal Controls*, p.244; Pogany, *Security Council*, p.121. For a somewhat different view see e.g. Bowett, *Self-Defence*, p.196: 'On balance . . . it is suggested that the preferable view, and one which is not excluded by the Charter, is that whether the necessary measures have been taken must be determined, objectively, as a question of fact, and that both the S.C. and the defending state are able to reach their own decisions on this.' During the Falklands crisis, in May 1982, the Argentine delegate argued before the Security Council that '[t]he determination of whether such measures have been effective must be reached objectively and cannot be left to the arbitrary judgment of the Government of the United Kingdom itself.' See S/PV. 2360th mtg., 21 May 1982, p.21. The British delegate, Sir Anthony Parsons, accepted that the determination 'must be an objective one . . . reached in the light of all the relevant circumstances'. See S/PV. 2362nd mtg., 22 May 1982, p.103. However, he insisted that the 'measures' contemplated by Article 51 must 'refer to measures which are actually effective to bring about the stated objective'. Ibid.; p.104. These words were first used in a letter from Sir Anthony to the President of the Security Council. See S/15016, 30 April 1982. Sir Anthony thus deliberately avoided acceptance of the ultimate authority of the Security Council to make such a determination.

148 A Soviet draft resolution, which condemned the US intervention and called for the immediate withdrawal of American troops from the Lebanon, failed to secure adoption. See S/4047, 15 July 1958.

149 Bowett, *Self-Defence*, p.207.

150   Ibid., p.218.
151   Ibid., pp.234-8.
152   Ibid., p.238. Other jurists who share Bowett's restrictive conception of the doctrine of collective self-defence include Higgins, *Development*, pp.208-10.
153   Goodrich, Hambro, Simons, *Charter*, p.348. See also McDougal and Feliciano, *World Public Order*, pp.247-53. Other writers, while discerning logical difficulties in the 'broad' view of collective self-defence, nevertheless favour it. See e.g. Brownlie, *Use of Force*, pp.329-31; Stone, *Legal Controls*, p.245; Kelsen, *United Nations*, pp.329-31; Skubiszewski; *Use of Force*, pp.768-9; Kunz, op. cit., note 134, p.875.
154   See generally Goodrich, Hambro, Simons, *Charter*, pp.342-3. See also Bowett, *Self-Defence*, pp.182-4, 215-16. The text of the Act of Chapultepec is reproduced at *AJIL*, vol. 39 (1945), p.108.
155   See e.g. Goodrich, Hambro, Simons, *Charter*, pp.349-51. See also Bowett,*Self-Defence*, pp.219-23.
156   See *UNTS*, vol. 34 (1949), p.243.
157   See *UNTS*, vol. 21 (1948), p.77.
158   SCOR 830th mtg., 16 July 1958, p.2.
159   SCOR 827th mtg., 15 July 1958, pp.18, 21.
160   This question is examined in Chapter 6.
161   Higgins, *Development*, p.211. See also E. Lauterpacht, 'Intervention by Invitation', *ICLQ*, vol. 7 (1958), p.102, at p.106; Brownlie, *Use of Force*, pp.325-7. See, however, Quincy Wright who argues that intervention in a civil conflict on behalf of the government is only lawful where the government can claim to represent the state and where the threat arises predominantly from external elements rather than from indigenous groups. See Q. Wright, 'United States Intervention in the Lebanon', *AJIL*, vol. 53 (1959), p.112, esp. at pp.119-25. Wright doubts whether either condition is satisfied by the events in Lebanon in 1958.
162   *Hansard*, H.C., vol. 591, col. 1372, 16 July 1958.
163   Ibid., col. 1517.
164   Measures taken in individual or collective self-defence are also subject to a requirement of proportionality. See Chapter 8, notes 105 and 261. However, the US intervention, which was confined to Lebanese territory and which was of little more than symbolic importance, can scarcely be viewed as disproportionate.
165   See, generally, Qubain, op. cit., note 73, pp.154-61.
166   Fifth Report of UNOGIL, S/4114, 17 November 1958, para. 20.
167   S/4113, 17 November 1958. The Security Council decided, on 25 November, to delete the Lebanese complaint from the list of matters of which it was seized. See SCOR 840th mtg., 25 November 1958, p.5.
168   For an assessment of the role and performance of UNOGIL, see e.g. Higgins, *I*, Part 3. See also G. Curtis, 'The UN Observation Group in Lebanon', *Int. Org.*, vol. 18 (1964), p.738; A.A. Al-Maryati, 'UN Observation Group in Lebanon', *Foreign Affairs Reports*, vol. XVI (1967), pp.41-4, 54-8.
169   See generally Hudson, op. cit., note 73, pp.297-325.
170   Salibi, *Crossroads*, pp.7, 9.
171   Ibid., p.11.
172   Hudson, op. cit., note 73, pp.325-8.
173   See generally on the Six Day War, W. Laqueur, *The Road to War* (1968).
174   Cobban, *PLO*, p.46.
175   Lebanon had wished to avoid Israeli reprisals. See e.g. Salibi, *Crossroads*, pp.25-8.

176 The Palestine Liberation Organisation was established in 1964 under the leadership of Ahmad Shuquairi. See generally Cobban, *PLO*, pp.28-30. Al Fatah's Yassir Arafat became Chairman of the PLO in February 1969. See generally ibid., pp.43-4. On the origins of Al Fatah, see ibid., pp.23-4.

177 These are chronicled in Khalidi, *Conflict and Violence in Lebanon*, p.164, note 40.

178 On the legal aspects of the Israeli operation see e.g. R.A. Falk, 'The Beirut Raid and the International Law of Retaliation', *AJIL*, vol. 63 (1969), p.415; Y.H. Blum, 'The Beirut Raid and the International Double Standard', *AJIL*, vol. 64 (1970), p.73. In so far as the Israeli operation constituted a forcible 'reprisal', it must be viewed as infringing international law. See e.g. Bowett who notes: '[f]ew propositions about international law have enjoyed more support than the proposition that, under the Charter of the United Nations, the use of force by way of reprisals is illegal.' See D. Bowett 'Reprisals Involving Recourse to Armed Force', *AJIL*, vol. 66 (1972), p.1. See also Higgins, *Development*, pp.217-18; Stone, *Legal Controls*, p.290; Feinberg, op. cit., note 86, p.97, note 52; Skubiszewski, *Use of Force*, p.754; Brownlie, *Use of Force*, p.281, and sources cited at note 4. The Declaration on Principles of International Law, adopted by the General Assembly in 1970, affirms: 'States have a duty to refrain from acts of reprisal involving the use of force.' Annex, GA Res. 2625 (XXV), 24 October 1970. Professor Brownlie has described the Declaration as 'a document of first importance' and has suggested that its legal significance 'lies in the fact that it provides evidence of the consensus among Member States of the United Nations on the meaning and elaboration of the principles of the Charter'. I. Brownlie (ed.), *Basic Documents in International Law* (3rd edn 1985), p.35. Dr Blum argues that 'raids of the Beirut type cannot be explained with reference to the international law of peace in general and the doctrine of peacetime reprisal in particular'. Blum, op. cit., p.78. However, the author readily acknowledges that the prevailing view is that a 'state of war' is incompatible with the UN Charter. Ibid., p.77, note 18. In these circumstances, it is difficult to see how the Israeli operation can be characterized other than as a forcible reprisal. However onerous or unfair, the 'international law of peace' represents the only standard by which the forcible measures of Israel, and of its antagonists, can be judged. See generally on the incompatibility of a 'state of war' with the requirements of the Charter, Higgins, *Development*, pp.214-15. See also Feinberg, op. cit., note 86, p.97; E. Lauterpacht, 'The Legal Irrelevance of the "State of War"', *Proceedings ASIL* (1968), p.58, at p.63.

179 Salibi, *Crossroads*, pp.34-5.

180 Ibid., pp.41-2.

181 See e.g. the account of Egypt's Foreign Minister, M. Riad, *The Struggle for Peace in the Middle East* (1981), pp.158-9.

182 For details of the Cairo Agreement see Chapter 5. The text is reproduced in the appendices. In fact, the Cairo Agreement failed to resolve the underlying tensions. Sections of the Maronite community rejected the Agreement from the outset as conceding too many rights to the Palestinians. On certain points, the Agreement was ambiguously worded. Thus, the text failed to sanction, explicitly, the launching of guerrilla operations against Israel from Lebanese soil. Inevitably, such ambiguities led to disputes over the interpretation of the Agreement.

183 Khalidi, *Conflict and Violence in Lebanon*, pp.41-2.

184 Salibi, *Crossroads*, p.49.

185 Ibid., pp.56-61.

186   See generally, on the clashes, Cobban, *PLO*, pp.48-52.
187   Salibi, *Crossroads*, p.65.
188   Bulloch, *Death of a Country*, pp.60-1, 68-9.
189   Salibi, *Crossroads*, p.65.
190   Ibid., p.66.
191   Bulloch, *Death of a Country*, p.70. Salam had initially called for the resignation of the commander of the army. However, when President Frangieh declined to exert pressure on the army commander to relinquish his post, the Prime Minister submitted his own resignation. He was replaced by Amin Hafez. See generally Salibi, *Crossroads*, pp.66-7.
192   Salibi, *Crossroads*, p.68.
193   See e.g. Khalidi, *Conflict and Violence in Lebanon*, p.164, note 44. The text is reproduced in the appendices.
194   Salibi, *Crossroads*, pp.69-70, 76.
195   Ibid., p.80.
196   Quoted in D.C. Gordon, *Lebanon* (1980), pp.86-7.
197   See generally Rabinovich, *War for Lebanon*, pp.34-5.
198   Ibid., pp.38-9.
199   Salibi, *Crossroads*, pp.92-3.
200   Salibi suggests that the army began to lose its reputation for neutrality during the Frangieh administration when Shihabist elements were systematically purged from the officer corps. See Salibi, *Crossroads*, p.95.

4 The Creation of the Symbolic Arab Security Force

On Sunday, 13 April 1975, unidentified gunmen shot and killed four men, including Pierre Gemayel's personal bodyguard, outside a church in Ain el-Roumaneh, a Christian suburb of Beirut. In retaliation, Phalangist militiamen ambushed a bus, travelling through the suburb later that day, killing twenty-seven Palestinian passengers.[1] These incidents proved the catalyst for civil war. Phalangist militiamen engaged Palestinian commandos in Beirut, while fighting spread to the northern port of Tripoli.[2] The Palestinian combatants were drawn, for the most part, from the Rejection Front and other radical factions. They were aided by elements of the National Movement, a coalition of Lebanese leftist organizations including the Progressive Socialist Party, the Communist Party, and various Nasserist and socialist factions.[3] The largest Palestinian guerrilla formation, Al Fatah, tried to avoid involvement in the conflict.[4]

The crisis, which showed signs of abating, was aggravated when Kamal Jumblatt, the head of the National Movement, announced that the Movement would no longer support any government in which Phalangist ministers were included.[5] Jumblatt's initiative prompted the resignation of the two serving Phalangist ministers, and of several sympathizers in the government, culminating in the resignation of the Prime Minister, Rashid Solh.[6]

Negotiations proceeded with a view to the formation of a new government. However, Jumblatt affirmed his continued opposition to the inclusion of Phalangist ministers, while the Phalange and its supporters insisted that the party must be represented.[7]

While the political wrangles continued, the security situation remained precarious. In various parts of Beirut, Phalangist militia clashed with Palestinian commandos. In the poorer Muslim quarters, Lebanese Sunni and Shia guerrillas fought Maronite militiamen.[8]

In late May, President Frangieh called on a retired officer of the gendarmerie, Brigadier General Nureddin Rifai, to form a government composed largely of army officers.[9] While the President's initiative was acclaimed by the Maronites, it was greeted with dismay by Sunni and Shia leaders, and by the Druzes.[10] The PLO were also alarmed at the prospect of a military government. Syria, as a token of its concern, despatched its Foreign Minister to Beirut.[11] Within a matter of days, Brigadier Rifai's government tendered its resignation. The President, succumbing to Muslim pressure, called on Rashid Karami to form a government.[12] Karami, who took on the defence portfolio as well as the premiership, announced the formation of a new government on 30 June. Karami's erstwhile opponent, Camille Chamoun, was appointed Minister of the Interior. Neither the Phalange, nor Jumblatt's parliamentary allies, were included in the Cabinet.[13]

Throughout this period the security situation continued to deteriorate, as the disturbances spread beyond Beirut. To the south of the capital, Shia gunmen supported by Palestinian guerrillas clashed with Maronite villagers.[14] To the north, Maronites in the coastal town of Jubayl severed the road linking Beirut with Tripoli. In the southern suburbs of Beirut, Maronite militia and Shia gunmen were locked in fierce battles.[15]

By the end of June, the fighting in Beirut had resulted in a virtual stalemate, although the Christian suburbs had endured disproportionate damage.[16] In the country at large, the Maronite community found itself under threat. In Tripoli, Christians had been forced to abandon their homes and property. In the predominantly Sunni Akkar region of northern Lebanon, and in the largely Shia Bekaa, Maronite villagers felt increasingly vulnerable.[17]

During its first months in office, the new government had tried to restore peace and security. With the support of both the Phalange and the PLO, Karami secured a truce which lasted for much of the summer.[18] However, Lebanon's assorted militias spent much of this period acquiring additional weapons in anticipation of renewed hostilities.[19] The government was hampered in its efforts to defuse tensions by the almost total lack of cooperation between the Prime Minister and the President. As a consequence, the Cabinet failed to meet for much of the summer.[20]

In late August, serious clashes occurred in Zahlé, in the Bekaa, and in Tripoli and Zghorta in the north. In all of these incidents,

Palestinian guerrillas supported Muslims who were pitted against Christian militiamen.[21]

Following a Cabinet meeting, on 9 September, a new army commander was appointed in an attempt to placate Lebanese Muslims. In addition, army units were introduced as a buffer between Tripoli and Zghorta.[22] However, the army itself was rapidly embroiled in the conflict around Tripoli, while fighting gradually enveloped the outskirts of Beirut.[23] On 15 September, serious clashes in the heart of the capital resulted in massive civilian casualties and in the large-scale destruction of business properties.[24] Efforts by the Prime Minister to achieve a ceasefire were unsuccessful.[25]

In the midst of the fighting the Syrian Foreign Minister, Abdul Halim Khaddam, and the Syrian Chief of Staff, Major-General Hikmat Shihabi, arrived in Beirut to negotiate a ceasefire. Following intensive mediation, a ceasefire was concluded and a Committee of National Dialogue was formed, composed of the principal Lebanese confessional leaders. However, the Committee discontinued its meetings in November.[26]

Referral to the Arab League

Following a request by Kuwait, an extraordinary session of the Council of the League of Arab States was convened, in Cairo, on 15 October 1975.[27] The meeting was attended at Foreign Minister level by the majority of member states. However, it was boycotted by Syria, Libya and the PLO.

The PLO was concerned that the Council, in considering the roots of the Lebanese crisis, would embark on a reappraisal of the Palestinian presence in the Lebanon. The Syrian boycott was prompted by the refusal of the League to examine the Lebanese conflict in the context of the wider Middle Eastern crisis and, in particular, the recent conclusion by Egypt of a second disengagement agreement with Israel.[28]

In the absence of Syria and the PLO, both of whom were essential to a resolution of the Lebanese crisis, the League Council was unable to make meaningful progress. After an inconclusive debate, the Council issued a communiqué, on 16 October, in which it expressed 'its profound distress at the succession of incidents in Lebanon' and called on all parties 'to exercise wisdom and restraint'.[29] The League Council did not meet again to consider the Lebanese situation until June, 1976.

The League's consideration of the Lebanese crisis has been interpreted by some commentators as 'interference' in the internal affairs of the Lebanon, contrary to Article 8 of the Pact.[30] Article 8, as will be recollected, states that '[e]ach member state shall respect the systems of government established in the other member states and regard them as exclusive concerns of those states. Each shall pledge to abstain from any action calculated to change established systems of government'. However, the better view would seem to be that the Lebanese crisis represented a threat to regional peace and security.[31] This was clearly the view of League members participating in the extraordinary session of the Council.

Nevertheless, the constitutional basis of the Council's resolution is difficult to gauge with any degree of precision. As noted in Chapter 1, the Council enjoys limited powers of arbitration and of mediation, in accordance with Article 5 of the Pact. In terms of the former, the parties to a dispute, provided they are League members, may 'have recourse to the Council for the settlement of this difference'.[32] Article 5 stipulates that '[i]n such a case, the states between whom the difference has arisen shall not participate in the deliberations and decisions of the Council'. The decision of the Council is 'enforceable and obligatory'.[33] However the jurisdiction of the Council, in exercise of its powers of arbitration, is limited to disputes which do not 'concern a state's independence, sovereignty, or territorial integrity'.[34]

Whereas reference of disputes to the Council for purposes of arbitration is voluntary, Article 5 affirms that '[t]he Council *shall* mediate in all differences which threaten to lead to war between two member states, or a member state and a third state, with a view to bringing about their reconciliation'.[35] When the Council is undertaking mediation, however, the parties to a dispute are not under any obligation to abide by the Council's decisions. It should also be emphasized that, whereas arbitration is only available in the case of disputes between member states, mediation may also take place in the context of disputes between members and non-members.

The present case cannot serve as an illustration of either arbitration or of mediation within the meaning of Article 5.[36] While its effects increasingly threatened regional peace, the conflict's origins were largely domestic in character.

Similarly, Article 6 would seem to be inapplicable. This states: '[i]n case of aggression or threat of aggression by one state against a member state, the state which has been attacked or threatened with aggression may demand the immediate convocation of the Council.' Lebanon had not been subjected to aggression, or even the threat of aggression, in October 1975. Thus, the Council's handling of the Lebanese crisis is illustrative of its pragmatic and flexible approach. As noted in Chapter 1, the Council is frequently willing to employ techniques, and address itself to disputes, without regard to a literal interpretation of the Pact.[37]

The fighting in Beirut, which had resumed early in October, intensified during the latter part of the month, as Muslim and Maronite militias clashed in the heart of the city. The fighting rapidly enveloped the coastal area of Ras Beirut, where many of the capital's hotels and foreign embassies were situated.[38] Hostilities also resumed in Zahlé and in Damour, to the south of the capital.[39] As the scale of the fighting grew, there were widespread fears that Syria and Israel would be drawn into the conflict.[40]

The Prime Minister's attempts to secure a ceasefire were hampered by his strained relations with President Frangieh and with the Interior Minister, Camille Chamoun. The President and the Interior Minister each headed sizeable militias which were actively involved in the fighting.[41] In addition, Karami was unable to convene the Lebanese Chamber of Deputies, as the disorders prevented a quorum of deputies from attending.[42]

Despite these difficulties, Karami established a Security Committee, on 28 October, composed of the principal confessional leaders.[43] After protracted negotiations with a PLO delegation headed by Yassir Arafat, the Committee announced a ceasefire. Agreement was also reached on the formation of a Higher Coordination Committee, charged with investigating breaches of the ceasefire, in which the PLO was represented together with the Lebanese Army and Security Forces, and the major Lebanese community leaders.[44]

During the course of November a papal delegate, Cardinal Bertoli, and M. Couve de Murville, a former French Prime Minister, tried to mediate between the Lebanese factional leaders.[45] These initiatives had the effect, in part, of reducing the rift between President Frangieh and Prime Minister Karami. The two leaders issued a joint appeal, on 29 November, for the cessation of violence and for national reconciliation based on economic, social and political reforms.[46] Nevertheless, in the first week of December, fighting resumed in Zahlé, Tripoli and Zghorta.[47] In the Chouf, Druze and Maronite militias exchanged artillery fire.

The security situation deteriorated further following the discovery, on 6 December, of the bodies of four Maronite militiamen in a Beirut suburb. In an orgy of vengeance, Maronite gunmen waylaid Muslims on the streets of the capital, killing over 200.[48] Predictably, the Maronite excesses led to an outbreak of fighting in various parts of the Lebanon. In central Beirut, Maronite militia strongholds came under attack from Muslim commandos operating in concert with Palestinian guerrillas.[49] Following pressure from Syria and the PLO, a ceasefire was concluded on 15 December.[50]

In the first week of January 1976, Maronite forces laid siege to the Palestinian refugee camps of Tal Zaatar and Jisr al-Pasha, in East Beirut. On 14 January, they occupied Dbayyeh, a refugee camp for Palestinian Christians, north of Beirut.[51] These developments finally prompted Fatah, the largest faction in the PLO, to enter the conflict in alliance with the Muslim-Leftist forces.[52] Fighting resumed along various fronts in the capital, while Maronite militiamen launched an attack on the predominantly Muslim slums of Qarantina, Maslakh and Naba'a, which dominated the strategically significant coastal road running north from Beirut.[53] Clashes between Maronites and Lebanese Leftists and their allies also occurred in Tripoli and Zghorta. After appeals from Lebanese Leftist leaders to President Assad of Syria, units of the Palestine Liberation Army (PLA), the regular military wing of the PLO, were despatched to the Lebanon.[54]

As the conflict intensified, a crucial struggle developed south of Beirut over Damour, the power-base of Interior Minister, Camille Chamoun. Damour fell to a combined force of Palestinian and Lebanese Leftist militias on 20 January. In revenge for the ruthless treatment of the population of Qarantina and Maslakh, which had fallen to the Maronites only two days previously, the inhabitants of Damour were treated with equal brutality.[55]

On 20 January, Syria's Foreign Minister, accompanied by two senior military figures, arrived in the Lebanon to negotiate a ceasefire. There was rapid agreement on the establishment of a six-member Higher Military Committee, empowered to conclude arrangements for a ceasefire, and to oversee its implementation.[56] The Committee was composed, in equal numbers, of Lebanese, Syrian and Palestinian representatives. As a reflection of Syria's increasing determination to shape events in the Lebanon, the two Palestinian delegates were Zuhair Muhsin, commander of Saiqa, a pro-Syrian Palestinian guerrilla movement, and a colonel in the Syrian-dominated Palestine Liberation Army.[57]

On 7 February, President Frangieh flew to Damascus for talks with Syrian officials. The Syrians emphasized the need for far-reaching economic and political reforms in the Lebanon, as a precondition for the restoration of peace and security.[58] On 14 February, President Frangieh outlined a new 'National Covenant' on Lebanese television.[59] President Frangieh affirmed that, in keeping with existing practices, the President should be a Maronite, the Prime Minister a Sunni Muslim, and the President of the Chamber of Deputies a Shia. However, in a departure from previous Lebanese conventions, the President proposed that seats in the Chamber of Deputies should be distributed 'on a fifty-fifty basis between Muslims and Christians', and that the appointment of all but the most senior civil servants should be 'on a basis of merit' rather than in accordance with confessional principles.[60] Significantly, President Frangieh noted that the Lebanon was an 'Arab' country, and he pledged to work for 'comprehensive social justice' and the provision of 'free compulsory education' for all. However, the Palestinians were reminded that 'the situation today requires closer adherence to agreements and greater punctiliousness in their implementation, especially in the case of the Cairo Agreement'.[61]

However, the 'National Covenant' failed to satisfy the aspirations of Lebanese Leftists and Palestinian guerrillas, while it antagonized sections of the Christian community.[62] In these circumstances, it proved impossible to form a government of national unity, one of Syria's foremost objectives.[63]

The prospects of national reconciliation receded further in the first weeks of March when large numbers of Muslim troops defected from the Lebanese army, declaring their allegiance to Lieutenant Ahmed Khatib's break-away Arab Army of Lebanon.[64] On 11 March, the Sunni army commander of the Beirut area, Brigadier Aziz Ahdab, proclaimed a state of emergency and demanded the resignation of President Frangieh and of his government within twenty-four hours.[65] Two days later, 68 of Lebanon's 99-member Chamber of Deputies also called on the President to resign.[66]

Despite the mounting pressure, President Frangieh announced that he would remain in office. Frangieh's intransigence prompted units of Lieutenant Khatib's Arab Army of Lebanon, supported by Druze militiamen, to launch a two-pronged attack on the presidential palace of Baabda. The Syrian government, anxious to prevent the violent overthrow of the Lebanese President, interposed units of Saiqa and the PLA between the palace and the rebel formations.[67]

Unable to occupy Baabda, Lebanese Leftist forces, supported by Palestinian commandos and units of the Lebanese Arab Army, attacked Phalangist positions in West Beirut. In fierce fighting, the Leftist forces occupied the strategically significant Holiday Inn.[68] On 25 March, units of the Lebanese Arab Army, using powerful field artillery, shelled the presidential palace, forcing the President to withdraw.[69]

Despite their opposition to the violent overthrow of President Frangieh, the Syrian leadership recognized that he was largely discredited. Accordingly, they persuaded him to accept an amendment to the Lebanese Constitution permitting the holding of presidential elections six months before his term of office was due to expire.[70] The Lebanese Cabinet, meeting on 22 March, endorsed the decision to hold presidential elections, while the Chamber of Deputies passed

· the necessary constitutional amendment in the second week of April.[71] On 8 May, Elias Sarkis, a former protégé of Fuad Shihab, was elected President of the Lebanon.[72]

Notwithstanding the election of President Sarkis, fighting continued throughout much of the Lebanon. In Beirut, artillery exchanges during a three-day period left 500 dead.[73] In the north, Saiqa and PLA units fought National Movement forces allied with Palestinian 'rejection front' guerrillas.[74] In Mount Lebanon, Druze and Palestinian forces clashed with Kataeb militia.[75]

Responding to the escalating crisis, the Syrian leadership decided, at the end of May, to despatch its regular armed forces.[76] On 1 June 1976, a Syrian force comprising 60 tanks and 2000 men, crossed into northern Lebanon, ostensibly to assist Christian villagers besieged by units of the Lebanese Arab Army.[77] On the same day, a substantially larger Syrian force entered the Bekaa, one column advancing towards Sofar in central Lebanon, while another headed for Sidon in the South.[78]

The fighting spread to Beirut and the coast, as Palestinian guerrillas attacked Syrian-backed Saiqa formations. In Sidon, the Syrians suffered a major reverse when several of their tanks were destroyed in the narrow streets of the city.[79]

The establishment of the Symbolic Arab Security Force

Syria's intervention in the Lebanon was condemned by the bulk of Arab states and by the Soviet Union, on whom Syria relied for arms and for economic assistance.[80] In separate statements, the PLO and Egypt called for an extraordinary session of the Council of the Arab League.[81] The Council met in Cairo, on the night of 8 June 1976, and adopted a seven-point resolution. The resolution called 'on all parties to cease fighting immediately and to consolidate such a ceasefire'.[82] In addition, the Council called 'on all the Lebanese parties to bring about comprehensive national conciliation under the auspices of the Lebanese President-elect, to ensure the maintenance of the unity of the Lebanese people and the unity of their territory and the country's sovereignty, security and stability'.[83]

The resolution provided for the immediate despatch to the Lebanon of 'a commission representing the League Council' with a mandate 'to cooperate with the parties concerned in following up the situation and ensuring security and stability in Lebanon'.[84] The Commission was to be composed of 'the Foreign Minister of Bahrein . . . the secretary of the Arab League and the heads of the Algerian and Libyan delegations'.[85]

Crucially, the Council decided to establish a 'symbolic Arab security force'. Thus, the member states resolved:[86]

> To form a symbolic Arab security force under the supervision of the general secretary of the Arab League to maintain security and stability in Lebanon, which force should start to perform its task immediately, replacing the Syrian forces. The task of this Arab security force should be brought to an end if the president-elect of Lebanon so requests.

At a further session of the Council of the Arab League, on the night of 9 June, the mandate of the Symbolic Arab Security Force was modified slightly. The Council decided that the Force should act 'within the framework of Lebanese sovereignty' and that the size of contingents should be determined by the Secretary-General of the Arab League 'according to the needs of the situation' and 'in accordance with the PLO'.[87] A spokesman for the Arab League indicated that contingents for the Force would be drawn from Algeria, Saudi Arabia, Libya, Sudan, Syria and the PLO.[88]

One of the objectives underlying the Arab League initiative, and the creation of the Symbolic Arab Security Force, had been to secure the withdrawal of the bulk of Syrian troops from the Lebanon.[89] However, after some prevarication, the Syrian government stated categorically that it would retain its forces in the Lebanon. Speaking on Sunday, 13 June, the Syrian Information Minister, Mr Ahmed Iskandar Ahmad commented:[90]

> when our troops entered the Lebanon, it was in order to impose security and stability and to create a climate favourable to political dialogue between the Lebanese. When all that has been achieved, there won't be a single Syrian soldier left. We will take all the time that is necessary.

Significantly, the Lebanese President, Suleiman Frangieh, supported the continued presence of Syrian troops, and opposed the deployment of the projected Arab League Force. In a memorandum, dated 9 June, addressed to the Secretary-General of the Arab League, President Frangieh stated: '[t]he Syrian military presence in the Lebanon is aimed at guaranteeing the proper application by the Palestinian resistance of the agreements which it concluded with the Lebanese authorities. It is provisional and will end when stability and security are restored in the country'.[91] In a further message to the Secretary-General of the Arab League, dated 10 June, President Frangieh declared: '[t]he resolutions taken yesterday and today by the League Council . . .

are null and void and unbinding and shall remain unenforced.'[92] The President argued that the Lebanon had not been represented at the extraordinary session of the League Council and that:[93]

> it is contrary to the League's Charter and to the very reasons which had prompted the creation of the League for an Arab League meeting to take place to discuss a Lebanese matter . . . and to attempt to make decisions binding on Lebanon without inviting Lebanon to attend or be represented at the meeting by a responsible person. The Lebanese Council of Ministers, which had the sole authority in those matters, had not charged anyone with representing Lebanon.

On the following day, a group of senior Maronite leaders, including the President, affirmed that 'Lebanon will oppose, by all means at its disposal and with all its potential, any Arab force that enters its territory against its wish and without its prior agreement'.[94]

Nevertheless, after discussions on 15 June with Mahmoud Riad, Secretary-General of the Arab League, President Frangieh changed his mind.[95] The President announced that he would permit the deployment of the Symbolic Arab Security Force, after he had received assurances from Mahmoud Riad that the deployment would 'take place . . . in agreement with the Lebanese authorities regarding all details, especially the size and nationality of the Arab troops which are to be sent to Lebanon'.[96] President Frangieh agreed to the introduction of the Force 'within the limits set by assurances and clarifications offered by the General-Secretary in the name of the League, provided this initiative is coordinated with the fraternal Syrian initiative currently under way and to which Lebanon had acceded'.[97]

Notes

1   Bulloch, *Death of a Country*, pp.37-8.
2   Salibi, *Crossroads*, pp.98-9.
3   Ibid., pp.76-7.
4   Cobban, *PLO*, pp.15-16, 66.
5   Khalidi, *Conflict and Violence in Lebanon*, p.47.
6   Ibid.
7   Salibi, *Crossroads*, pp.102-3.
8   Ibid., pp.103-4.
9   Rabinovich, *War for Lebanon*, p.44.
10   Salibi, *Crossroads*, pp.107-8.
11   Ibid., p.108.
12   Rabinovich, *War for Lebanon*, p.44.
13   For the composition of the Cabinet, see e.g. Salibi, *Crossroads*, p.112.
14   Ibid., p.110.

15 Ibid., pp.110-11.
16 Ibid., p.116.
17 Ibid., pp.116-17.
18 Khalidi, *Conflict and Violence in Lebanon*, p.48.
19 On the Christian side, the militias included, in addition to the Kataeb or Phalange, Tony Frangieh's 'Zghorta Liberation Army', and Chamoun's PNL militia. On the Muslim side, the formation of a new Shia Muslim militia, 'Amal', was announced by the Imam Musa Sadr. See e.g. Rabinovich, *War for Lebanon*, p.45. Amal members received support and training at Al Fatah camps in the Lebanon. See Salibi, *Crossroads*, p.119.
20 Salibi, *Crossroads*, p.120.
21 Khalidi, *Conflict and Violence in Lebanon*, p.48.
22 Ibid., pp.48-9.
23 Salibi, *Crossroads*, pp.124-5.
24 Khalidi, *Conflict and Violence in Lebanon*, pp.48-9.
25 Salibi, *Crossroads*, p.128.
26 See generally Dawisha, *Syria and the Lebanese Crisis*, pp.91-2.
27 In accordance with Article 11 of the Pact of the League of Arab States, the Council may 'convene in extraordinary session upon the request of two member states of the League whenever the need arises'.
28 On the status of the PLO within the Arab League see, Chapter 1, notes 55-8 above, and the accompanying text. On the reasons for the non-participation of Syria, Libya and the PLO, see e.g. *Keesing's* (1976), pp.27767-8.
29 The text of the communiqué is reproduced in *al-Nahar*, 17 October 1975. It is available, in English, in *IDP* (1975), p.493.
30 See e.g. Kourula, *Peacekeeping and Regional Arrangements*, p.105.
31 Hassouna, *Regionalism*, p.319.
32 Article 5.
33 Ibid.
34 Ibid.
35 My emphasis.
36 For a detailed analysis of these concepts, as embodied in the League Pact, see Chapter 1, notes 123-41, and the accompanying text.
37 See above, Chapter 1, note 141, and the accompanying text.
38 Salibi, *Crossroads*, p.131.
39 Khalidi, *Conflict and Violence in Lebanon*, p.49.
40 Dawisha, *Syria and the Lebanese Crisis*, pp.92-3.
41 See note 19 above.
42 Salibi, *Crossroads*, p.133.
43 Ibid.
44 Dawisha, *Syria and the Lebanese Crisis*, p.93.
45 Salibi, *Crossroads*, pp.141-2.
46 For details see e.g. *Keesing's* (1976), p.27768.
47 Salibi, *Crossroads*, pp.145-6.
48 Randal, *Tragedy of Lebanon*, pp.84-5.
49 Salibi, *Crossroads*, pp.146-8.
50 Ibid.
51 Khalidi, *Conflict and Violence in Lebanon*, p.51.
52 Cobban, *PLO*, pp.68-9.
53 Salibi, *Crossroads*, pp.151-2.
54 This was acknowledged by President Assad in a speech broadcast on Syrian radio on 20 July 1976. The text of the broadcast is available, in English, in Rabinovich, *War for Lebanon*, p.201. See, in particular, ibid., pp.210-11. On

the role of the PLA within the PLO, see e.g. Cobban, *PLO*, p.13. Units of the PLA had previously entered Lebanese territory from Syria during the fighting in October. Salibi, *Crossroads*, p.132. The legality of the Syrian initiative is extremely doubtful. *Prima facie* the Syrian decision to introduce units of the PLA into the Lebanon amounted to a breach of Article 2(4) of the UN Charter which proscribes any 'threat or use of force against the territorial integrity or political independence of any State'. As noted in Chapter 3, Article 2(4) has frequently been interpreted by the General Assembly as proscribing not merely an attack by regular forces, but also support for armed bands which are infiltrated into another state. See Chapter 3, note 139, and the accompanying text. President Assad, in his radio broadcast of 20 July 1976, explained his decision to despatch PLA units as having been motivated by concern at the prospect of a 'dangerous massacre' of Lebanese Muslims by Maronite militias, and by his desire 'to save the [Palestinian] resistance'. See Rabinovich, *War for Lebanon*, pp.211-12. The former objective practically amounts to the assertion of a right of humanitarian intervention. This doctrine has been extensively discussed in Chapter 2. In the view of the present writer, it has no place in contemporary international law. See Chapter 2, note 73. The latter objective, the protection of the Palestinian 'resistance', is also of doubtful legality. In effect, it amounted to forcible Syrian assistance for the Palestinian insurgents involved in the Lebanese civil conflict. As will be explained in Chapter 6, the law relating to intervention in civil conflicts is in a state of some uncertainty. While some publicists continue to recognize a right of military assistance to governments, a significant proportion consider aid to either the government, or to the insurgents, as impermissible intervention. However, at no time has there been support for the view that a third party may intervene to assist insurgents. Such action has consistently been regarded as unlawful intervention. Thus, the General Assembly's Declaration on the Principles of International Law, affirms that 'no State shall organize, assist, foment, finance, incite or tolerate subversive, terrorist or armed activities directed towards the violent overthrow of the regime of another State, or interfere in civil strife in another State'. See GA Res. 2625 (XXV), 24 October 1970. For further discussion of the law relating to intervention in civil conflicts, and for references to appropriate authorities, see Chapter 6.

55   For a somewhat lurid account of the fall of Damour, see J. Becker, *The PLO* (1984), Chapter 22.

56   For the terms of reference of the Higher Military Committee see *al-Nahar*, 23 January 1976. The text is reproduced, in English, in *IDP* (1976), p.363. See, generally, Dawisha, *Syria and the Lebanese Crisis*, pp.118-19; Salibi, *Crossroads*, pp.158-9.

57   Dawisha, *Syria and the Lebanese Crisis*, p.119. On Saiqa, see e.g. Cobban, *PLO*, pp.157-61. On the PLA, see ibid., p.12.

58   Dawisha, *Syria and the Lebanese Crisis*, pp.119-20. For the text of the joint statement issued by the two heads of state, on 7 February 1976, see *al-Baath*, 8 February 1976. The text is reproduced, in English, in *IDP* (1976), p.196.

59   For the text of the President's message, see *al-Nahar*, 15 February 1976. Excerpts are available, in English, in *IDP* (1976), p.370.

60   Ibid.

61   On the Cairo Agreement, see Chapter 3, note 182, and the accompanying text.

62   See generally Dawisha, *Syria and the Lebanese Crisis*, pp.120-1.

63   Ibid.

64   See e.g. Khalidi, *Conflict and Violence in Lebanon*, p.53. Lieutenant Khatib, formerly an officer in the Lebanese army, had deserted in late January to

form the largely Muslim Lebanese Arab Army. See e.g. Gilmour, *Lebanon*, p.132.
65 For the text of Brigadier Ahdab's communiqué, see *al-Nahar*, 12 March 1976. The text is available, in English, in *IDP* (1976), p.384.
66 *Keesing's* (1976), p.27771.
67 Syria was opposed to the forcible removal of the Lebanese President, and was unwilling to acquiesce in a rebel initiative which it had not sanctioned. See in particular Dawisha, *Syria and the Lebanese Crisis*, p.124. See also Khalidi, *Conflict and Violence in Lebanon*, p.54.
68 Bulloch, *Death of a Country*, pp.123-5.
69 Ibid., p.123.
70 Dawisha, *Syria and the Lebanese Crisis*, p.125.
71 Khalidi, *Conflict and Violence in Lebanon*, pp.55-6. The convening of the Lebanese Chamber of Deputies was facilitated by the declaration of a ceasefire. This was due, in large measure, to massive Syrian pressure on the Lebanese National Movement. Syria severed arms supplies to Lebanese Leftists and Syrian troops were reinforced along the Lebanese border. In addition, a Syrian armoured column advanced into Lebanese territory, while Syrian naval vessels enforced a blockade of Lebanese ports used by the National Movement. See generally Dawisha, *Syria and the Lebanese Crisis*, pp.128-30.
72 Khalidi, *Conflict and Violence in Lebanon*, p.56.
73 Bulloch, *Death of a Country*, p.138.
74 Dawisha, *Syria and the Lebanese Crisis*, pp.133-5.
75 Bulloch, *Death of a Country*, p.138.
76 See generally on the reasons underlying Syrian intervention, Dawisha, *Syria and the Lebanese Crisis*, pp.134-5. See also Rabinovich, *War for Lebanon*, p.54. See also President Assad's own explanation, given in a speech broadcast by Radio Damascus on 20 July 1976. For the text of the speech, see e.g. Rabinovich, *War for Lebanon*, p.201. In the broadcast, Assad argues that his overriding objective was to stop the fighting in the Lebanon, and thereby prevent the country from breaking up into confessional cantons. See ibid., pp.207-8. In addition, President Assad emphasized Syria's common cultural, geographical and historical links with the Lebanon: 'through history, Syria and Lebanon have been one country and one people. The people in Syria and Lebanon have been one through history. Genuine joint interests ensued.' Ibid., pp.205-6. For an alternative explanation of Syria's intervention in the Lebanon, emphasizing domestic Syrian considerations, see F.H. Lawson, 'Syria's Intervention in the Lebanese Civil War, 1976: a Domestic Conflict Explanation', *Int. Org.*, vol. 38 (1984), p.451.
77 Bulloch, *Death of a Country*, p.143.
78 Khalidi, *Conflict and Violence in Lebanon*, pp.58-9. The Syrian intervention cannot be justified under international law. As noted above, Syria's decision to despatch units of the PLA constituted a breach of Article 2(4) of the UN Charter. See note 54 above. *A fortiori*, the intervention by regular Syrian troops in the Lebanon violated international law. This conclusion is not affected by the fact that the PLA were introduced to fight the Maronite militias, whereas the Syrian army was deployed to counter the Palestinian-Leftist forces. In both instances, the Syrian action, which was taken without reference to the Lebanese authorities, amounted to a 'use of force against the territorial integrity or political independence' of the Lebanon within the meaning of Article 2(4). Following the introduction of regular Syrian troops, in June, President Frangieh expressed some support for their continued presence. See

note 91 below, and the accompanying text. However, it must be emphasized that the Syrian government did not seek the *prior* approval of the Lebanese authorities for the deployment of Syrian troops. President Frangieh's subsequent attitude cannot validate the Syrian presence retrospectively. Nor is it clear that the consent of the Lebanese President would have been sufficient to authorize the intervention of Syrian troops in the Lebanese civil conflict. As noted above, there is increasing support for the view that no foreign assistance is permissible for *either* the government *or* the insurgents involved in a civil war. See note 54 above. There is also some doubt as to whether the Lebanese President, a Maronite Christian with his personal militia, could be regarded as representing the Lebanese authorities in their entirety. In view of the confessional character of appointments to the Lebanese government, it is far from clear that Muslim or Druze ministers welcomed the Syrian intervention which was directed against the Palestinian-Leftist alliance.

79   Bulloch, *Death of a Country*, pp.146-51.
80   Dawisha, *Syria and the Lebanese Crisis*, pp.136-7.
81   For the texts of the messages from the PLO and Egypt to the Secretary-General of the League of Arab States, requesting an extraordinary session of the Council, see, respectively, *Wafa*, 2 June 1976, 2nd Bulletin, pp.4-5; *al-Ahram*, 4 June 1976. Both texts are available, in English, in *IDP* (1976), pp.425-6.
82   League Council Resolution No. 3456, 9 June 1976. The resolution is reproduced in *al-Ahram*, 9 June 1976. It is available, in English, in *IDP* (1976), p.431. A French translation may be found in *Le Monde*, 10 June 1976, p.2. The following quotations are taken from the English-language translation referred to above.
83   Ibid.
84   Ibid.
85   Ibid.
86   Ibid. An earlier draft of the resolution had referred to the 'withdrawal' of Syrian forces. After objections from the Syrian Foreign Minister, the term 'replacement' was used instead. See *The Times*, 11 June 1976, p.1.
87   League Council Resolution No. 3457, 10 June 1976. For details see e.g. *Le Monde*, 11 June 1976, p.1.
88   *Le Monde*, 11 June 1976, p.1.
89   See e.g. G. Feuer, 'La Force Arabe de Sécurité au Liban', *AFDI*, vol. 22 (1976), p.51, at p.53. See also Bulloch, *Death of a Country*, pp.151-2; Khalidi, *Conflict and Violence in Lebanon*, p.59. PLO Chairman Yassir Arafat argued that, following the Council's resolution, Syria could only retain a military presence in Lebanon which was equivalent in size to the other national contingents in the Security Force. See *Le Monde*, 12 June 1976, p.3.
90   *Le Monde*, 15 June 1976, p.2 (my translation).
91   *Le Monde*, 10 June 1976, p.2.
92   See *al-Safir*, 11 June 1976. The message is reproduced, in English, in *JPS*, vol. 6 (1976/77), p.170.
93   Ibid. Lebanon's Ambassador to Cairo attended the Council meeting. However, President Frangieh subsequently claimed that he had only been there in an unofficial capacity. See e.g. *Fiches du Monde Arabe*, 4 February 1981, No. 1812. Article 7 of the Pact states: '[u]nanimous decisions of the Council shall be binding upon all member states of the League; majority decisions shall be binding only upon those states which have accepted them.' Consequently, member states are only bound by resolutions which they have accepted. The question of attendance is, therefore, not directly relevant, other than as evidence of non-acceptance. For a more detailed consideration of the rules

governing voting in the League Council, see Chapter 1, notes 78-81, and the accompanying text.
94 For the text of the communiqué, see *al-Nahar*, 12 June 1976. The text is available, in English, in *IDP* (1976), p.432.
95 *Keesing's* (1976), p.28119.
96 See communiqué issued by the Office of the Presidency of Lebanon, 16 June 1976, in *al-Nahar*, 17 June 1976. The text is available, in English, in *IDP*, 1976, p.433.
97 Ibid.

5 The Functions and Powers of the Arab League Force in the Lebanon

The 'Symbolic Arab Security Force'

The Arab League Force in the Lebanon was originally designated as a 'Symbolic Arab Security Force'. In accordance with a resolution adopted by the League Council, on 9th June 1976, the Force was empowered to 'maintain security and stability in Lebanon'.[1] The resolution stated that the Force 'should start to perform its task immediately, replacing the Syrian forces'.[2]

The Arab League Force was not authorized to remain in the Lebanon without host-state consent. Thus, the resolution of 9 June emphasized '[t]he task of this Arab security force should be brought to an end if the president-elect of the republic of Lebanon so requests'.[3] The clarity of this provision may be contrasted with the uncertainty surrounding the mandate of the United Nations Emergency Force, which was deployed in Egypt in 1956.[4] Following an Egyptian request for the prompt removal of UNEF, in May 1967, there was some controversy as to whether Egypt had the right, unilaterally, to demand the withdrawal of the UN Force.[5]

The subordination of the Symbolic Arab Security Force to the ultimate authority of the Lebanese government was emphasized further in a resolution adopted by the League Council on 10 June. Thus, the Council resolved that the Force should act 'within the framework of Lebanese sovereignty'.[6]

The Arab Deterrent Force

Following the Riyadh and Cairo Summit Conferences of October 1976, the Symbolic Arab Security Force was transformed into the Arab Deterrent Force. Thus, the Resolution adopted by the Six-Party Arab Summit Conference, convened in Riyadh, decided that 'existing Arab security forces should be expanded to 30 000 men so that they might become a deterrent force operating inside Lebanon'.[7] The functions and powers of the Arab Deterrent Force (ADF) were set out in the Resolution and Schedule adopted by the Riyadh Summit Conference on 18 October 1976.[8] The Resolution of the Riyadh Conference defined the functions of the Arab Deterrent Force in the following terms:[9]

(a) Ensuring observance of the cease-fire and termination of hostilities, disengaging belligerent troops and deterring any violation of the agreement;
(b) Implementing the Cairo Agreement and its annexes;[10]
(c) Maintaining internal security;
(d) Supervising the withdrawal of armed troops to positions they held prior to 13 April 1975 and removing all military installations in accordance with the schedule set out in the enclosed annex;
(e) Supervising the collection of heavy weaponry such as artillery, mortars, rocket-launchers, armoured vehicles, etc., by the parties concerned;
(f) Assisting the Lebanese authorities when necessary with respect to taking over public utilities and institutions prior to their re-opening as well as guarding public military and civilian establishments.

The Schedule adopted by the Six-Party Arab Summit Conference elaborated, in considerable detail, the manner in which the Force was to accomplish these objectives. The Summit Conference had emphasised that the Schedule should be considered 'an integral part' of the Riyadh Resolution.[11]

The Schedule envisaged the declaration of a final cease-fire and the 'termination of fighting in all Lebanese territories by all parties as from 6.00 a.m. on 21 October 1976 (D-Day)'.[12] Following the establishment of a cease-fire, and 'the creation of buffer-zones in areas of tension',[13] the Schedule provided that the Arab Deterrent Force would establish checkpoints 'in order to consolidate the ceasefire and the termination of fighting'.[14]

As noted above, the Resolution adopted by the Riyadh Summit Conference required the Arab Deterrent Force to supervise the 'withdrawal of armed troops to positions they held prior to 13 April

1975' and the 'collection of heavy weaponry . . . by the parties concerned'.[15] In addition, the Resolution entrusted the Force with responsibility for 'removing all military installations'.[16] The Schedule laid down the following time-table for discharging these obligations:[17]

(a)   Mount Lebanon: within five days (D-Day + 5).
(b)   Southern Lebanon: within five days (D-Day + 5).
(c)   Beirut and outskirts: within seven days (D-Day + 7).
(d)   Northern Lebanon: within ten days (D-Day + 10).

The Schedule also entrusted the Arab Deterrent Force with responsibility for facilitating the re-opening of Lebanon's principal roads. Thus, the Schedule stated that four of Lebanon's 'international highways shall be reopened within 5 days (D-Day + 5)'.[18] These were the following:[19]

– Beirut/Al Masnaa
– Beirut/Tripoli/the Borders
– Beirut/Tyre
– Beirut/Sidon/Marjayoun/Al Masnaa

The Schedule provided that '[c]heckpoints and patrols shall be established along unsafe routes, and shall consist of units from the deterrent security force as agreed by the parties concerned and the commander of the said force'.[20]   The Force's responsibility for facilitating travel on Lebanon's major roads was consistent with the ADF's principal function of '[e]nsuring observance of the cease-fire and termination of hostilities'.[21] This is, at any rate, how the first Commander of the Deterrent Force, Colonel Ahmed al-Hajj, viewed the matter.[22]

As noted above, the Resolution of the Riyadh Summit Conference charged the Arab Deterrent Force with '[a]ssisting the Lebanese authorities when necessary with respect to taking over public utilities and institutions prior to their re-opening as well as guarding publics military and civilian establishments'.[23] The Schedule adopted by the Summit Conference emphasized that '[t]he legitimate Lebanese authorities shall take over public, military and civilian utilities and establishments'.[24] The Arab Deterrent Force was to facilitate this process in the following manner:[25]

(a)   after the removal of armed troops and non-employees, the Arab security force shall be assigned to guarding such utilities and establishments and facilitating their operation by employees who shall begin work within 10 days (D-Day + 10);

(b)   the utilities and establishments shall be handed over to an official central Lebanese commission which shall, in turn, be responsible for forming a sub-committee in each utility or establishment to make an inventory of its contents and to take over.

Once again, these responsibilities may be viewed as consistent with the duty of the Arab Deterrent Force to ensure the observance of the ceasefire and the termination of hostilities.[26] In addition, they may be seen as contributing to the maintenance of internal security.

As noted previously, the Resolution of the Riyadh Summit Conference designated the implementation of 'the Cairo Agreement and its annexes' as one of the 'principal tasks' of the Deterrent Force. Responsibility for the implementation of these texts was also entrusted to a newly-constituted committee composed of Saudi, Egyptian, Syrian and Kuwaiti representatives.[27] In accordance with the Riyadh Resolution, the committee would 'ensure co-ordination with the President of Lebanon in respect of the implementation of the Cairo Agreement and its annexes', and would function for an initial 90-day period.[28] The Schedule adopted by the Riyadh Summit Conference stipulated:[29]

> As a second stage, [after the declaration of a ceasefire, establishment of checkpoints, withdrawal of armed troops, etc.] the Cairo Agreement and its annexes shall be implemented, particularly those provisions concerning the existence of weapons and ammunition in refugee camps and the exit of those armed Palestinian forces that entered the country after the beginning of the incidents. The implementation of the agreement is to be completed within 45 days, beginning on the date of the formation of the Arab deterrent security force.

The Cairo Agreement was concluded by Lebanese and PLO officials in November 1969 after a period of fighting.[30] The PLO pledged 'non-interference in Lebanese affairs', while the Lebanese authorities undertook 'to facilitate . . . Fedayeen action'.[31] This was interpreted, by the Palestinians, as permitting guerrilla operations against Israel. In addition, the Cairo Agreement envisaged that steps would be taken to 'organis[e] the presence of arms and their limitation in the camps',[32] although the Agreement omitted to specify the levels, or types, of arms which could be retained.

The Cairo Agreement did not require the withdrawal of all PLO guerrillas from the Lebanon, despite the reference in the Schedule of the Riyadh Conference to implementation of 'those provisions concerning . . . the exit of . . . armed Palestinian forces that entered the country after the beginning of the incidents'. Indeed, the Cairo Agreement had recognized '[t]he right of work, residence, and movement of Palestinians *presently* residing in Lebanon'.[33] However, the Agreement did provide for a census of all Palestinian guerrillas 'operating in Lebanon', and for the introduction of regulations governing, *inter alia*, the entry and departure of guerrillas from the country.[34]

A series of Annexes to the Cairo Agreement, drawn up by the PLO and the Lebanese authorities between January 1970 and May 1973, specified, in some detail, the types of arms that could be retained in the Palestinian refugee camps, and principles governing the presence of PLO guerrillas in the Lebanon.[35] Thus, an agreement concluded between the PLO and Lebanese military personnel in May 1973, known as the 'Melkart Understanding' after the Beirut hotel in which it was negotiated, stipulated that 'Fedayeen', i.e. guerrillas, were no longer permitted in the refugee camps, the defence of which was to be entrusted to a 'militia' composed of civilian residents.[36] The militia would be provided with 'individual light weapons'.[37] However, the agreement emphasized that '[t]here are to be no medium or heavy arms in the camps; for example: mortars, rockets, cannons, anti-tank weapons, etc.'[38]

In addition, the Melkart Understanding placed an explicit moratorium on guerrilla operations against Israel. Thus, the PLO agreed that '[a]ll operations from Lebanese territory are frozen' and that Palestinian guerrillas were forbidden to leave Lebanon 'for a foreign country in order to undertake Fedayeen operations'.[39]

Thus, the Cairo Agreement and its Annexes were inconsistent on the crucial question of whether guerrilla operations could be mounted against Israel from southern Lebanon. The Cairo Agreement implied that such operations were permissible. The Annexes stated, categorically, that they were forbidden. The 1976 Riyadh and Cairo Summit Conferences, which called for the implementation of the Cairo Agreement and its Annexes, failed to resolve this question. Indeed, it is doubtful whether the leaders attending the Summit Conferences were even aware of the contradiction.

As noted previously, the Cairo Agreement itself did not provide for the withdrawal of Palestinian guerrillas from the Lebanon, beyond emphasizing that only Palestinians already in the Lebanon enjoyed a right of 'residence'.[40] However, during the fighting in May 1973, several hundred Palestinian guerrillas crossed into the Lebanon from Syria. Accordingly, the Melkart Understanding, which was eventually negotiated by the PLO and the Lebanese authorities, required 'the restitution of all reinforcements offered to the Lebanon from abroad'.[41]

During the course of the civil war which began in April 1975, contingents of the Palestine Liberation Army entered Lebanon to assist the Palestinian-Leftist militias.[42] In calling for the implementation of the Cairo Agreement and its Annexes, particularly of the provisions concerning 'the exit of those armed Palestinian forces that entered the country after the beginning of the incidents', the Schedule of the

Riyadh Conference was no doubt referring to the PLA units which had crossed into the Lebanon early in 1976.[43]

The change in nomenclature of the Arab League Force also merits consideration. Constituted as 'the Symbolic Arab Security Force', in June 1976, with a mandate 'to preserve security and stability in Lebanon',[44] it was transformed by the Riyadh and Cairo Resolutions[45] into the 'Arab Deterrent Force' with the functions outlined above.

The term 'deterrent', from the Arabic 'al-Rad', is indicative of a significant extension of the Force's powers. This transformation, of what was a conventional peacekeeping mission into a force with mandatory and coercive powers, is confirmed by the text of the Riyadh Resolution. The Resolution called for an increase in the size of the 'existing Arab security forces . . . so that they might become a *deterrent* force operating inside Lebanon'.[46] The Resolution stated that one of the 'principal tasks' of the Force would be to 'deter' any violation of the ceasefire.[47]

On his assumption of office Colonel al-Hajj, the first Commander of the Arab Deterrent Force, emphasized the potentially coercive character of the new Force. Colonel al-Hajj declared that the ADF 'shall carry out their tasks justly and firmly and shall work for the interests of all without partiality or distinction'.[48] However, he warned that '[i]n calling upon everyone to facilitate the execution of their mission, [the Force] declare their resolve to use *deterrent force* whenever security so requires'.[49] Similarly, at a press conference after the conclusion of the Cairo Summit Conference, the League's Secretary-General, Mahmoud Riad, had stated that the ADF would have the power 'to enforce peace'.[50]

Endorsement by the League of Arab States

A plenary Arab Summit Conference was convened in Cairo, on 25 October. Of the 21 members of the League, 14 were represented by Heads of State, while Yassir Arafat attended on behalf of Palestine.[51] With the exception of Libya, which declined to participate in the initial sessions of the Summit Conference, the remaining member states were represented by government ministers, or by senior political advisers.[52]

On the following day, the Summit Conference adopted a series of resolutions in which, *inter alia,* it 'approve[d] the statement., resolutions and annexes' of the Six-party Arab Summit Conference.[53] However, Iraq did not assent to this provision, while Libya did not participate in the Conference session at which the resolutions were adopted.[54]

As noted in Chapter 1, Arab Summit Conferences are treated as equivalent to sessions of the League Council.[55] Consequently, the resolution of the Cairo Summit Conference, approving the 'resolutions and annexes' of the Riyadh summit, amounted to a decision by the League of Arab States to establish the Arab Deterrent Force, endowed with the functions and powers laid down in the Resolution and Schedule of the Riyadh Conference. As such, the Resolution of the Cairo Summit Conference was binding on those members of the League who had accepted it.[56]

The Chtaura Agreement

The 'Chtaura Agreement', concluded in July 1977 by Lebanese, Syrian and PLO delegates, placed certain additional duties upon the Arab Deterrent Force.[57] In essence, the agreement provided for strict Palestinian compliance with the provisions of the Cairo Agreement and its Annexes, particularly the Melkart Understanding. Accordingly, Palestinian guerrillas would be withdrawn from a six-mile strip along the border with Israel, to specified areas in southern Lebanon. Guerrilla operations against Israel were forbidden, while any heavy weapons remaining in the Palestinian camps would be surrendered.[58]

In accordance with the agreement, units of the ADF were to establish checkpoints at the entrances to the Palestinian refugee camps, and the ADF was empowered to 'stage surprise raids' on illegal arms caches.[59] Previously, the Arab Deterrent Force had not been authorized to enter the Palestinian camps.

These new responsibilities were consistent with the functions of the Arab Deterrent Force, as laid down in the Resolution and Schedule adopted by the Riyadh Summit Conference. Thus, the Riyadh Summit had authorized the ADF to supervise the 'collection of heavy weaponry', and to oversee the implementation of the Cairo Agreement and its Annexes.[60] Accordingly, the Chtaura Agreement, while entrusting particular tasks to the Deterrent Force, did not modify its essential mission.

It is perhaps more surprising that the ADF, which was created by the League of Arab States, should have implemented the Chtaura Agreement, even though it was never formally endorsed by the Council of the Arab League. However, it should be borne in mind that Lebanon was a party to the Chtaura Agreement and that, under the terms of the Riyadh Resolution, the Lebanese President had been placed in overall command of the Arab Deterrent Force.[61] In addition, the military Commander of the ADF, also a Lebanese national, participated in the negotiations at Chtaura.[62]

The Beiteddine Conference

The Beiteddine Conference, held in October 1978, was attended by the Foreign Ministers of Lebanon, Syria, Saudi Arabia and Kuwait. In addition, delegates were sent by the United Arab Emirates, Qatar and Sudan.[63] These comprised all of the states then contributing funds or troops to the Arab Deterrent Force, and also the host-state, Lebanon.

The Conference adopted a series of proposals which provided, *inter alia,* for the collection of all weapons retained contrary to the Cairo Agreement and its Annexes, the curbing of 'armed manifestations', and strict application of the resolutions adopted by the Riyadh and Cairo Conferences of October 1976.[64] In addition, the Conference called for the ending of 'information campaigns', and the prohibition of illegal radio, television and press operations.[65] Various decisions were also taken concerning the redeployment of ADF units in Beirut.[66]

The Beiteddine Conference affirmed the continuing importance of the Arab Deterrent Force, to which the Conference 'expressed its appreciation'. The proposals adopted by the Conference either reproduced, or were consistent with, the original mandate of the ADF as expressed in the Resolution and Schedule adopted by the Riyadh Summit Conference.

Perhaps the most controversial proposal adopted by the Beiteddine Conference concerned the ending of 'information campaigns' and the prohibition of illegal media. These measures, for whose implementation the ADF assumed some responsibility, could perhaps be justified as a means of maintaining 'internal security' in accordance with the Resolution of the Riyadh conference.[67]

Notes

1 League Council Resolution No. 3456, 9 June 1976.
2 Ibid.
3 Ibid
4 On the establishment of UNEF see e.g. Pogany, *Security Council,* p.78. See also Higgins, *I*, Part 2.
5 See generally Pogany, *Security Council,* pp.85-6. See also Higgins, *I*, pp.362-7; J. Dehaussy, 'La Crise du Moyen-Orient et l'O.N.U.', *RGDIP,* vol.95 (1968), p.853, at pp.861-2.
6 League Council Resolution No. 3457, 10 June 1967.
7 Para. 2, Resolution adopted by the Six-Party Arab Summit Conference (Riyadh, 1976); For further details concerning the transformation of the Symbolic Arab Security Force into the Arab Deterrent Force, see Chapter 8.
8 See, respectively, Resolution adopted by the Six-Party Arab Summit Conference (Riyadh, 1976); Schedule adopted by the Six-Party Arab

Summit Conference (Riyadh, 1976). These texts, and related documents, are reproduced in the appendices. In addition to the texts cited in this book, which are based on a UN text, other English-language translations of the Resolution and Schedule adopted by the Riyadh Conference are available in *Keeesing's* (1976), pp.28122-3; *IDP* (1976), pp.492-3. For the Arabic text of the Resolution and Schedule see *al-Ahram,* 19 October 1976.

9   See para. 2, Resolution adopted by the Six-Party Arab Summit Conference (Riyadh, 1976).

10 On the background to the Cairo Agreement see Chapter 3, notes 174-81, and the accompanying text. For the text of the Cairo Agreement in Arabic, see *al-Nahar,* 20 April 1970. For English-language translations see e.g. *Fiches du Monde Arabe,* 20 October 1976, No. 575; Khalidi, *Conflict and Violence in Lebanon,* p.185; Lukacs, *Documents,* p.215. The complete text of the Annexes to the Cairo Agreement are reproduced in *Fiches du Monde Arabe,* 20 October 1976, No. 575, Supplement (38 pp.). The text of the 'Melkart Understanding', which constitutes a part of the Annexes, is reproduced in Lukacs, *Documents,* p.216. For an analysis of the legal implications of the Cairo Agreement, see e.g. G. Feuer, 'Les Accords Passé par les Gouvernements de Jordanie et du Liban avec Les Organisations Palestiniennes (1968-1970)', *AFDI,* vol. XVI p.177, esp. at pp.193-4. The Cairo Agreement and the Melkart Understanding are reproduced in the appendices.

11 See para. 9, Resolution adopted by the Six-Party Arab Summit Conference (Riyadh, 1976).

12 Para. 1, Schedule adopted by the Six-Party Arab Summit Conference (Riyadh, 1976). See also para. 1, Resolution adopted by the Six-Party Arab Summit Conference (Riyadh, 1976), in which the date of the commencement of the ceasefire is also given.

13 Para. 2, Schedule adopted by the Six-Party Arab Summit Conference (Riyadh, 1976).

14 Ibid.

15 Paras. 2(d),(e), Resolution adopted by the Six-Party Arab Summit Conference (Riyadh, 1976).

16 Ibid.,para. 2(d).

17 Para. 3, Schedule adopted by the Six-Party Arab Summit Conference (Riyadh, 1976).

18 Ibid., para. 4(a).

19 Ibid.

20 Ibid., para. 4(b).

21 Para. 2(a), Resolution adopted by the Six-Party Arab Summit Conference (Riyadh, 1976).

22 See below, note 48.

23 Ibid., para. 2(f). Resolution adopted by the Six-Party Arab Summit Conference (Riyadh, 1976).

24 Para. 5, Schedule adopted by the Six-Party Arab Summit Conference (Riyadh, 1976).

25 Ibid.

26 Para. 2(a), Resolution adopted 'by the Six-Party Arab Summit Conference (Riyadh, 1976).

27 Ibid., para. 4.

28 Ibid.

29 Para. 7, Schedule adopted by the Six-Party Arab Summit Conference (Riyadh, 1976).

30 See note 10 above.
31 Cairo Agreement, op. cit., note 10.
32 Ibid.
33 Ibid. It is not clear from the text of the Agreement whether this provision relates solely to Palestinian civilians, or whether it also extends to Palestinian guerrillas. However, it has generally been interpreted as including both categories. See e.g. Feuer, op. cit., note 10, p.193. The use of the term 'presently' suggests that Palestinians who enter the Lebanon, subsequent to the conclusion of the Cairo Agreement, do not enjoy an automatic right of residence.
34 Cairo Agreement, op. cit., note 10.
35 Unlike the Cairo Agreement, the Annexes are not widely available. However, an English-language translation, which has yet to be authenticated, has been published in *Fiches du Monde Arabe*. See note 10 above.
36 Melkart Understanding, op. cit., note 10.
37 Ibid.
38 Ibid.
39 Ibid.
40 See notes 33-4 above and the accompanying text.
41 This quotation is taken from the English-language translation of the Melkart Understanding reproduced in *Fiches du Monde Arabe*. See supra, note 10.
42 See Chapter 4, note 54 and the accompanying text.
43 The Schedule of the Riyadh conference, in calling for 'the exit of those armed Palestinian forces that entered the country after the beginning of the incidents', does not specify which 'incidents' are at issue. Presumably, however, it is a reference to the 'incidents' of April 1975. If so, the withdrawal of Palestinian forces that entered the Lebanon *after* April 1975 can scarcely be based on the provisions of the Cairo Agreement, or its Annexes, which were concluded *before* the eruption of the Lebanese civil war in 1975.
44 Para. 3, League Council Resolution No. 3456, 9 June 1976. The Resolution is reproduced in *IDP* (1976), p.431.
45 See Resolution adopted by the Six-Party Arab Summit Conference (Riyadh, 1976); Resolutions adopted by the Arab Summit Conference (Cairo, 1976).
46 Para. 2, Resolution adopted by the Six-Party Arab Summit Conference (Riyadh, 1976).
47 Ibid., para. 2(a).
48 See *al-Nahar,* 10 November 1976. The text of the statement is reproduced, in English, in *IDP* (1976), p.506.
49 Ibid.
50 *The Times,* 27 October 1976, p.8.
51 See e.g. *Keesing's,* (1976), p.28123.
52 For details see e.g. *Le Monde.* 26 October 1976, p.3.
53 See para. 1, Resolution I, Resolutions adopted by the Arab Summit Conference (Cairo, 1976).
54 A Libyan delegate did, however, participate in the subsequent sessions of the Conference. See *Le Monde,* 27 October 1976, p.2.
55 See Chapter 1, note 89, and the accompanying text.
56 Article 7 of the Pact of the Arab League states: 'Unanimous decisions of the Council shall be binding upon all member states of the League; majority decisions shall be binding only upon those states which have accepted them.'
57 For details see e.g. Gilmour, *Lebanon,* p.150. See also Khalidi, *Conflict and Violence in Lebanon,* p.119.

58   Ibid.
59   Keesing's (1977), p.28735.
60   Para. 2(b)(e), Resolution adopted by the Six-Party Arab Summit Conference (Riyadh, 1976).
61   Ibid., para. 2.
62   See Chapter 8.
63   Ibid.
64   For the text of the statement issued by the Beiteddine Conference, see e.g. *IDP* (1978), p. 561.
65   Ibid.
66   See Chapter 8.
67   Syria was acutely sensitive to criticism of its role in the Lebanon. Syrian troops of the ADF occupied a number of newspaper offices in Beirut which had been critical of Syrian actions, shortly after their deployment in the capital. Subsequently, the Maronite community opposed the continued presence of Syrian troops in the Lebanon, expressing its views through its own media organs. See Chapter 8.

6 The Legal Basis of the Arab League Force in the Lebanon

The immediate basis, in law, of the Arab League Force in the Lebanon are the Council resolutions of 9 and 10 June 1976, and the resolutions of the Riyadh and Cairo Summit Conferences. As noted in previous chapters, the League Council, meeting in extraordinary session, established the Symbolic Arab Security Force in June 1976.[1] In October, a six-party Arab Summit Conference, convened in Riyadh, decided that 'existing Arab security forces should be expanded to 30 000 men so that they might become a deterrent force operating inside Lebanon'.[2] A plenary Arab Summit, meeting in Cairo, endorsed the resolutions of the Riyadh Conference, translating them into decisions of the League of Arab States.[3] However, the ultimate legal basis of the Arab League Force in the Lebanon must be found in the Pact of the Arab League, and in the Charter of the United Nations.[4]

Any analysis of the constitutionality of the Arab League Force in the Lebanon must be preceded by an evaluation of its character, i.e. was the Force an example of international peacekeeping, of collective security, or of enforcement action by a regional organization? Only then can the legal basis of the Force be properly determined.

The Nature of the Arab League Force in the Lebanon

The Arab League Force in the Lebanon has been widely character-ized as an example of regional 'peacekeeping'. This characterization has been applied not only to the first phase of the Force, before the Riyadh and Cairo Summits, but also to the second phase, when the pan-Arab operation became known as the Arab Deterrent Force. Thus, Dr Hassouna has commented:[5]

> It must be emphasized that in spite of the transformation of the force – in size, level of equipment, scope of mandate and pattern of supervision – its basic nature remained that of a regional peace-keeping force . . .

However it may be useful to recall, at this juncture, that there is no universally accepted definition of peacekeeping. This is due, at least in part, to the fact that peacekeeping has developed on an *ad hoc* basis. Unlike the maintenance of international peace, peacekeeping was not listed amongst the functions of the United Nations, or of the various regional organizations.[6] Nevertheless, a rough consensus has emerged amongst political scientists concerning the nature of 'peacekeeping'. The term is associated, in the main, with host-state consent, the absence of coercion, and political impartiality.[7]

In its original form, before the Riyadh and Cairo Summit Conferences, the Arab League Force readily complied with these criteria. Thus, the Council resolution establishing the Symbolic Arab Security Force emphasized that host-state consent was a prerequisite for the existence of the Force.[8] Similarly, while charged with 'maintain[ing] security and stability' in the Lebanon, the Arab League troops were not authorized to use force in circumstances other than self-defence.[9]

The available evidence also suggests that, at least in conception, the Symbolic Arab Security Force was politically impartial. Thus, one of the objectives underlying the creation of the Force was to replace Syrian troops in the Lebanon who had intervened in the civil conflict in favour of the Maronites.[10] As an additional safeguard, the Secretary-General of the Arab League indicated that the size and nationality of the various contingents would be determined in cooperation with the Lebanese authorities.[11]

However, once the Symbolic Arab Security Force had been transformed into the Arab Deterrent Force it no longer conformed so readily with traditional notions of peacekeeping. The resolution adopted by the Riyadh mini-Summit authorized the Arab Deterrent Force to 'deter' violations of the ceasefire.[12] At the conclusion of the Cairo Summit Conference, the League Secretary-General indicated that the ADF would be empowered 'to "enforce" peace'.[13] On assuming his office, the first Commander of the Force, Colonel al-Hajj, emphasized the resolve of the ADF 'to use deterrent force whenever security so requires'.[14]

Prima facie, the Arab Deterrent Forcé cannot be reconciled with a 'narrow' view of peacekeeping, which excludes resort to armed force in circumstances other than self-defence. However, the 'narrowness' of this view, and hence the exclusion of the ADF, may be more apparent than real. Ultimately, it depends on the ambit of the doctrine of self-defence.

UN Secretary-General Hammarskjold, for example, assumed that peacekeeping operations are, by definition, restricted to the use of force in self-defence. This assumption influenced the Secretary-General's attitude to the mandate and functions of ONUC, the UN Operation in the Congo.[15] However, it is significant that the range of functions vested in ONUC, which the Secretary-General believed to be authorized by the principle of self-defence, was striking in its breadth. Thus, a Security Council resolution, adopted on 21 February 1961, authorized ONUC to use force, if necessary, 'to prevent the occurrence of civil war'.[16]

There is little difference between a mandate to use force to prevent the *occurrence* of civil war, as in the case of ONUC, and a mandate to use force to 'deter' a *resumption* of civil conflict, as illustrated by the ADF. Thus, a 'broad' view of the doctrine of self-defence may permit recognition of the ADF as a peacekeeping force, even by those adhering to the 'narrow' view of peacekeeping.

However, the 'narrow' view of peacekeeping, which confines the use of force to self-defence, may be unnecessarily restrictive. The *Certain Expenses Case* suggests that a broader construction is legitimate.

In its Advisory Opinion in the *Certain Expenses Case,* the International Court reviewed the powers which had been vested in ONUC. As noted above, these included the capacity to use force, if necessary, 'to prevent the occurrence of civil war'.[17] They included, in addition, authority to use 'the requisite measure of force, if necessary, for the immediate apprehension, detention pending legal action and/or deportation of all foreign military and paramilitary personnel and political advisers not under the United Nations Command, and mercenaries'.[18]

The Court did not attempt to argue that such measures were founded on a right of self-defence. The argument is, at best, tenuous.[19] Instead, the Court noted:[20]

> the operations of ONUC did not include a use of armed force against a State which the Security Council, under Article 39, determined to have committed an act of aggression or to have breached the peace. The armed forces which were utilized in the Congo were not authorized to take military action against any State. The operation did not involve 'preventive or enforcement measures' against any State under Chapter VII . . .

Thus, the Court drew a distinction between the use of force as a *sanction*, against a state which has committed an act of aggression or has threatened international peace, and the use of force to maintain law and order.[21] The distinction is noted by Oscar Schachter, legal adviser to Hammarskjold during the Congo operation, in a pseudonymously written article:[22]

> The kind of military action which the Council authorized in the Congo was restricted essentially to the maintenance of internal law and order, the purpose of which was to enable the Belgian troops to be speedily withdrawn. While this was a use of armed force, it was essentially of a police or 'criminal law' character, and in that sense seems fundamentally different from the type of enforcement measure which had been envisaged as the military sanctions of Article 42. Certainly, the expectation at San Francisco was that Article 42 would be resorted to for military action of an international character – that is to say, directed against the troops of a state or another governmental authority which bore responsibility for a breach of peace or act of aggression. Use of troops for internal security purposes at the request of the territorial state does not have this kind of international coercive character . . .

Thus, the Advisory Opinion of the International Court supports the conclusion that peacekeeping operations may use force in civil conflicts, outside the parameters of self-defence, for the purpose of preserving (or restoring) internal order. A prerequisite of such an operation is host-state consent.[23] In the light of the foregoing, the characterization of the ADF as a 'peacekeeping' operation is at least tenable. Applying the 'narrow' view of peacekeeping, i.e. that force may only be used in self-defence, it is significant that the mandate of the ADF is scarcely distinguishable from that of ONUC. The latter was authorized to use force, if necessary, to prevent the occurrence of civil war.[24] The former was mandated to 'deter' violations of a ceasefire.[25] If the functions of ONUC can be reconciled with the concept of self-defence, as argued by Hammarskjold, the powers of the Arab Deterrent Force are also consistent with the doctrine.

Applying a 'broad' view of peacekeeping, it is unnecessary to argue that peacekeeping operations are restricted to the use of force in self-defence. On this view, peacekeeping forces may use armed force provided that the consent of the host-state has been obtained, that the purpose of the coercion is to promote internal order, and that the nature of the forcible assistance does not amount to intervention in a civil conflict.[26]

Intervention in civil conflicts

Peacekeeping forces such as ONUC and the Arab League Force in the Lebanon, which operate against a background of civil conflict, raise delicate questions concerning the permissibility of intervention in civil wars. There has been extensive debate, for example, as to whether the activities of ONUC amounted to an unlawful intervention in the civil strife in the Congo.[27] Similar questions must be faced in relation to the operations of the Arab League Force in the Lebanon.

The law concerning intervention in civil conflicts is in a state of some uncertainty. While a number of publicists continue to recognize a right of military assistance to governments, a significant proportion consider aid to either the government, or to the insurgents, as impermissible intervention.[28] An intermediate viewpoint, which has attracted a number of adherents, is that assistance to a government ceases to be lawful once the insurgents have attained a certain measure of support.[29] Different considerations apply where the insurgents are receiving support from a third party. In such circumstances, assistance to the government is often characterized as collective self-defence.[30]

Whatever view one adopts of the current law concerning intervention in civil conflicts, it is difficult to accept that the mandate of the Arab League Force in the Lebanon amounted to 'intervention' in any but the most unavoidable sense.[31] As originally constituted, the Symbolic Arab Security Force was explicitly required to act 'within the framework of Lebanese sovereignty'.[32] Even after its transformation into the Arab Deterrent Force, in accordance with the Resolution of the Riyadh Conference, it did not involve assistance to either the government, or to the insurgents, in waging an armed conflict. As noted previously, the functions of the ADF included 'observance of the ceasefire . . . termination of hostilities, disengaging belligerent troops and deterring any violation of the agreement'.[33] It is also significant that the Lebanese and Syrian Presidents, and the Chairman of the PLO, consented to the establishment of the Arab League Force in the Lebanon, and to its subsequent evolution into the Arab Deterrent Force. Thus, the principal parties to the Lebanese conflict had approved the creation, and subsequent modification, of the Force.[34]

It is even doubtful whether the situation in the Lebanon can be characterized as a civil war in the conventional sense. A significant proportion of the Palestinian guerrillas active in the Lebanon had entered the country after the commencement of the fighting. Few of the remainder possessed Lebanese nationality. Since June 1976, thousands of regular Syrian troops had also become embroiled in the conflict.

In these circumstances, it seems reasonable to conclude that the establishment, successively, of the Symbolic Arab Security Force and the Arab Deterrent Force did not amount to intervention in a civil war. It is far from clear that the functions of the Force, in either phase of its existence, constituted 'intervention', or that the disturbances were a 'civil conflict' in the normal sense of that term.[35] The Arab League Force in the Lebanon should be viewed, instead, as a lawful measure to assist the restoration of Lebanese unity and sovereignty, and thereby arrest a serious threat to regional peace.

The Authority of the Arab League to establish a peacekeeping force in the Lebanon

In the absence of express legal authority, two types of argument can be advanced to justify the establishment of peacekeeping forces by international organizations. These are (a) that particular treaty provisions may be interpreted as authorizing peacekeeping operations; and (b) that there is a presumption that an organization is acting *intra vires.*

Examples of the former type of argument can be found in analyses of the peacekeeping activities of the United Nations.[36] Due to the frequent failure of UN organs to specify particular Charter provisions as underpinning their actions, such arguments often have a speculative flavour.

Authority for the latter proposition, in the context of UN peacekeeping, can be found in the Advisory Opinion of the International Court of Justice in the *Certain Expenses Case.* The Court held that 'when the Organization takes action which warrants the assertion that it was appropriate for the fulfilment of one of the stated purposes of the United Nations, the presumption is that such action is not *ultra vires* the Organization'.[37] The Court went on to observe:[38]

> In the legal systems of States, there is often some procedure for determining the validity of even a legislative or governmental act, but no analogous procedure is to be found in the structure of the United Nations. Proposals made during the drafting of the Charter to place the ultimate authority to interpret the Charter in the International Court of Justice were not accepted; . . . As anticipated in 1945, therefore, each organ must, in the first place at least, determine its own jurisdiction. If the Security Council, for example, adopts a resolution purportedly for the maintenance of international peace and security and if, in accordance with a mandate or authorization in such a resolution, the Secretary-General incurs financial obligations, these amounts must be presumed to constitute 'expenses of the Organization'.

That particular treaty provisions permit the establishment of peacekeeping forces

The Pact of the Arab League does not provide *expressly* for peacekeeping operations. Nevertheless, there are various provisions of the Pact, and of the Treaty of Joint Defence, which can be construed as authorizing the establishment of peacekeeping forces. In particular, Article 2 of the Pact states that one of the purposes of the League shall be to co-ordinate the policies of members 'in order to achieve cooperation between them and to safeguard their independence and sovereignty'. The purposes of the Organisation include, in addition, 'a general concern with the affairs and interests of the Arab countries'.[39]

The Treaty of Joint Defence, which is an integral part of the League's system of collective security, is also pertinent.[40] The preamble notes the desire of the contracting states to cooperate, *inter alia,* for the 'maintenance of security and peace' and to 'consolidate stability and security'. Article 3 is of particular importance. This notes that 'the Contracting States shall hold consultations whenever there are reasonable grounds for the belief that the territorial integrity, independence, or security of any one of the parties is threatened'. In the event of 'the threat of war or the existence of an international emergency', the Contracting States undertake to 'unify their plans and defensive measures, as the situation may demand'.[41]

Thus, the establishment of peacekeeping forces, such as the Arab League Force in the Lebanon, is consistent with both the Pact and with the Treaty of Joint Defence. The creation of the Force can be viewed as a means of fulfilling one of the purposes of the League, that is of safeguarding the 'independence and sovereignty' of member states. This was, without doubt, the principal objective of the Arab League in establishing and maintaining the Force.[42]

The establishment of the Arab League Force in the Lebanon can also be seen as a means of giving expression to 'a general concern with the affairs and interests of the Arab countries'.[43] By June 1976, the Lebanese conflict had escalated to a point where it threatened regional peace.

Article 3 of the Pact states that the Council is charged with 'the realisation of the objectives of the League'. For politically important issues, Arab Summit Conferences frequently assume the functions of the Council.[44] Thus, the Council resolutions of June 1976, and the Cairo Summit Conference in October of the same year, represented the appropriate constitutional means to establish the Arab League Force.

The provisions of the Treaty of Joint Defence are also relevant. The Arab League Force was clearly a means of 'consolidat[ing] stability and security' as understood by the preamble, while the situation in the Lebanon can be characterized as 'an international emergency' within the meaning of Article 3. Accordingly, the establishment of the Arab League Force in the Lebanon amounted to the Contracting States 'unify[ing] their plans . . . as the situation may demand'.[45]

The presumption that action is intra vires

As noted above, the International Court of Justice, in the *Certain Expenses Case*, held that 'when the Organization takes action which warrants the assertion that it was appropriate for the fulfilment of one of the stated purposes of the United Nations, the presumption is that such action is not *ultra vires* the Organisation.[46] The Court placed particular emphasis on the absence of an 'ultimate authority' to interpret the Charter, and on the fact that 'each organ must, in the first place at least, determine its own jurisdiction'.[47]

Although these arguments were advanced with reference to the United Nations, they can be applied, by analogy, to the League of Arab States.[48] The purposes of the League, as expressed in Article 2 of the Pact, include the coordination of the policies of member states 'to safeguard their independence and sovereignty'. By June 1976, the 'independence and sovereignty' of the Lebanon was threatened by the escalating civil conflict, and by the intervention of third parties. Consequently, the establishment of the Arab League Force was 'appropriate for the fulfilment of one of the stated purposes' of the League.

Unlike the United Nations, the League does not even possess a judicial organ.[49] Thus, there is no 'ultimate authority' to interpret the Pact, other than the Council and the Conferences of Arab Kings and Heads of State.

Compatibility of the Arab League Force in the Lebanon with the UN Charter

The UN Charter recognizes the right of member states to establish regional arrangements for the maintenance of international peace and security. Thus, Article 52(1) states:

> Nothing in the present Charter precludes the existence of regional arrangements or agencies for dealing with such matters relating to the maintenance of international peace and security as are appropriate for regional action, provided that such arrangements or agencies and their activities are consistent with the Purposes and Principles of the United Nations.

However, Article 53(1) imposes a significant limitation on the authority of regional organizations:

> The Security Council shall, where appropriate, utilise such regional arrangements or agencies for enforcement action under its authority. But no enforcement action shall be taken under regional arrangements or by regional agencies without the authorisation of the Security Council . . .

A number of questions arise concerning the compatibility of the Arab League Force in the Lebanon with the UN Charter:

1 Did the establishment of the Arab League Force, particularly after its transformation into the ADF, amount to 'enforcement action' within the meaning of Article 53(1)?
2 If question (1) is answered in the *affirmative*, some analysis of the meaning of Security Council 'authorisation' will be necessary, in order to determine whether the establishment of the Arab League Force breached the requirements of Article 53.
3 If question (1) is answered in the *negative*, it will be necessary to determine whether the matter dealt with, that is the civil conflict in the Lebanon, was 'appropriate for regional action' as understood by Article 52, and whether the relevant 'arrangements' and their 'activities' were 'consistent with the Purposes and Principles of the United Nations'.[50]

The concept of 'enforcement action'

As noted previously, the Advisory Opinion of the International Court of Justice, in the *Certain Expenses Case*, offers some guidance as to the meaning of 'enforcement action'. The Court held that 'enforcement action' must mean 'such action as is solely within the province of the Security Council'.[51] Such 'action' can take the following forms:[52]

> it is the Security Council which is given a power to impose an explicit obligation of compliance if for example it issues an order or command to an aggressor under Chapter VII. It is only the Security Council which can require enforcement by coercive action against an aggressor.

The reasoning of the Court suggests that 'enforcement action' may be of two types. A measure may constitute 'enforcement action' *either* because it is mandatory *or* because it is coercive.[53] However, as previously noted, the Court found that ONUC did not amount to 'enforcement action', even though it had been authorized to use force in circumstances which could not be reconciled with the concept of self-defence. In effect, the Court distinguished between the use of force as a sanction, and the use of force to preserve law and order within a state:[54]

> the operations of ONUC did not include a use of armed force against a State which the Security Council, under Article 39, determined to have committed an act of aggression or to have breached the peace. The armed forces which were utilised in the Congo were not authorised to take military action against any State. The operation did not involve 'preventive or enforcement measures' against any State under Chapter VII and therefore did not constitute 'action' as that term is used in Article 11.

There are significant similarities between ONUC and the Arab Deterrent Force. Both operations were authorized to use force to assist in the pacification of what were, to some degree, civil conflicts. Neither was mandated to use force as a sanction, in the sense of Article 42 of the Charter. In view of the finding of the Court that ONUC did not constitute 'enforcement action', it seems reasonable to conclude that the Arab Deterrent Force was also a 'peacekeeping' operation. *A fortiori*, the Symbolic Arab Security Force, the first phase of the Arab League operation in the Lebanon, did not amount to 'enforcement action'. As will be recollected, the Symbolic Arab Security Force lacked either mandatory or coercive powers.[55]

It has been suggested that Security Council authorization is a prerequisite for peacekeeping, as well as for enforcement action, by regional organizations.[56] However, this argument is unconvincing. It can only be reconciled with the requirements of Article 53(1) if the distinction between 'peacekeeping' and 'enforcement action' is ignored. While this argument was advanced by certain states in the *Certain Expenses Case*, it was rejected by the Court in its Advisory Opinion.[57] Crucially, the argument is unsupported by state practice. There has been no criticism of the Arab League for 'failing' to obtain Security Council authorization for the establishment, successively, of the Symbolic Arab Security Force and the Arab Deterrent Force.

Was the Lebanese conflict 'appropriate for regional action'?

There can be little doubt that the Lebanese conflict was 'appropriate for regional action' within the meaning of Article 52. As noted above, the conflict had ceased to be of a wholly domestic character by June 1976. The infiltration of armed Palestinian elements from Syria, and the deployment of regular Syrian forces, had rendered the situation a threat to regional peace.

The appropriateness of 'regional action' was also confirmed by the fact that the states embroiled in the Lebanese conflict, and the PLO, were represented in the League of Arab States.[58] Consequently, none of the states parties to the Lebanese conflict were excluded from the League.[59]

Were the relevant arrangements and their activities consistent with the purposes and principles of the United Nations?

In essence, two distinct questions arise. Article 52 must be understood as requiring that *both* the 'arrangements' *and* their 'activities' are consistent with the Purposes and Principles of the United Nations.[60]

Despite an Egyptian initiative at the San Francisco conference, the UN Charter does not offer a definition of 'regional arrangements' for the purposes of Chapter VIII.[61] Nevertheless, it is broadly accepted that the Arab League constitutes a 'regional arrangement' within the meaning of Article 52 of the Charter. In part, this is reflected in the writings of jurists.[62] In part, it can be deduced from the practice of the UN itself.

As will be recalled, Lebanon informed the Security Council in 1958 that the UAR was fomenting civil disturbances in its territory.[63] The Security Council, although seised of the Lebanese complaint, complied with Iraqi and Lebanese requests that the Arab League should first be given the opportunity to effect a peaceful settlement.[64] This amounted to *de facto* recognition of the League as a 'regional arrangement' for the purposes of Chapter VIII of the Charter.

The 'activities' of the League, in establishing the pan-Arab Force in the Lebanon, were also consistent with 'the Purposes and Principles of the United Nations', foremost of which is the maintenance of international peace and security.[65] As noted above, the Lebanese conflict increasingly threatened regional order, while the essence of the Force's mandate, at all stages of its existence, was to ensure the maintenance of a ceasefire. Thus, the Arab League Force in the Lebanon was an 'activity' consistent with 'the Purposes and Principles of the United Nations'.

Notes

1 See Chapter 4, notes 86-7, and the accompanying text.
2 Para. 2, Resolution adopted by the Six-Party Arab Summit Conference (Riyadh, 1976).
3 Resolution I, Resolutions adopted by the Arab Summit Conference (Cairo 1976).
4 It is, perhaps, misleading to suggest that authority for the establishment of the

Arab Deterrent Force must be found in the UN Charter. Regional organizations, such as the Arab League, do not derive their powers, or their legitimacy, from the United Nations. See e.g. Kelsen, *United Nations*, pp.321-4. Nevertheless, Articles 52-4 of the UN Charter place important constraints on the autonomy of regional organizations. These constraints are examined below.

5   Hassouna, *Regionalism*, p.321. See also Kourula, *Peacekeeping and Regional Arrangements*, p.111; Rikhye, *Peacekeeping*, p.133.

6   Despite the absence of express legal authority, peacekeeping operations have been mounted by the United Nations, by the Organization of American States, by the Organization of African Unity and by the League of Arab States. For an overview see e.g. Rikhye, *Peacekeeping*, esp. Chapters 1 and 5.

7   See e.g. Rikhye, *Peacekeeping*, p.2. See also L. Fabian, *Soldiers Without Enemies* (1971) p.16; D Wainhouse, *International Peacekeeping at the Crossroads* (1973), p.1; I. Rikhye, M Harbottle and B. Egge, *The Thin Blue Line* (1974), p.10.

8   The resolution establishing the Symbolic Arab Security Force stated that the Force's mission would be 'brought to an end' at the request of the Lebanese President-elect. *A fortiori*, the Force could not commence its operations without the consent of the Lebanese authorities. See League Council Resolution No. 3456, 9 June 1976.

9   This can be inferred from the fact that the Force was transformed into the Arab Deterrent Force, which was expressly mandated to use force to 'deter' violations of the ceasefire. See generally Chapter 5, notes 44-50, and the accompanying text.

10   See Chapter 4, note 89, and the accompanying text.

11   Chapter 4, note 96, and the accompanying text.

12   Para. 2(a), Resolution adopted by the Six-Party Arab summit conference (Riyadh, 1976).

13   *The Times*, 27 October 1976, p.8.

14   *IDP* (1976), p.506.

15   See e.g. Bowett, *UN Forces*, pp.200-3.

16   SC Res. S/4741, 21 February 1961.

17   Ibid.

18   SC Res. S/5002, 24 November 1961. This resolution was adopted *after* Hammarskjold's death, in September 1961.

19   See e.g. Bowett, *UN Forces*, pp.201-3.

20   *ICJ Rep.* (1962), p.151, at p.177.

21   See e.g. Higgins, *III*, p.58.

22   E.M. Miller, 'Legal Aspects of the United Nations Action in the Congo', *AJIL*, vol. 55 (1961), p.1, at p.8. See also Higgins *Development*, pp.236-7; Bowett, *UN Forces*, p.271. Arguably, the passage from the Advisory Opinion in the *Certain Expenses Case* can be read as supporting an alternative distinction, i.e. between coercion *of a state* and coercion *within a state*. On this view, the former is 'enforcement action', whereas the latter may qualify as 'peacekeeping'. See e.g. Abi-Saab, *Congo*, p.104, note 165. The quotation from Professor Schachter's article, cited above, is also consistent with this alternative interpretation.

23   In the absence of consent, the introduction of peacekeeping troops would infringe the 'territorial integrity and political independence' of the host-state, contrary to Article 2(4) of the Charter. Thus, the International Court was careful to note that ONUC was established in response to 'the appeal from the Government of the Congo'. *ICJ Rep.* (1962) p.175.

24   See note 16 above.

25 See note 12 above. Despite the similarities there are, of course, significant differences between the two forces. ONUC was established by the UN, whereas the Arab League Force in the Lebanon was created by the Arab League. Justification for the former must therefore be found in Chapters VI and VII of the Charter, whereas the constitutionality of the latter is governed by Chapter VIII. It follows, therefore, that the Court's view of 'enforcement measures', for the purposes of Chapter VII, is not necessarily conclusive as to the meaning of 'enforcement action', as understood by Chapter VIII. Nevertheless, these terms are generally seen as synonymous. See e.g. Goodrich, Hambro, Simons, *Charter*, p.365. See also A. Chayes, *The Cuban Missile Crisis* (1974), pp.60-1; Kourula, *Peacekeeping and Regional Arrangements*, p.115. Even the International Court seems to have used these terms interchangeably. See *ICJ Rep.* (1962), pp.171, 177.

26 Bowett clearly subscribes to this 'broad' view of peacekeeping. While recognizing that the functions of ONUC could not be justified as self-defence, he views ONUC as a genuine peacekeeping operation. With reference to the coercive powers assumed by ONUC, Bowett argues:

> clinging to the 'self-defence' concept . . . was unfortunate in the context of measures to prevent a civil war . . . What was really required was the assertion of a right (which is not the right of self-defence but a more general right to maintain peace between the rival factions) to act against any unit which began military action in defiance of the Security Council Resolutions . . . (Bowett, *UN Forces*, p.202).

27 See e.g. Higgins, *Development*, pp.228-31. See also Bowett, *UN Forces*, pp.191-200; Abi-Saab, *Congo*, pp.57-65, 97-107, 129-31.

28 While recognizing the 'diverse and contradictory trends in the practice of states', Brownlie concludes that the traditional customary law right of assistance to governments has not been superseded. See Brownlie, *Use of Force*, p.327. For a similar conclusion, albeit with comparable reservations, see e.g. Skubiszewski, *Use of Force*, p.750. In terms of recent state practice, it is noteworthy that the right of military assistance to the lawful government was recently affirmed by the US as a partial justification for its intervention in Grenada. See e.g. letter, dated 10 February 1984, from the legal adviser of the Department of State to Professor E. Gordon, Chairman of the Committee on Grenada of the American Bar Association's Section on International Law and Practice. The letter is reproduced in *AJIL*, vol. 78 (1984), p.661. See, in particular, at p.662. For the view that assistance to either the government or to the insurgents is impermissible, see e.g. Q. Wright, 'Subversive Intervention', *AJIL*, vol. 54 (1960), p.521, at p.529. See, also, D.W. Bowett, 'The Interrelation of Theories of Intervention and Self-Defense', in J.N. Moore (ed.), *Law and Civil War in the Modern World* (1974), p.38, at pp.41-2.

29 See e.g. E. Lauterpacht, 'Intervention by Invitation', *ICLQ*, vol. 7 (1958), p.102, at p.104. See also R. Higgins 'The Legal Limits to the Use of Force by Sovereign States: United Nations Practice', *BYIL*, vol. 34 (1961) p.269, at pp.308-9.

30 In 1958, for example, US military assistance to the Lebanese government was characterized as collective self-defence. As will be recalled, the Lebanese authorities argued that the insurgents in the Lebanon were receiving support from the United Arab Republic. For details see Chapter 3, note 117, and the accompanying test. See, also, E. Lauterpacht, 'The Contemporary Practice of the United Kingdom in the Field of International Law', *ICLQ*, vol. 8 (1959), p.146, at pp.149-51.

31　Thus, commenting on ONUC, Abi-Saab notes that, merely by virtue of its existence, the Force had some impact on the civil conflict in the Congo:

> Maintenance of law and order, especially in a situation of relative chaos and a power vacuum, inevitably had an impact on the internal political balance. The mere existence of a large U.N. Force in the Congo did affect the internal political situation, if only by radically changing the context within which the political struggle for power took place. In these circumstances every act of omission or commission by the Force had a potential effect on the internal situation. (Abi-Saab, *Congo*, p.65)

32　League Council Resolution No. 3457, 10 June 1976.

33　See note 12 above.

34　The Presidents of Lebanon and Syria, and the Chairman of the PLO, had participated in the Riyadh and Cairo Summit Conferences which established the ADF. For details see Chapter 8. The three leaders had, albeit with greater difficulty, accepted the establishment of the Symbolic Arab Security Force, in June 1976. For details see Chapter 4.

35　This analysis is based on the functions and powers granted to the Arab League Force in the Lebanon. Consequently, it does not take into account the *actual* behaviour of the Force in so far as it deviated from its mandate.

36　See e.g. Bowett, *UN Forces*, pp.274-312. See also the 'Constitutional Basis' chapters in Higgins, *I-IV*.

37　*ICJ Rep.* (1962), p.151, at p.168.

38　Ibid.

39　Art. 2, League Pact.

40　It may be objected that the Treaty of Joint Defence is not relevant to peacekeeping as the Treaty was concluded, chiefly, to improve the League's system of collective security. However, Dr Hassouna has argued persuasively that there is an organic link between the League's collective security functions and its peacekeeping activities. See Hassouna, *Regionalism*, p.317.

41　Art. 3, Treaty of Joint Defence.

42　The Council resolution establishing the Arab League Force in the Lebanon called on the parties to the Lebanese conflict to achieve comprehensive national reconciliation 'to ensure the maintenance of the unity of the Lebanese people and the unity of their territory and the country's sovereignty, security and stability'. See League Council Resolution No. 3456, 9 June 1976. See also the Statement adopted by the Six-Party Arab Summit Conference (Riyadh, 1976), which noted the agreement of the participating leaders to 'preserve the security, safety, independence and sovereignty of Lebanon'. Similarly, the Preamble of the Resolution adopted by the Six-Party Arab Summit Conference (Riyadh, 1976) recognized the 'national commitment to preserve the unity, security and sovereignty of Lebanon', while the communiqué adopted by the Arab Summit Conference (Cairo, 1976) recognized that the 'Arab Kings and Heads of State are unanimous in their commitment to maintain Lebanon's national unity and territorial integrity'.

43　Art. 2, League Pact.

44　See Chapter 1, notes 86-9, and the accompanying text.

45　Art. 3, Treaty of Joint Defence. This provision has been relied upon by a number of Syrian jurists as providing a legal basis for the Arab League Force in the Lebanon. See Ben Amara, above p.ix, note 10, pp.125-6.

46　See note 37 above.

47　Ibid.

48　The arguments advanced in the *Certain Expenses Case*, with respect to the

United Nations, have been applied to the peacekeeping functions assumed by the Organization of African Unity. See G.J. Naldi, 'Peace-Keeping Attempts by the Organisation of African Unity', *ICLQ*, vol. 34 (1985), p.593, at note 2.

49 Article 19 of the Pact anticipates the creation of an 'Arab Tribunal of Arbitration'. However, this has not materialized.

50 A literal construction of the Charter suggests that Article 52 imposes constraints on the types of disputes that may be dealt with, on the sorts of regional organizations that are competent to deal with them, and on the methods which may be employed. There has been widespread acceptance of this view. Thus, states participating in measures authorized by regional organizations have frequently argued not only that their actions do not amount to 'enforcement action', within the meaning of Article 53, but also that their activities are consistent with the requirements of Article 52. See e.g. the US justifications of the OAS-sponsored naval quarantine of Cuba, in 1962, and of the OECS-approved intervention in Grenada, in 1983. On Cuba, see *Department of State Memorandum: Legal Basis for the Quarantine of Cuba*, 23 October 1962. The text is reproduced in Chayes, op. cit., note 25, p.141. See, in particular, ibid., pp.143-6. On Grenada, see letter from the Legal Adviser of the Department of State, etc., op. cit., note 28, at pp.663-4. See, in addition, Syria's arguments in the UN Security Council concerning the collective Arab intervention in Palestine, in May 1948. See SCOR 299th mtg., pp.13-15; SCOR 301st mtg., p.12. See also Goodrich, Hambro, Simons, *Charter*, pp.357-60.

51 *ICJ Rep.*, (1962), p.151, at p.165.

52 Ibid., p.163.

53 The US has contended that unless a measure is mandatory it does not constitute 'enforcement action'. This was, for example, the US position with regard to the 'voluntary' naval quarantine of Cuba authorized by the Organization of American States. See *Department of State Memorandum etc.*, op. cit., note 50, at pp.146-8. For a critique of the US position, see e.g. A. Eide, 'Peace-Keeping and Enforcement by Regional Organisations'. *Journal of Peace Research*, vol. 3 (1966), p.125, at p.140.

54 *ICJ Rep.*, (1962), p.151, at p.177.

55 See Chapter 5, notes 1-6, and the accompanying text.

56 See e.g. Kourula, *Peacekeeping and Regional Arrangements*, pp.116-18. See also Eide, op. cit., note 53, at pp.141-2.

57 *ICJ Rep., Pleadings* (1962), at pp.177-8, 270-1.

58 On the significance of this factor see e.g. Goodrich, Hambro, Simons, *Charter*, p.358. Palestine became a full member of the League in September 1976. See Chapter 1, note 58, and the accompanying text.

59 Of course, the various confessional groupings in the Lebanon lacked individual representation in the League.

60 See e.g. Goodrich, Hambro, Simons, *Charter*, p.355.

61 For the text of the Egyptian definition of 'regional arrangements', see UNCIO *Documents*, vol. 12, p.857.

62 Both Arab and non-Arab jurists have recognized the League as a regional organization, for the purposes of Chapter VIII of the Charter. See e.g. Hassouna, *Arab League*, pp.11-12; A. Moussa, 'Rapports entre les Nations Unies et La Ligue des Etats Arabes', *REDI*, vol. 29 (1973), p.67, at pp.69-70, 72-3; Kourula, *Peacekeeping and Regional Arrangements*, p.102; Eide, op. cit., note 53, at p.136.

63 See Chapter 3, note 108, and the accompanying text.

64 Ibid., note 110.

65 See Art. 1(1), UN Charter.

7 Composition, Organization, Control and Finance of the Arab League Force in the Lebanon

Composition of the Arab League Force

As noted in Chapter 4, the Council, in a resolution adopted on 10 June 1976, entrusted the Secretary-General of the League with responsibility for deciding all details concerning the composition of the Symbolic Arab Security Force.[1] The Secretary-General was required to make his decisions 'according to the needs of the situation' and 'in accordance with the PLO'.[2] A spokesman for the Arab League indicated that contingents for the Force would be drawn from Algeria, Saudi Arabia, Libya, Sudan, Syria and the PLO.[3]

However, after President Frangieh had demonstrated his opposition to the introduction of the Arab League Force on Lebanese territory, the Secretary-General reached an accommodation with the Lebanese President. It was decided that the agreement of the Lebanese authorities would be necessary concerning all details, including 'the size and nationality' of the Arab contingents.[4]

The first units of the Symbolic Arab Security Force arrived in Beirut on 21 June. These comprised two 500-man contingents despatched by Libya and Syria.[5] Additional Libyan and Syrian troops arrived during the following weeks, together with small contingents from Sudan and Saudi Arabia.[6] The Syrian contingent included a battalion of PLA troops, comprising some 600 men. By mid-July, the Symbolic Arab Security Force was estimated to comprise 2500 men.[7]

President Frangieh called for the withdrawal of the Libyan

contingent, on the grounds that the Libyan regime was closely aligned with the Palestinian guerrillas.[8] The President declared that 'Libya is in no way suitable to participate in the Arab peace-keeping force which is expected to have a neutral position in this conflict'.[9] However, the Lebanese Prime Minister, Rashid Karami, informed the League Council that the President had exceeded his constitutional powers in bringing these views to the attention of the League without having obtained the prior approval of the Lebanese government.[10] The Libyan contingent remained in the Lebanon until the end of November, when it was withdrawn on the instructions of the Libyan government.[11]

The composition, and size, of the Arab League Force in the Lebanon changed dramatically following the decision of the Riyadh summit conference, in October 1976, that 'existing Arab security forces should be expanded to 30 000 men so that they might become a deterrent force operating inside Lebanon'.[12] As previously noted, the plenary Arab summit conference, meeting in Cairo, approved the Resolution of the Riyadh conference, transforming it into a decision of the League of Arab States.[13]

On 26 October, during the Cairo Summit Conference, the Secretary-General of the League, Mahmoud Riad, announced that Libya, the PLO, Saudi Arabia, Sudan, Syria, North and South Yemen, and the United Arab Emirates had agreed to contribute troops to the Arab Deterrent Force.[14] However, Algeria, Morocco, Tunisia and Egypt declined to furnish contingents.[15]

There was bitter disagreement amongst the Arab Kings and Heads of State participating in the Cairo Summit concerning the size of the national contingents. The PLO demanded that Syrian units should not exceed 10 000 men,[16] whereas Syria insisted that her troops should account for at least half of the Deterrent Force, i.e. 15 000 men.[17] A meeting of Arab Foreign Ministers, convened on the night of 25 October, failed to resolve these differences; nor could a series of private talks between Arab leaders on the final day of the Summit Conference.[18] In the absence of prior agreement, Secretary-General Riad announced, at the conclusion of the Conference, that the Lebanese President, Elias Sarkis, would determine the size of each national contingent.[19]

Despite Palestinian objections, President Sarkis agreed that Syria should contribute the bulk of the Arab Deterrent Force – up to 25 000 men.[20] Palestinian hopes of ensuring the inclusion of substantial non-Syrian contingents were frustrated by Egypt's refusal to contribute any troops to the Arab Deterrent Force,[21] and by Syrian opposition to the participation of PLO formations.[22]

The Libyan, Saudi and Sudanese contingents of the Symbolic Arab Security Force, which had remained in place in the Lebanon, were integrated into the Arab Deterrent Force.[23] However, these were limited in size. The Libyans had deployed 700 men in the Lebanon as against 1000 Sudanese troops, and a Saudi contingent of 1200 men.[24] The United Arab Emirates despatched 1000 troops, South Yemen agreed to provide 700 men, while an additional 1000 soldiers were sent by Saudi Arabia.[25]

On 29 November, Libya announced that its troops would be withdrawn from the Lebanon. Libya declared that its decision was prompted by the failure of the Arab League Force to comply with the resolutions of the Riyadh and Cairo Summit Conferences.[26] In reality, it is likely that the Libyan withdrawal was motivated by concern at the extent of Syrian influence in the Lebanon.[27]

The small South Yemeni contingent was withdrawn in December 1977.[28] Thereafter, during 1978 and 1979, the other non-Syrian units in the Arab Deterrent Force were progressively withdrawn. In October 1978, Sudan announced that it would terminate its participation in the Force. Sudanese troops were eventually withdrawn from the Lebanon in February 1979.[29] In March, Saudi Arabia withdrew its contingent from the ADF, while the United Arab Emirates removed their troops at the end of April 1979.[30]

The governments concerned justified their decision by claiming that the troops were required for national defence. Thus, the Saudis stated that they had been compelled to recall their contingent because of an outbreak of fighting between the neighbouring states of North and South Yemen.[31] In reality, the withdrawal of the Sudanese, Saudi and UAE contingents can be ascribed to the realization that the Lebanese factions had shown little inclination for national reconciliation, and that the ADF was therefore incapable of fulfilling its mandate.[32] In addition, the three governments were perturbed by the increasingly violent behaviour of the Syrian troops. From July to October 1978, Syrian forces clashed intermittently with Maronite militiamen in Beirut. The Syrians, who made frequent use of their artillery, caused hundreds of fatalities amongst the civilian population.

According to reports from Maronite sources, Syria deployed some 3600 troops of the Palestine Liberation Army in the Lebanon, in March 1979, as part of its ADF contingent. The troops, who were positioned chiefly in the central sector of Beirut, were commanded by Syrian officers.[33] There were no further changes in the composition of the Arab League Force before its mandate expired in July 1982.

Organization and control of the Arab League Force

In accordance with the Council resolution of 9 June 1976, the

Symbolic Arab Security Force was placed 'under the supervision' of the League's Secretary-General, Mahmoud Riad.[34] An Egyptian officer, Major-General Muhammad Hassan Ghoneim, was appointed Commander of the Force.[35]

By contrast, the Resolution of the Six-Party Arab Summit Conference, which transformed the Symbolic Arab Security Force into the Arab Deterrent Force, stated that the Deterrent Force would operate 'under the personal command of the President of the Lebanese Republic'.[36] As noted above, the decision of the Riyadh Conference was endorsed by the plenary Arab Summit Conference, meeting in Cairo.[37]

President Sarkis notified the Arab League that, in order to counter Syrian influence over the Deterrent Force, its Commander must be a Lebanese national.[38] Accordingly, on 5 November, the Lebanese President appointed Colonel Ahmed al-Hajj, a Lebanese Sunni Muslim, as Commander of the Force.[39] A number of factors may have influenced the selection of Colonel al-Hajj. The Colonel had avoided any involvement in the Lebanese civil war. In addition, he had participated in the intermittent Lebanese–Palestinian negotiations that had occurred since 1969.[40] Colonel al-Hajj was therefore well-qualified to oversee the implementation of the Cairo Agreement and its Annexes, one of the principal tasks of the Arab Deterrent Force.[41]

The PLO protested at the appointment of a Lebanese as Commander of the Deterrent Force.[42] However, President Sarkis refused to be swayed by the Palestinian objections, reminding his critics that he would exercise personal control over the operation.[43] At a ceremony in Beirut, on Monday, 8 November, General Ghoneim, the Egyptian Commander of the Symbolic Arab Security Force, formally transferred his powers to Colonel al-Hajj.[44]

The Deputy Commander Lieutenant-Colonel Georges Garib, and the bulk of the senior staff, were also selected from the ranks of Lebanese officers who had refrained from participating in the civil conflict. A Syrian officer, General Naji Jamil, and a Saudi, General Ali El Chaer, were also assigned to assist Colonel al-Hajj.[45]

The headquarters of the Arab Deterrent Force were established in Museum Street, in the centre of Beirut, in a building formerly occupied by the Lebanese Ministry of Health. The HQ was divided into a number of branches concerned with operations, logistics, intelligence and personnel. An additional branch was headed by the Force's Inspector-in-Chief.

There was no attempt to integrate the various contingents of the Arab Deterrent Force, each of which had its own nationally appointed Commander.[46] Nominally, every contingent was subject to the overall authority of Colonel al-Hajj and of the Lebanese President. In practice, the large Syrian contingent, under its Commander General Ali Aslam, frequently received its instructions from the Syrian government.[47]

In November 1978, following the outbreak of particularly vicious fighting between Syrian troops of the ADF and Maronite militias, which resulted in substantial civilian casualties, the Lebanese President, Elias Sarkis, acknowledged that he did not exercise effective control over the Arab Deterrent Force. However, the President tried to argue, somewhat unconvincingly, that his lack of authority over the ADF was actually consistent with the understandings reached at the Riyadh mini-Summit:[48]

> When the participants at the Riyadh Conference decided that this force should be placed at the disposal of the Lebanese head of state they were intending to create a juridical and institutional link which would not amount to effective military command.

A corps of Lebanese liaison officers was created to provide the units of the pan-Arab force with information about local conditions. Liaison officers were attached to all units of battalion size, and also to some units of company strength. In addition, a Syrian liaison officer was assigned to Colonel al-Hajj's staff at the Beirut headquarters.

Colonel al-Hajj was replaced as Commander of the Arab Deterrent Force by Lieutenant-Colonel Sami al-Khatib, also a Lebanese national, on 11 April, 1977.[49] Colonel al-Hajj's resignation has been attributed to dissatisfaction with the performance of the Arab Deterrent Force.[50] His successor, Lieutenant-Colonel al-Khatib remained in his post until March 1983 when the Lebanese President, Amin Gemayel, dissolved the Command of the Arab Deterrent Force.[51]

Financing the Arab League Force

The Council resolutions establishing the Symbolic Arab Security Force, in June 1976, do not indicate how the operation was to be financed. In view of the modest size of the force, which did not exceed 2500 men by mid-July, the expenses incurred by the operation were met out of the League's general budget.[52]

The Resolution adopted by the Riyadh Summit Conference, in October 1976, transformed both the functions and size of the Arab League Force in the Lebanon. The Resolution stated that 'existing Arab security forces should be expanded to 30 000 men so that they might become a deterrent force operating inside Lebanon'.[53]

In view of the greatly increased size of the Arab Deterrent Force, the costs of maintaining the operation were correspondingly augmented.

Nevertheless, neither the Resolution nor the Schedule adopted by the Riyadh Summit indicated how the Force would be funded. However, these matters were dealt with, in some detail, in Resolution III of the plenary Arab Summit Conference, which was convened in Cairo, in October 1976:[54]

The Arab Summit Conference:

With a view to providing the financial resources required to maintain the Arab security forces in Lebanon, forces established in accordance with the second resolution adopted at the Riyadh Summit Conference,

Having reviewed the relevant report of the Military Secretariat of the League of Arab States,
Decides the following:

1   A special fund shall be set up to meet the requirements of the Arab security forces in Lebanon;

2   Each member State of the League of Arab States shall contribute a certain percentage to the fund, to be determined by each State according to its capabilities;

3   The President of the Republic of Lebanon shall supervise the fund, and, in consultation with the General Secretariat of the League of Arab States and those States contributing at least 10 per cent, shall work out general rules governing payments from the fund and its liquidation when its term expires; the present regulations for the Arab security force shall remain in effect until new regulations are drawn up;

4   The fund shall be set up for a six-month period, renewable by a decision of the Council of the League of Arab States; the Council shall meet for this purpose at the request of the President of the Republic of the Lebanon.

Thus, each member of the League was free, in principle, to determine the extent of its financial contribution. This policy may be contrasted, in particular, with the more centralized procedures of the United Nations.[55]

Agreement was reached, at the Cairo Summit Conference, that the 'special fund' for the initial six-month period should be set at $90 million.[56] Kuwait and Saudi Arabia undertook to provide 20 per cent each of this sum, while the United Arab Emirates and Qatar agreed to contribute 15 and 10 per cent, respectively.[57] It was envisaged that the remainder would be paid by other members of the League. However, as no other state volunteered funds for the upkeep of the Arab Deterrent Force, Saudi Arabia and Kuwait have contributed the balance.[58]

The composition of the Beiteddine Conference, in October 1978, indicates that the four above-mentioned states continued to bear sole responsibility for funding the Arab League Force in the Lebanon. The Beiteddine Conference was attended by delegates from every state which was contributing either troops or funds to the Force.[59] Syria and Sudan, each of which maintained a contingent in the Lebanon, participated in the Conference; the only other delegates were from Saudi Arabia, Kuwait, the United Arab Emirates and Qatar.[60]

In February 1982, the National Assembly of Kuwait voted to discontinue its financial support for the Arab Deterrent Force.[61] Kuwait's annual contribution to the upkeep of the ADF amounted to $48 000 000.[62] The Kuwaiti decision was prompted by concern at Syrian 'excesses' in the Lebanon, and also by disapproval of the massive use of force by Syrian troops in quelling an insurrection by Muslim fundamentalists in the Syrian city of Hama.[63]

Previously, in March 1979, Saudi Arabia, Kuwait, the United Arab Emirates and Qatar had threatened to cease funding the Arab Deterrent Force. At a meeting of the League Council which decided to extend the mandate of the ADF for only three months, as compared to the customary six, the four states declared their intention of terminating their financial contributions when the new mandate expired, on 27 July 1979.[64] However, the ADF's mandate was subsequently extended by the League Council at six-monthly intervals, until July 1982, and the four Gulf states maintained their contributions to the operation, with the exception of a four-month period at the beginning of 1981.[65]

On 20 January 1981, the League Council adopted a resolution renewing the mandate of the ADF for six months. However, the resolution noted that the states contributing funds to the Force would withhold further financial assistance.[66] The states concerned resumed their funding of the ADF towards the end of May.[67]

In July 1982, the mandate of the Arab Deterrent Force expired. An Arab Summit Conference, convened in Fez in September 1982, took note of 'the decision of the Lebanese Government to terminate the functions of the Arab deterrent forces in Lebanon'.[68] The League's apparent acceptance of the termination of the ADF's mandate, despite initial Syrian opposition, was due in part to the emphatic desire of the Gulf states to cease funding the operation.[69] In March of the following year, the Lebanese President, Amin Gemayel, issued a decree dissolving the Command of the Force.[70]

Notes

1 League Council Resolution No. 3457, 10 June 1976.
2 Ibid.
3 *Le Monde*, 11 June 1976, p.1.
4 See Chapter 4, note 96, and the accompanying text.
5 *Fiches du Monde Arabe*, 4 February 1981, No. 1812.
6 *Keesing's* (1976), p. 28119.
7 Ibid.
8 See cable from President Frangieh of Lebanon to General-Secretary Riad of the Arab League, 30 June 1976, in *al-Nahar*, 1 July 1976. The text is available, in English, in *IDP* (1976), p.436.
9 Ibid.
10 For the text of the Prime Minister's statement see *al-Nahar*, 2 July 1976. For an English-language translation see *IDP* (1976), p.438.
11 *Keesing's* (1976), p.28124.
12 Para. 2, Resolution adopted by the Six-Party Arab Summit Conference (Riyadh, 1976).
13 Para. 1, Resolution I, Resolutions adopted by the Arab Summit Conference (Cairo, 1976).
14 Keesing's (1976), p.28123.
15 *Kuwait Times*, 27 October 1976; *International Herald Tribune*, 27 October 1976.
16 *International Herald Tribune*, 27 October 1976.
17 *Kuwait Times*, 27 October 1976.
18 *International Herald Tribune*, 27 October 1976.
19 Ibid.
20 *Fiches du Monde Arabe*, 2 August 1978, No. 1024.
21 *The Times*, 26 October 1976, p.8.
22 *The Times*, 28 October 1976, p.10.
23 *Keesing's*, (1976), p.28123.
24 *Fiches du Monde Arabe*, 2 August 1978, No. 1024.
25 Ibid. According to League sources the UAE and Yemeni contingents were limited to 500 men apiece. I am also indebted to the League for information concerning the additional 1000 troops sent by Saudi Arabia.
26 *Keesing's* (1976), p.28124.
27 Libya and Iraq were the only League members who did not endorse the establishment of the Arab Deterrent Force at the Cairo Summit Conference. See Chapter 8.
28 *Fiches du Monde Arabe*, 2 August 1978, No. 1024.
29 *Keesing's* (1979), p.30005.
30 *Fiches du Monde Arabe*, 1 April 1981, No. 1862.
31 See e.g. *Middle East Economic Digest Arab Report*, 14 March 1979, p.2.
32 Ibid.
33 *Fiches du Monde Arabe*, 1 April 1981, No. 1862.
34 League Council Resolution No. 3456, 9 June 1976.
35 *Fiches du Monde Arabe*, 4 February 1981, No. 1812.
36 Para. 2, Resolution adopted by the Six-Party Arab Summit Conference (Riyadh, 1976).
37 Para. 1, Resolution I, Resolutions adopted by the Arab Summit Conference (Cairo, 1976).
38 *The Times*, 28 October 1976, p.10.

39   *Le Monde,* 6 November 1976, p.3.
40   Ibid.
41   Para. 2(b), Resolution adopted by the Six-Party Arab Summit Conference (Riyadh, 1976).
42   *Le Monde,* 6 November 1976, p.3.
43   *Le Monde,* 7/8 November 1976, p.4.
44   *Le Monde,* 9 November 1976, p.6.
45   *Le Monde,* 6 November 1976, p.3.
46   *Fiches du Monde Arabe,* 2 August 1978, No. 1024.
47   Ibid.
48   *Le Monde,* 28 November 1978, p.10.
49   *Keesing's* (1977), p.28735.
50   For details of the ADF's performance see Chapter 8.
51   *Le Monde,* 2 April 1983, p.3.
52   Information supplied by the Arab League. In accordance with Article 13 of the League Pact, the Secretary-General is responsible for preparing the draft budget of the League and for submitting it to the Council 'for approval before the beginning of each fiscal year'. The Council 'shall fix the share of the expenses to be borne by each state of the League', while individual shares 'may be reconsidered if necessary'. Ibid. Decisions concerning the adoption of the budget may be made by majority vote. Art. 16.
53   Para. 2, Resolution adopted by the Six-Party Arab Summit Conference (Riyadh, 1976).
54   Resolution III, Resolutions adopted by the Arab Summit Conference (Cairo, 1976).
55   In December 1961, following the refusal of certain UN Members to pay their share of the costs of UNEF and ONUC, as determined by the General Assembly, the Assembly sought an advisory opinion from the International Court of Justice. See GA Res. 1731 (XVI), 20 December 1961. The question at issue was whether the expenditure on UNEF and ONUC constituted 'expenses of the Organization' within the meaning of Article 17(2) of the Charter. This provides that: '[t]he expenses of the Organization shall be borne by the members as apportioned by the General Assembly'. In a majority opinion, the Court found that the expenditure did amount to 'expenses of the Organization' for the purposes of Article 17(2):

> At the outset of this opinion, the Court pointed out that the text of Article 17, paragraph 2, of the Charter could lead to the simple conclusion that 'the expenses of the Organization' are the amounts paid out to defray the costs of carrying out the purposes of the Organization. It was further indicated that the Court would examine the resolutions authorizing the expenditures referred to in the request for the advisory opinion in order to ascertain whether they were incurred with that end in view. The Court has made such an examination and finds that they were so incurred. The Court has also analysed the principal arguments which have been advanced against the conclusion that the expenditures in question should be considered as 'expenses of the Organization within the meaning of Article 17, paragraph 2, of the Charter of the United Nations', and has found that these arguments are unfounded. Consequently the Court arrives at the conclusion that the question submitted to it in General Assembly resolution 1731 (XVI) must be answered in the affirmative.

ICJ Rep. (1962), p.1, at p.179. See, generally, on the financing of UN peacekeeping operations, the 'finance' sections in Higgins, *I-IV.*

56 *Fiches du Monde Arabe*, 2 August 1978, No. 1024.
57 Ibid.
58 Ibid.
59 *Fiches du Monde Arabe*, 8 November 1978, No. 1107.
60 Ibid.
61 *Keesing's* (1983), p.31924.
62 Ibid. In 1981, the annual budget of the Arab Deterrent Force amounted to $180 000 000. *Keesing's* (1983), p.31922.
63 *Keesing's* (1983), p.31924.
64 *Le Monde*, 29 March 1979, p.6.
65 On the subsequent extension of the ADF's mandate, see Chapter 8.
66 League Council Resolution No. 4011, 20 January 1981.
67 *The Times*, 25 May 1981, p.5.
68 Resolution II, para. 3, Resolutions adopted by the Arab Summit Conference (Fez, 1982). The resolutions are reproduced in the Annex to S/15510, 15 December 1982.
69 *Le Monde*, 11 September 1982, p.3.
70 *Keesing's* (1983), p.32164. For additional information concerning the funding of the ADF see Isselé, op. cit., p.ix, note 10, esp. at p.216, note 150.

8 The Performance of the Arab League Force in the Lebanon

June 1976 – November 1976

The first units of the Symbolic Arab Security Force arrived in Beirut on 21 June. These comprised two 500-man contingents despatched by Libya and Syria.[1] Additional troops from Libya and Syria arrived during the following weeks, together with small contingents from Sudan and Saudi Arabia.[2] An Egyptian, Major-General Muhammad Hassan Ghoneim, was appointed Commander of the Force, which was estimated to comprise 2500 men by mid-July.[3]

Initially, the Arab League troops took up positions around Beirut's international airport, to the south of the city.[4] As a result of their deployment, the airport was re-opened and regular Syrian troops were withdrawn from Beirut.[5]

Although President Frangieh had finally consented to the introduction of the Arab League Force, he notified the League's Secretary-General that the continued presence of Syrian troops in the Lebanon was 'essentially part of Lebanese sovereignty' and that '[i]t is outside the jurisdiction of the Arab League to consider the bilateral relations between Lebanon and Syria'.[6]

The Lebanese President also observed that, due to the political alignment of the Libyan regime with the Palestinian guerrillas in the Lebanon, 'Libya is in no way suitable to participate in the Arab peace-keeping force which is expected to have a neutral position in this conflict'.[7] President Frangieh called for the withdrawal of Libyan troops from the Arab Security Force.[8] However, Rashid Karami, the Lebanese Prime Minister, informed the League that President Frangieh had exceeded his constitutional powers in bringing these views to the attention of the League without having obtained the prior approval of the Lebanese government.[9] No further action was taken by the President to secure the removal of the Libyan troops.

The effectiveness of the Symbolic Arab Security Force was limited by a number of factors. Amongst these were its modest size, and the refusal of Lebanese Christians to permit units of the Force to deploy in Christian-held East Beirut.[10] The Force was therefore unable 'to preserve security and stability', as envisaged by the Council resolution of 9 June.[11]

The resolution of 9 June had also envisaged that the Arab League Force would 'replace' Syrian troops in the Lebanon.[12] However, no progress was made in realizing this objective. As noted above, President Frangieh declared that the matter was outside the jurisdiction of the Arab League. President Assad asserted that Syrian troops would only be withdrawn at the request of the Lebanese President.[13]

In fact, Syrian troop concentrations in the Lebanon were steadily increased during June.[14] By mid-August, Syria was believed to have deployed a total of 20 000 men in the Lebanon.[15] Of these, only a fraction were integrated in the Symbolic Arab Security Force.[16]

The League Council's call for a ceasefire, in its resolution of 9 June, went largely unheeded. On 16 June, the US Ambassador to the Lebanon was murdered. On 22 June, Maronite forces launched a co-ordinated attack on the Palestinian refugee camps of Tal Zaatar and Jisr al-Pasha, and on the Muslim enclave of Nabaa, situated in predominantly Christian East Beirut.[17] Jisr al-Pasha fell to the Christian militia on 30 June; Nabaa was occupied on 6 August. On 12 August, after a protracted siege, Tal Zaatar fell to the Christian forces. Hundreds of the inhabitants were slaughtered.[18] The Symbolic Arab Security Force, which had been prevented from entering East Beirut by the Christian militias, was powerless to intervene.

Despite the fall of Tal Zaatar, a serious blow to the morale of the Palestinian-Leftist forces, fighting continued in Beirut, and in the Dhour Shuwair region north of the Beirut – Damascus highway.[19] On 23 September, during a brief interlude in the fighting, Elias Sarkis was inaugurated as President of the Lebanon. In his inaugural address, President Sarkis spoke of his hopes for a dialogue leading to national reconciliation. In addition, he emphasized Lebanon's sovereignty, noting that the continued presence of Syrian troops would depend on Lebanese consent:[20]

I am in a position to declare that the future of their presence here and all that relates to it is subject to the constitutional Lebanese authorities which, in accordance with their responsibilities, may adopt whatever position they regard appropriate to the overriding Lebanese interest in the light of prevailing circumstances.

However, the limited character of President Sarkis' authority was exposed at the end of September, when Syrian troops launched a brief offensive against a combined Palestinian – National Movement force east of Beirut.[21] On 12 October, the Syrians renewed their offensive against Palestinian – Leftist positions east of Beirut and in the vicinity of Sidon.[22]

The Syrian offensive was halted only after the intercession of the government of Saudi Arabia. On 15 October, a Saudi envoy was despatched to Damascus to persuade the Syrian President to attend a summit conference in Riyadh, to be convened on the following day.[23] The Saudis also extended invitations to the heads of state of the Lebanon, Egypt and Kuwait, and to the Chairman of the PLO.[24]

The Summit Conference, which was held in Riyadh from 16 to 18 October, decided, *inter alia,* that 'all parties should definitively cease fire and terminate fighting in all Lebanese territories as from 6.00 a.m. on 21 October 1976' and that 'the Palestine Liberation Organization shall affirm its respect of the sovereignty and security of the Lebanon, as well as its non-interference in Lebanese internal affairs'.[25] In addition, the Resolution declared that 'the Arab States participating in the Conference pledge their respect for the sovereignty, security, and territorial integrity of Lebanon, as well as the unity of its people'.[26]

Crucially, the Conference decided that 'existing Arab security forces should be expanded to 30 000 men so that they might become a deterrent force operating inside Lebanon under the personal command of the President of the Lebanese Republic'.[27] The functions of the Force included '[e]nsuring observance of the ceasefire and termination of hostilities, disengaging belligerent troops and deterring any violation of the agreement' and 'maintaining internal security'.[28]

As noted in Chapter 5, the transformation of the Symbolic Arab Security Force into the Arab Deterrent Force involved a major change in the Force's powers, as well as of its size and functions. The term 'deterrent', from the Arabic 'al-Rad', signified a readiness to use force in order to preserve the ceasefire.[29]

The Riyadh Conference was followed by a Summit Conference of Arab heads of state, convened in Cairo, on 25 October.[30] On the following day, the Conference adopted a series of resolutions in which, *inter alia*, it 'approve[d] the statement, resolutions and annexes' adopted at the Riyadh Conference, and established a fund 'to meet the requirements of the Arab security forces in Lebanon'.[31] The resolutions were endorsed by nineteen of the twenty-one member states. Only Iraq and Libya declined to approve the establishment of the Arab Deterrent Force.[32]

On 5 November, President Sarkis appointed Colonel Ahmed al-Hajj, a Lebanese Sunni Muslim, Commander of the Force.[33] A number of factors may have influenced the selection of Colonel al-Hajj. The Colonel had avoided any involvement in the Lebanese civil war. In addition, he had participated in the intermittent Lebanese – Palestinian negotiations that had been held since 1969.[34] Colonel al-Hajj was therefore well-qualified to oversee the implementation of the Cairo Agreement and its Annexes, one of the principal tasks of the Arab Deterrent Force.[35]

At a ceremony in Beirut, on Monday 8 November, General Ghoneim, the Egyptian Commander of the Symbolic Arab Security Force, formally transferred his powers to Colonel al-Hajj.[36] In an announcement issued on the following day, Colonel al-Hajj confirmed that the Arab Deterrent Force was empowered to use force in order to realise its objectives. Thus, the Colonel warned that the ADF 'declare their resolve to use deterrent force whenever security so requires'.[37]

The composition of the Arab League Force in the Lebanon changed, dramatically, as a result of the Riyadh and Cairo Summit Conferences. In part, the changes reflected the need to expand the Force to 30 000 men, in accordance with the resolutions adopted at the Summits.[38] In part, the changes in the Force's composition, particularly the increasing preponderance of the Syrian contingent, reflected the political manoeuvrings of the interested parties.

On 26 October, during the Cairo Summit Conference, the Secretary-General of the League, Mahmoud Riad, announced that Libya, the PLO, Saudi Arabia, Sudan, Syria, North and South Yemen, and the United Arab Emirates had agreed to contribute troops to the Arab Deterrent Force.[39] However, Algeria, Morocco, Tunisia and Egypt declined to furnish contingents.[40]

There was bitter disagreement amongst the Arab kings and heads of state participating in the Cairo Summit concerning the size of the national contingents. The PLO demanded that Syrian units should not exceed 10 000 men,[41] whereas Syria insisted that her troops should account for at least half of the Deterrent Force, i.e. 15 000 men.[42] A meeting of Arab Foreign Ministers, convened on the night of 25 October, failed to resolve these differences; nor could a series of private talks between Arab leaders on the final day of the Summit Conference.[43] In the absence of prior agreement, Secretary-General

Riad announced, at the conclusion of the Conference, that the Lebanese President, Elias Sarkis, would determine the size of each national contingent.[44]

Despite Palestinian objections, President Sarkis agreed that Syria should contribute the bulk of the Arab Deterrent Force – up to 25 000 men.[45] Palestinian hopes of ensuring the inclusion of substantial non-Syrian contingents were frustrated by Egypt's refusal to contribute any troops to the Arab Deterrent Force,[46] and by Syrian opposition to the participation of PLO formations.[47]

The Libyan, Saudi and Sudanese contingents of the Symbolic Arab Security Force, which had remained in place in the Lebanon, were integrated into the Arab Deterrent Force.[48] However, these were limited in size. The Libyans had deployed 700 men in the Lebanon as against 1000 Sudanese troops, and a Saudi contingent of 1200 men.[49] The United Arab Emirates despatched 1000 troops, while South Yemen agreed to provide 700 men.[50]

November 1976 – March 1978

During the first weeks of November 1976, Syrian troops advanced from their positions in the north and east of the Lebanon, as part of the newly-constituted Arab Deterrent Force. Initially, ADF units occupied Aley, to the east of Beirut, gradually extending their control over suburbs in the north and south of the capital.[51]

Leaders of both the Palestinian-Leftist alliance, and of the Maronite community, had indicated that they would not oppose the presence of Arab peacekeeping troops in territories under their control.[52] As a result, the initial deployment of ADF troops was accomplished without significant resistance.

On 15 November, a large Syrian force advanced into central Beirut, taking up positions along the dividing line between the Muslim and Christian sectors of the city.[53] Within a matter of days, Syrian units occupied the coastal cities of Tripoli and Sidon, both of which had been under Palestinian-Leftist control.[54]

However, Syrian troops were unable to make significant progress south of Sidon, because of the threat of Israeli intervention.[55] The Litani river, some 20 miles south of Sidon, constituted a 'red line' beyond which Israel would not countenance Syrian or other non-Lebanese forces.[56] Due to Israeli pressure, the southernmost ADF outpost was established at Zahrani, ten miles north of the Litani.[57]

Arguably, the most important function assigned to the Arab Deterrent Force, by the Riyadh Resolution, was the supervision of 'the collection of heavy weaponry'.[58] The Commander of the Arab Deterrent

Force, Colonel al-Hajj, made strenuous efforts to discharge this part of his mandate.[59] However, both sides remained deeply suspicious of one another, and were reluctant to surrender their weapons before their adversaries had been disarmed.

By 13 January, the ADF had collected a quantity of heavy weapons from various Maronite and Palestinian-Leftist militias.[60] However, despite an enthusiastic announcement on Beirut Radio that the Deterrent Force had accomplished this aspect of its mission, it was widely understood that the militias retained the bulk of their weapons.[61]

Despite these difficulties, the ADF made a significant contribution to the restoration of a climate of normalcy in the Lebanon during the first months of its existence. In addition to collecting a quantity of heavy weapons and establishing its presence in the cities, the ADF set up checkpoints along Lebanon's major roads, many of which had been closed by the fighting.[62] Units of the Palestine Liberation Army, which had entered Lebanon during the civil war, were withdrawn under ADF supervision.[63] The militias disappeared from public view, while Beirut's airport and harbour resumed their normal functions.

In an interview with Walter Cronkite, in May 1977, President Assad expressed some satisfaction with the progress of the Arab Deterrent Force. The President commented '[t]he situation in Lebanon is good and has been stable for a long time, since the entry of the [Arab Deterrent] Forces, apart from some clashes that have taken place in a restricted area on the Israeli frontier'.[64] President Assad emphasized that the continued presence of the Arab League Force in the Lebanon 'depends on the wishes of the legitimate Lebanese authorities'. He expressed the hope that:[65]

> they may be able to dispense with our help as soon as possible. But it depends on how long they will need to set up a Lebanese force capable of establishing security, and this depends on many factors, most of them related to Lebanon and her legitimate authorities. I do not want to give an inaccurate estimate on this matter, but it seems to me that this will take more than a year.

However, as noted above, the ADF was unable to enter southern Lebanon because of the threat of Israeli counteraction. As the security situation improved in central and northern Lebanon, it began to deteriorate in the south.

Paradoxically, the reduction of tension in the north released thousands of Palestinian guerrillas who returned to their bases in southern Lebanon. The guerrillas were confronted by newly-constituted Christian militias, armed and financed by Israel.[66] Fighting occurred intermittently during the latter part of 1976, and in the early months of

1977. The Christian forces, receiving occasional artillery support from Israel, gradually gained the upper hand.[67] In the spring of 1977, the Palestinian-Leftist militias launched a successful counter-offensive.[68] A ceasefire was eventually achieved on 19 July.[69]

In an effort to arrest the cycle of violence, Syrian, Lebanese and PLO delegates met in the Lebanese town of Chtaura, on 20 July, together with Colonel Sami al-Khatib, who had succeeded Colonel al-Hajj as Commander of the Arab Deterrent Force.[70] After a second round of talks, on 25 July, the 'Chtaura Agreement' was concluded.

In essence, this provided for strict compliance by the Palestinian guerrillas with the provisions of the Cairo Agreement and its Annexes, particularly the Melkart Understanding of May 1973. Palestinian guerrillas would be withdrawn from frontier zones bordering on Israel to specified areas in southern Lebanon. Lebanese army troops were to be sent to the border region, while guerrilla operations against Israel were forbidden. Any heavy weapons remaining in the Palestinian camps would be removed.[71]

The Arab Deterrent Force was given additional responsibilities under the Chtaura Agreement. Units of the ADF were to be deployed at the entrances to the refugee camps, and the ADF was empowered to 'stage surprise raids' on illegal arms caches.[72] Previously, the Arab Deterrent Force had not been authorized to enter the Palestinian camps.

A time-table was drawn up for the implementation of the Agreement. As a first stage, troops of the Deterrent Force took up positions around the principal Palestinian camps on 30 July.[73] There was also some progress in implementing the second phase, concerning the surrender of heavy weapons.[74] However, the third stage of the Agreement, involving the withdrawal of Palestinian guerrillas from the border areas, and their replacement by Lebanese army troops, was not carried out, largely because fighting had resumed between Christian militias and Palestinian-Leftist forces in southern Lebanon.[75]

As the hostilities intensified, Israel provided artillery support for the Christian forces, while Syrian elements of the ADF reportedly allowed Palestinian reinforcements to pass unhindered through their lines.[76] A ceasefire, concluded under US auspices, was achieved in late September. However, it remained precarious.

Security conditions in central and northern Lebanon also deteriorated. On 16 March, Kamal Jumblatt, the charismatic leader of the Palestinian-Leftist alliance was killed by unknown gunmen.[77] An additional 4000 troops of the Arab Deterrent Force were deployed in the Chouf, where Jumblatt's Druze supporters were concentrated.[78] Despite this precaution, over 100 Christians were killed in an orgy of vengeance.[79] A further outbreak of intercommunal fighting occurred in the village of Brieh, in August. Displaying the ruthlessness that was to be its hallmark, ADF units reportedly shelled the village in order to arrest the fighting.[80]

In Beirut, and in northern Lebanon, there were a number of incidents. On 3 January, a large bomb exploded in Ashrafiyeh, in Christian East Beirut, precipitating a massacre of scores of Muslims in the eastern part of the city.[81] During February, Syrian units of the ADF intervened to halt fighting between rival Palestinian factions in the capital.[82] In May, there were repeated clashes between ADF troops and Christian villagers in the north, following the murder of two men from the Deterrent Force.[83] In the previous month, ADF troops had fought with Palestinian guerrillas in a Beirut suburb after the death of two Syrian soldiers.[84] Following delays in the implementation of the Chtaura Agreement, there was a further wave of violence throughout the country.[85]

Although units of the ADF entered Beirut on 15 November, they had refrained from taking up positions in the Christian eastern sector. However, following the explosion in Ashrafiyeh, units of the Arab Deterrent Force were deployed in the suburb.[86] ADF troops also occupied adjacent coastal areas, and the hills surrounding Beirut.[87]

By contrast, the ADF had, from the outset, established itself in the Muslim western sector of the city, with the exception of the Palestinian refugee camps.[88] Unaccustomed to the invective of the Arab world's freest press, Syrian troops occupied several newspaper offices located in West Beirut, which had been critical of the Syrian presence, in an effort to impose their own form of censorship.[89] A Syrian spokesman protested that it was 'inconceivable that Syrian soldiers should accept the insults of the press'.[90]

The ceasefire which had been established in southern Lebanon, in late September, was shattered early in November when fighting resumed between Palestinian-Leftist forces and Christian militias.[91] The scale of the conflict increased when Katyusha rockets were fired into Israel, prompting massive reprisals.[92] After a brief lull, there was a general resumption of hostilities in southern Lebanon in January 1978.[93]

The threat of Israeli intervention continued to prevent the Arab Deterrent Force from advancing into southern Lebanon. Crucially, the likelihood of the Palestinian guerrillas withdrawing from the border regions, which was to have been the final phase of the Chtaura Agreement, receded as each outbreak of violence increased Palestinian intransigence.[94]

In the central and northern sectors of the Lebanon, units of the Arab Deterrent Force succeeded in pacifying a number of incidents during the closing months of 1977.[95] However, on 7 February 1978,

Syrian soldiers of the Deterrent Force clashed with Christian troops of the Lebanese army in Fayadiyah, in the eastern sector of Beirut.

The violence was sparked off by a seemingly trivial incident. The Syrian troops had been attempting to erect a checkpoint close to a Lebanese army barracks occupied by Christian soldiers. An argument between members of the two forces escalated into an exchange of gunfire in which more than a dozen Syrians were killed.[96]

Stung by their losses, and by the affront to their authority, Syrian troops shelled the Lebanese barracks setting it on fire. Syrian soldiers, spoiling for a fight, clashed with Maronite militiamen loyal to Camille Chamoun's National Liberal Party, and bombarded the Christian suburb of Ashrafiyeh.[97] Order was finally restored on 9 February. It was estimated that a hundred Syrians had been killed in the fighting, as against Lebanese losses of fifty.[98]

The incident was indicative of the tense relations between the Syrian troops of the Arab League Force and Lebanon's Maronite community. Although the Syrians had originally intervened in the Lebanon, in June 1976, to safeguard the Maronites, the gratitude of the latter was inevitably ephemeral. The psychology of their relationship is explored with some acuity by Walid Khalidi:[99]

> The presence of any 'foreign' force, however friendly and legitimate, is bound to generate over time cumulative tensions between the members of this force and the host country . . . To the Maronites, the Syrians had at first seemed saviours, which indeed they had been. But from the beginning, the Maronites had been allergic to Syrian deployment in their own territories. As the Maronites saw it, the principal, if not exclusive, task of the Syrians was to tame and disarm the PLO and the National Movement.

In addition to the divergence of Syrian and Maronite objectives, and the ruffled sensibilities of the latter, there were more practical difficulties. Khalidi notes that the 'mere juxtaposition of the Sarkis administration and the ADF forces in the same territory created problems which were compounded by the inevitable confusions and misunderstandings arising from parallel or interlocking prerogatives and chains of command'.[100] In the circumstances, it is surprising not that the incident should have occurred, but rather that it, or something very similar, had not happened sooner.

In the aftermath of the Fayadiyah incident, a Lebanese – Syrian tribunal was constituted to try those responsible for the fighting, and a joint commission was established to examine the causes of the bloodshed.[101] In addition, after consultations between Lebanese and

Syrian ministers, it was agreed that members of the Lebanese security forces should be attached to all roadblocks manned by ADF units in Beirut.[102]

At the beginning of March, fighting broke out between Christians, in the Beirut suburb of Ain el-Roumaneh, and Muslims, in the neighbouring suburb of Chiah. The clashes were brought to a halt after the forceful intercession of ADF units'.[103]

March 1978 – November 1978

The future course of events in the Lebanon was transformed by a PLO raid into Israel. On 11 March, Palestinian guerrillas originating in the Lebanon penetrated Israel's coastal defences. Landing on the coast south of Haifa, the guerrillas seized a civilian bus and its passengers. In the eventual confrontation with Israeli security forces, 31 Israelis lost their lives.[104] The incident proved the catalyst for a major Israeli operation designed to eliminate the PLO from southern Lebanon.[105] On 14 March, some 25 000 Israeli troops swept across the border, while Israeli jets and warships bombarded Palestinian fortifications.[106] Israel accepted a ceasefire on 21 March, its forces having occupied almost the whole of Lebanon south of the Litani.[107]

Responding to the crisis, the UN Security Council adopted a resolution, on 19 March, calling for 'strict respect for the territorial integrity, sovereignty and political independence of Lebanon' and providing for the immediate establishment of a United Nations Interim Force (UNIFIL).[108] The mandate of the force was defined as 'confirming the withdrawal of Israeli forces, restoring international peace and security and assisting the Government of Lebanon in ensuring the return of its effective authority in the area'.[109]

The first troops of the newly-constituted UN force began to arrive in the Lebanon on 22 March.[110] However, Israel did not commence its withdrawal from the Lebanon for some weeks. After mounting international pressure, Israeli forces were finally pulled back from the Lebanon on 13 June. However, control of a narrow strip of Lebanese territory north of the border was left in the hands of Major Haddad, a former Lebanese army officer who led a Christian militia in southern Lebanon.[111]

Syria's response to the establishment of UNIFIL was equivocal. The authorities in Damascus recognized that the introduction of the UN force would accelerate the withdrawal of Israeli troops from the Lebanon. However, the creation of UNIFIL also represented a tacit acknowledgement of the limited role that the Arab Deterrent Force, and Syria, could fulfil in the Lebanon.[112]

Although the threat of Israeli intervention had prevented the Deterrent Force from ever advancing beyond the Litani, the ADF had been conceived as an instrument for the restoration of peace and security throughout the Lebanon. Thus, the Riyadh Resolution had entrusted the Deterrent Force with responsibility for ensuring observance of the ceasefire and the maintenance of internal security in all regions of the country.[113] It was therefore difficult for the Syrian regime to accept that a UN force should assume some of these functions in southern Lebanon.

There were certain discrepancies between the mandate of UNIFIL and the Resolution of the Riyadh Conference which had served as a basis for reconciliation between the warring factions in the Lebanon. The Riyadh Resolution had called for implementation of the Cairo Agreement and its Annexes, and had committed the Lebanese authorities to 'guarantee[ing] security to the Palestine Liberation Organization with respect to its presence and activities in Lebanese territory' in accordance with the above-mentioned texts.[114]

In reality, the Cairo Agreement and its Annexes were themselves inconsistent. The former bound the Lebanese authorities to 'facilitate . . . Fedayeen action', which was interpreted by the Palestinians as permitting guerrilla operations across the border. The latter, notably the Melkart Understanding of May 1973, stated explicitly that '[a]ll operations from Lebanese territory are frozen' and that guerrillas were forbidden to leave Lebanon 'for a foreign country in order to undertake Fedayeen operations'.[115] The Chtaura Agreement of July 1977 reaffirmed the moratorium on guerrilla operations.[116]

Nevertheless, the Cairo Agreement and its Annexes had tried to preserve a balance between the interests of the Lebanon and those of the Palestinian guerrillas. However, the Security Council initiative, in establishing UNIFIL, disregarded the interests of the guerrillas in favour of securing a *modus vivendi* between Israel and the Lebanon. Thus, in Resolution 426 the Security Council stated that UNIFIL will 'use its best efforts to prevent the recurrence of fighting and to ensure that its area of operation is not utilized for hostile activities of any kind'.[117]

Israel's incursion into southern Lebanon had an additional impact on efforts to restore national cohesion in the wake of the protracted civil war. Lebanon's confessional leaders took note of the fact that Syria had not even attempted to oppose the Israeli forces. The perceived weakness of Syria tempted some Maronites, particularly Camille Chamoun and Bashir Gemayel, to challenge Syrian hegemony over central and northern Lebanon. Through a series of provocations against Syrian forces they hoped to 'rattle the garrison troops' and to 'impress upon the Lebanese, the Arab states, and the world at large that the Syrian contingent was in fact an occupying army and not, as President Assad claimed, a peacekeeping force serving in Lebanon at the invitation of Lebanese President, Elias Sarkis, and with the approval of the Arab League'.[118]

Meeting in Cairo, at the end of March, the Arab League Council 'condemn[ed] the Israeli aggression against Lebanon' and called for an Arab summit conference 'to mobilize all Arab strength and resources to confront the aggressive Israeli defiance'.[119] On 28 March, the Council voted to extend the mandate of the Deterrent Force for a further six months.[120] The mandate of the ADF had been renewed, previously, at six-monthly intervals since its establishment by the Riyadh and Cairo Summit Conferences, in October 1976.[121]

The Riyadh and Cairo Conferences had not, in fact, created the Force for six months, or for any other specific term. However, the Cairo Summit had instituted a 'special fund' to finance the ADF for an initial six-month period, which could be extended by the League Council at the request of the Lebanese President.[122] In effect, the continued existence of the ADF was subject to regular approval by the League Council, acting on the initiative of the President of the Lebanon.

The extension of the ADF's mandate, in March 1978, had not been a unanimous decision. In the previous November, Egypt's President Sadat had visited Israel, profoundly angering many Arab leaders. In retaliation, the hard-line Arab states decided to boycott Council sessions held in Cairo.[123] As a result, delegates from Syria, Iraq, Libya, South Yemen and Algeria were absent from the Council meeting, in March 1978, which voted to extend the ADF's mandate.[124]

This situation was not without irony as Syria, while declining to approve the extension of the ADF's mandate, contributed the largest contingent to the Force and was anxious to ensure the retention of its troops in the Lebanon. In an interview published a month before the Council meeting, the Syrian Information Minister had stated bluntly that Syrian troops would be maintained in the Lebanon whether or not the ADF's mandate was renewed:[125]

> The Syrian contingent in the Arab Deterrent Forces will remain in Lebanon as long as Lebanon's legal authorities wish it to remain, and as long as its mission – the mission of maintaining the security and stability of Lebanon – continues to exist.

With the exception of Syria, the troop-contributing states became increasingly uneasy with the course of events in the Lebanon. As noted above, Libya withdrew its troops in November 1976. A small South Yemeni contingent, comprising around 700 men, was withdrawn in December 1977.[126]

During 1978 and 1979, the other non-Syrian contingents of the ADF were progressively withdrawn. In October 1978, Sudan announced its intention to terminate its participation in the Force. However, in response to requests from Lebanese leaders, Sudanese troops remained in the Lebanon until February, 1979.[127] During the early months of 1979, Saudi Arabia and the United Arab Emirates also declared that their contingents would be withdrawn from the Lebanon.[128]

Although none of these contingents was numerically significant, they were important in preserving the pan-Arab character of the Deterrent Force. After their withdrawal, the ADF appeared, increasingly, as an expression of Syrian authority. Paradoxically, their removal was the result, at least in part, of the tendency of the sizeable Syrian contingent to act independently of the nominal chain of command in the Arab Deterrent Force.[129] Between July and October 1978, there were fierce clashes between Syrian troops and Maronite militiamen in Beirut. The Syrians, who made frequent use of their artillery, caused hundreds of fatalities amongst the civilian population.

The withdrawal of the non-Syrian contingents also reduced the effectiveness of the ADF as a conventional peacekeeping operation. The numerical strength of the Syrians, combined with their sheer ruthlessness of purpose, meant that they frequently used considerable force to achieve their objectives. By contrast, the relatively small non-Syrian units exercised more restraint, conforming to traditional stereotypes of peacekeeping. Their presence was therefore acceptable in areas where Syrian troops had clashed repeatedly with local militias, causing considerable resentment amongst the local population.

The usefulness of the non-Syrian contingents was illustrated when fighting broke out between Muslim and Christian militias in Ain el-Roumaneh, in the eastern sector of the city, in the second week of April 1978. The intercession of Syrian units of the ADF, equipped with artillery, resulted in considerable loss of life and destruction of property, particularly amongst Christians. As a token of their determination, the Syrian units had issued a 'shoot to kill' order, warning the militias that anyone found armed in the suburbs of Chiah and Ain el-Roumaneh would be shot on sight.[130]

Following the restoration of calm, it was decided that Sudanese troops should replace the Syrian units which had previously been stationed in Ain el-Roumaneh.[131] The Syrians were redeployed across the 'green line' in the Muslim western sector of the city.

In June, mounting tensions between Lebanon's Maronite leaders culminated in an attack by Phalangist militia on the home of Tony Frangieh, eldest son of former President Suleiman Frangieh. In the assault, carried out at Ehden in northern Lebanon, Tony Frangieh, together with his wife, daughter and over thirty supporters, were killed by the Phalange.[132]

The attack on the Frangiehs, who enjoyed close links with President Assad and who had recently severed their connection with the increasingly pro-Israeli Maronite leaders of the Lebanese Front, led to the deployment of ADF troops in northern Lebanon and to a further heightening of tension.[133] In the first week of July, fighting erupted in Beirut between Maronite militiamen and Syrian units of the ADF. Syrian artillery bombardments of the Christian suburbs of Ashrafiyeh and Ain el-Roumaneh left over 100 dead.[134]

Lebanese President Elias Sarkis threatened to resign, protesting that the Arab Deterrent Force, of which he was the nominal head, had carried out operations without his sanction or foreknowledge.[135] In an interview published in *Le Monde*, President Sarkis subsequently acknowledged that he did not exercise effective control over the Force: '[w]hen the participants at the Riyadh Conference decided that this force should be placed at the disposal of the Lebanese head of state they were intending to create a juridical and institutional link which would not amount to effective military command'.[136] The President admitted that he was 'profoundly shocked' by the events in Beirut.[137]

Bashir Gemayel, the Phalangist militia leader, implored Israel to intervene militarily.[138] However, Israel confined its response to a low-altitude overflight of Beirut by several jets.[139]

On 7 July, an uneasy ceasefire was achieved in the capital. The security situation improved further when, on 11 July, Syrian units of the ADF reduced their presence in Christian East Beirut.[140] However, the ceasefire was shattered in the third week of July when fighting resumed between Syrian troops and Maronite militias in the suburbs of Beirut. Further, intense artillery bombardments by Syrian gunners left scores dead, and many more wounded.[141] A ceasefire was restored on 9 August, partially as a result of pledges by the ADF to withdraw some of its remaining units from the eastern sector of Beirut.[142]

In late August, fighting developed between Phalangist supporters in northern Lebanon and Syrian troops belonging to the Arab Deterrent Force.[143] Once again, Bashir Gemayel appealed for military assistance from Israel. However, the Begin government, which was preparing for the Camp David talks with Egypt, declined to offer any direct help.[144]

Beirut relapsed into violence as Syrian troops fought Christian militiamen. The general resumption of fighting prompted Camille Chamoun and Bashir Gemayel to oppose a renewal of the ADF's mandate, which was due to expire on 28 October.[145] However, more moderate Maronite figures, together with a majority of Muslim leaders, called for an extension of the mandate of the Deterrent Force.[146]

In a message broadcast on 22 September, President Elias Sarkis expressed his continued commitment to the ADF whose presence was 'necessary to the salvation of the fatherland and the security of the state'.[147] However, the Lebanese authorities did not submit a formal request for an extension of the Force's mandate. Consequently, the Arab League Council, which met in ordinary session from 12 to 14 September, did not consider the matter.[148]

Despite his public pronouncements, President Sarkis' enthusiasm for the Arab Deterrent Force had become increasingly qualified. While recognizing that the continued presence of Arab League troops was essential until the Lebanese army had been reconstructed, he favoured their replacement by Lebanese soldiers in the Maronite heartland of Mount Lebanon. A security plan, containing these proposals, was promulgated on 28 June.[149] However, Syria had rejected this initiative, calling instead for the deployment of ADF units in all parts of the Lebanon.[150]

As September drew to a close, the fighting in Beirut intensified. The Syrians used unprecedented force against Christian targets in Beirut, and in the villages in the hinterland.[151] The fighting continued, despite appeals from the US and from France for a ceasefire.[152] With unintentional irony, Camille Chamoun and Pierre Gemayel called for the replacement of the ADF by an international peacekeeping force.[153] Following a unanimous Security Council resolution appealing for an immediate cessation of hostilities, the Syrians finally agreed to a ceasefire on 7 October.[154] It was estimated by the Red Cross that, in this latest round of fighting, 400 Christians had been killed and that 5000 apartments had been destroyed.[155]

On 6 October, President Sarkis, at the head of a Lebanese delegation, travelled to Damascus for urgent talks with Syria's President Assad. Three days later, Elias Sarkis left Damascus to hold consultations with Arab leaders in Saudi Arabia, the United Arab Emirates and Kuwait, before returning to Syria for a final round of talks with Hafez Assad.[156] As a result of these soundings, it was decided to convene a conference in the Lebanon, at foreign minister level, of all states contributing either funds or troops to the Arab Deterrent Force.

The Conference, which was convened on 15 October at Beiteddine, some twenty miles south-east of Beirut, was attended by the Foreign Ministers of Lebanon, Syria, Saudi Arabia and Kuwait. In addition, delegates were sent by the United Arab Emirates, Qatar and Sudan.[157] Elias Sarkis presided over the conference, while the Lebanese Prime Minister, Salim Hoss, was also in attendance.

After extensive discussion, and the consideration of memoranda submitted by the Phalange, the National Movement, and by various other Lebanese factions, the Conference issued a statement, on 17 October, noting that a comprehensive solution of the Lebanese crisis must ensure 'the unity, sovereignty and territorial integrity of Lebanon' and the 'elimination of all impediments to the establishment of a strong central authority capable of reconstructing the institutions of the state'.[158] The Conference called for the reconstruction of the Lebanese army 'on a balanced national basis, to enable it to perform its role of ensuring national security and to carry out the tasks now being performed by the Arab Deterrent Forces'.[159] However, the Conference recognized that, in the interim, the ADF would continue to be an important element in preserving peace and security.[160] Thus, the Conference 'expressed its appreciation of the delicate and difficult circumstances in which the Arab Deterrent Forces are performing their tasks in Lebanon and of the burdens they have to bear in these circumstances'.[161]

The Conference decided, in addition, that 'armed manifestations' must be halted, that all weapons retained contrary to the Cairo Agreement and its Annexes must be collected, and that the Resolutions adopted by the Riyadh and Cairo conferences of October 1976 must be strictly applied.[162] The Conference also called for the ending of 'information campaigns', and the 'enforcement of the Printed Matter Law and the banning of all illegal information media, whether visual, oral or intended to be read, with a view to maintaining the unity of the country'.[163] Finally, the Conference decided to establish a 'follow-up committee', consisting of Saudi, Syrian and Kuwaiti representatives, to 'be placed at the disposal of the [Lebanese] President' and to perform such tasks as the President may request it to undertake 'within the framework' of the principles agreed at the Beiteddine Conference.[164]

On 20 October, in accordance with understandings reached at Beiteddine, Syrian troops withdrew from a series of positions they had previously occupied in Ashrafiyeh and Qarantina, in East Beirut, while their places were taken by Saudi units of the Arab Deterrent Force.[165] However, Syrian troops remained in Sin el-Fil, Tal Zaatar, and other key points in the eastern sector of the city.[166]

In return for a partial Syrian withdrawal from East Beirut, the Lebanese government had agreed to request a renewal of the ADF's mandate.[167] Meeting in extraordinary session on 26 October, the League Council extended the mandate of the Deterrent Force for a further six months.[168] However, Syria, Iraq, Algeria, Libya and South Yemen declined to attend the Council meeting, which was held in Cairo, while Egypt abstained.[169]

November 1978 – March 1980

Following the Beiteddine Conference, the security situation improved markedly in the Lebanon. In November, there were renewed clashes between Syrian troops and Maronite militia in Beirut, while a truck containing ADF troops exploded in Aley, some miles to the east of the capital.[170] Nevertheless, in comparison with the furious battles that had raged before the Conference, this represented a significant reduction in the level of violence.

The pattern of intermittent clashes between Syrian units of the ADF and Maronite militias continued in the new year. In addition, there were armed confrontations between various Maronite factions. In view of the recurrent fighting between Syrian troops and Christian militiamen, President Sarkis proposed that Lebanese troops should replace ADF units in the centre of Beirut.[171] When the Saudi contingent of the ADF was withdrawn, in March 1979, the Syrian authorities permitted Lebanese troops to be deployed at three points in the eastern sector of the capital where the Saudis had been stationed.[172] However, Syria declined to withdraw its forces from the centre of Beirut.

At the end of April, the United Arab Emirates withdrew its contingent from the ADF.[173] The Sudanese had departed early in February. With the loss of the UAE troops, only the Syrian contingent remained in the Arab Deterrent Force. However, there were reports, in March, that Syria had deployed some 3600 soldiers of the Palestine Liberation Army in central Beirut, under the command of Syrian officers.[174]

In contrast to the rhetoric of the Beiteddine Conference, the withdrawal of the Sudanese, Saudi and UAE contingents revealed the diminishing confidence of Arab states in either the Deterrent Force, or in the prospects of national reconciliation in the Lebanon. This was confirmed by the decision of the League Council, on 25 March, to extend the mandate of the Force for three months only.[175]

In addition, Saudi Arabia, Kuwait, the United Arab Emirates and Qatar, who collectively funded the ADF, announced that they would cease their financial support for the operation when the new mandate expired, on 27 July.[176] The announcement by the Gulf states prompted speculation that the Arab Deterrent Force would be disbanded, and that the presence of Syrian troops in the Lebanon would be based, thereafter, on a bilateral arrangement with Damascus.[177]

In the midst of considerable uncertainty about the future of the Deterrent Force, Lebanese leaders renewed their calls for the replacement of ADF troops in Beirut by soldiers of the Lebanese Army. President

Sarkis suggested this course of action during talks with President Assad in May.[178] Prime Minister Hoss repeated the proposal when visiting Damascus in June. However, the Syrian authorities refused to accede to the Lebanese request.

The Syrian reaction is difficult to reconcile with the Resolution of the Riyadh Summit Conference, which had stipulated that the ADF should act 'under the personal command of the President of the Lebanese Republic', or with the fact that the Commander of the Deterrent Force, Colonel Sami al-Khatib, was a Lebanese national. However, as noted previously, President Sarkis acknowledged after the Syrian-Maronite clashes of 1978 that he did not exercise effective military control over the ADF.

At Lebanon's request, the mandate of the ADF was renewed, successively, on 28 June 1979 and on 23 January 1980 for six-month periods, despite the earlier threat by the Gulf states to discontinue their financial support for the Force.[179] A further six-month extension was approved by the Council on 26 July 1980.[180]

The decision by Saudi Arabia and by the other Gulf states to continue funding the Deterrent Force, despite their earlier announcement that they would terminate their financial contributions in July, may have stemmed from a number of considerations. Although the Gulf states viewed Syrian excesses in the Lebanon with evident distaste, it remained clear that the Lebanese army was not yet ready to assume the functions of the Deterrent Force. In addition, a purely bilateral arrangement between Syria and the Lebanon, under which Syrian troops would have continued to maintain law and order, would have eliminated whatever modest influence the moderate Arab states could bring to bear on Syria.

The decision to continue funding the Arab Deterrent Force may also have reflected the political and military weakness of the Gulf states, and their undoubted fear of Syrian reprisals. It is noteworthy that, when Kuwait finally withdrew its financial support for the ADF, in February 1982, a Kuwaiti jet was highjacked the next day. The authorities in Kuwait were convinced that Syria was responsible for the incident.[181]

Relations between the Lebanese and Syrian governments, which had been strained by conflicting attitudes concerning the deployment of ADF units, deteriorated further over the issue of Palestinian guerrilla operations in southern Lebanon. A PLO raid into Israel, in January 1979, followed by a bomb explosion in a Jerusalem market, had brought massive Israeli reprisals, precipitating an escalating cycle of violence. Despite Lebanese requests, Syria refused to exert pressure on the PLO to halt its attacks against Israel. The Syrian authorities welcomed PLO militancy in southern Lebanon as a means of exerting pressure on the pro-Israeli enclave which Major Haddad's militia had established along the border with Israel.[182]

The Syrian attitude is difficult to reconcile with either the Riyadh Summit (1976) or the Beiteddine conference (1978) both of which, with Syrian concurrence, had called for the implementation of the Cairo Agreement and its Annexes. As noted above, these entailed the cessation of all guerrilla operations against Israel launched from Lebanese territory.

The cycle of Palestinian raids and Israeli reprisals threatened, increasingly, to engulf the Syrian troops of the Arab Deterrent Force. On 19 January, Israeli soldiers crossed into Lebanon to attack PLO positions. Briefly, the Israeli force thrust north beyond the Litani river, entering territory in which the ADF was deployed.[183] In April, following a Palestinian raid into Israel in which four civilians were killed, Israel launched massive reprisals against Palestinian targets in southern Lebanon, many of which were close to ADF positions.[184]

The Syrian contingent of the Arab Deterrent Force was composed of infantry, supported by artillery and tanks. Syria was precluded from deploying ground-to-air missiles anywhere in the Lebanon, under the terms of its 'red line' agreement with Israel which also proscribed Syrian penetration south of the Litani river.[185]

However, following Israel's massive intervention in the Lebanon, in March 1978, Syria supplied its ADF units with anti-aircraft guns, while Syrian fighter aircraft were also introduced to provide air cover for the ADF.[186] On 26 April, Syrian jets were scrambled after Israeli planes appeared over Beirut.[187] On 27 June, Israeli aircraft, on a bombing mission north of Sidon, were intercepted by Syrian jets. In the ensuing dog-fight, five Syrian Mig-21s were reportedly destroyed.[188] In a further confrontation in September, four Syrian jets were shot down by Israeli aircraft south of Beirut.[189]

Although the Syrian aircraft were not integrated into the Arab Deterrent Force, they were deployed so that the ADF could operate freely north of the Litani. As noted previously, Israel had consistently prevented the Arab Deterrent Force from advancing south of the river, at times even in the face of US opposition.[190] However, through its regular attacks on Palestinian targets as far north as Tripoli, Israel eroded the credibility and effectiveness of the ADF even in the central and northern sectors of the Lebanon.

In January 1980, the Syrian government announced that its troops serving in the Arab Deterrent Force would be redeployed. In accordance with the new plan, Syrian units would be withdrawn from Beirut, and from various positions in the west of the Lebanon. Henceforth, Syrian troops would be concentrated in the Bekaa, and in other areas east of Beirut.[191]

Neither the President of the Lebanon, nor the Lebanese Commander of the ADF, were consulted about the proposed redeployment. This was acknowledged by President Assad, in an interview published in March. Defending the lack of consultation with the Lebanese authorities, the Syrian President asserted:[192]

> Certainly we have never consulted anyone about our defence policy in the past, and we do not intend to do so now or in the future . . . the decision is relating to developments in the area and I do not believe that this requires us to take a decision jointly with others in this regard.

On 22 January, without prior notification, Syrian troops abandoned their positions along the coast between Beirut and Zahrani, moving to the Bekaa.[193] On 3 February, Syrian concentrations in northern Lebanon and in West Beirut were reduced. The Syrian presence in East Beirut, already confined to Tal Zaatar, Jisr al-Pasha, Dekwaneh and Sin el-Fil, was cut by half.[194] On the same day, Syria declared that its troops would be withdrawn entirely from the Lebanese capital.[195]

Following an urgent visit to Damascus, on 4 February, the Lebanese Prime Minister received assurances that the further withdrawal of Syrian troops from Beirut would be postponed until the Lebanese authorities were able 'to fill any vacuum which might arise'.[196] Two days later, the Lebanese Cabinet announced that the army would be deployed in particularly sensitive areas vacated by Syrian troops.[197]

Acting in concert with the Lebanese authorities, Syria removed its remaining troops from East Beirut, and from neighbouring suburbs, on 6 March. Their positions were immediately taken over by units of the Lebanese army.[198] However, several thousand Syrian troops remained in West Beirut, where they continued to perform their normal functions.

General Khoury, Commander of the Lebanese army, visited Damascus on 9 March to propose that Lebanese troops should replace Syrian forces in all sectors of Beirut.[199] However, the Syrian government chose to ignore its earlier pledge to withdraw completely from the Lebanese capital. In all probability, this had never been more than a feint, intended to concentrate the minds of Lebanese politicians. The retention of a sizeable Syrian presence in Beirut was essential for the maintenance of Syrian prestige and authority in the Lebanon.[200]

Various explanations have been offered for the Syrian decision, announced in January 1980, to redeploy its forces in the Lebanon. In part, it reflected Syrian impatience with the Lebanese, who had failed to take any meaningful steps towards national reconciliation, and who continued to rely on the presence of Syrian troops. By withdrawing its forces from Beirut and from other population centres, Syria hoped that the Lebanese factions would be compelled to resolve their political differences. This motive is apparent in a commentary broadcast on Syrian radio: 'Syria has performed its full pan-Arab duty. It is up to the Lebanese sides and state to do their duty . . . Perhaps the decision to redeploy forces will be a national factor prompting all sides to seek means which will consolidate stability and peace throughout Lebanon'.[201]

In addition, the Syrian redeployment was probably motivated by strategic considerations. By concentrating its forces in the Bekaa, Syria was assuring additional protection for its most vulnerable flank in the event of hostilities with Israel. Thus, in an interview published in March, President Assad commented that the Syrian redeployment was 'a possible and appropriate measure that could give us some margin of freedom of movement' in the event of Israeli aggression.[202] The President also observed that the decision concerned Syria's 'defence policy'.[203]

However, the Syrian initiative was also prompted by domestic, political and security considerations. The secular Ba'ath regime was facing a series of debilitating attacks from members of the fundamentalist Muslim Brotherhood.[204] The relative proximity of the Bekaa meant that, in the event of a crisis, security forces in Syria could be speedily reinforced by units from the Arab Deterrent Force.

Finally, the protracted Syrian 'occupation' of the Lebanon had undermined the discipline of Syrian troops. Released from the rigours of life in Syria, an increasing number had turned to gambling and drugs, to the consternation of Ba'ath officials in Damascus.[205]

Israel interpreted the Syrian redeployment in the Lebanon as a possible threat to its security, placing Israeli forces on alert.[206] Prime Minister Begin denied that Israel had any intention of attacking Syria. However, he expressed his 'commitment to help the Christians in Lebanon'.[207] Emboldened by Israeli support, the right-wing Lebanese Forces called for the withdrawal of Syrian troops from the Lebanon.[208]

In northern Lebanon, serious clashes occurred in February between the Phalange and militiamen loyal to Suleiman Frangieh, whose son had been murdered at the instigation of Bashir Gemayel some eighteen months earlier.[209] Syrian troops of the ADF intervened in the fighting, in opposition to the Phalange. The clashes continued for several days, resulting in some 30 deaths.[210] The feud between the Frangiehs and the Gemayels was believed to be responsible for an explosion in Beirut, later that month, in which Bashir Gemayel's baby daughter was killed.[211]

April 1980 – June 1982

The security situation in southern Lebanon, which had been pacified briefly by a ceasefire established in October 1979, deteriorated steadily. In April 1980, a Palestinian attack on a kibbutz in northern Israel, in which several children were taken hostage, resulted in a resurgence of violence.[212] In a series of raids on Palestinian positions in the Lebanon, Israeli forces struck at PLO camps both inland and along the coast, far to the north of the notional 'red line' dividing Syrian and Israeli spheres of influence.[213] As Israel thrust repeatedly into the Lebanon, Syrian jets were scrambled to challenge Israeli planes. In dogfights over southern Lebanon, on 24 and 31 August, three Syrian MiGs were reportedly shot down.[214]

In December 1980, the first clash occurred between Syrian troops of the ADF and Israeli forces. During an assault on Palestinian positions north of the Litani river, a number of Syrian soldiers were killed. According to one version, three Syrians died during Israeli shelling of the village of Rihane, some miles to the north of Marjayoun;[215] according to another report, four Syrian soldiers were killed in a raid by Israeli commandos.[216]

Both versions agree that the attack on members of the Arab Deterrent Force was unintentional. In an effort to calm the situation, Mordechai Zippori, Israel's Deputy Defence Minister, apologized for the incident, declaring that Israel had no wish to harm Syrian forces in the Lebanon.[217] The Syrian response was confined to a heavy artillery bombardment of Marjayoun, occupied by the Israeli-backed militia of Major Haddad.[218]

As Palestinian guerrillas fought Israeli troops and their Lebanese Christian allies in southern Lebanon, a number of major developments occurred in the central and northern sectors of the country. On 7 July, Phalangist militia loyal to Bashir Gemayel attacked offices and camps belonging to the rival National Liberal Party militia, led by Dany Chamoun.[219] The assault was completely successful, resulting in the collapse of Chamoun's 'Tiger' militia. As a consequence of the fighting, all Christian militias in central Lebanon were integrated into the 'Lebanese Forces' with a unified command structure.[220] The military and political potential of the Maronites, under the dynamic if ruthless leadership of Bashir Gemayel, appeared to have increased significantly. In October, the Lebanese Forces attacked a group of 'Tiger' militiamen who had taken refuge in Ain el-Roumaneh, after the fighting in July. In four days of heavy fighting, the remnants of Dany Chamoun's militia were finally routed.[221]

The failure of ADF units to intervene in the clashes between the Christian militias was interpreted in some quarters as evidence of tacit Syrian support for Bashir Gemayel. However, in December 1980, there was a serious outbreak of fighting in Zahlé involving Syrian troops and members of the Phalange.[222] The Syrian – Phalangist confrontation, which had originated in a Syrian attempt to arrest fighting between rival Christian militias, exemplified the difficulties of maintaining peace in the Lebanon, and the propensity of the Syrian 'peacekeepers' to escalate the level of violence once they had come under attack.

There were also outbreaks of fighting between members of Lebanon's traditionally underprivileged Shia community, who had become increasingly radicalized, and their former Palestinian allies.[223] In July, ADF units intervened to halt clashes between Lebanese supporters of the secular Ba'ath regime in Iraq and Shia fundamentalists.[224] In August, Syrian troops acted to stop fighting between rival Muslim factions in the northern port of Tripoli.[225]

In March 1981, fighting of unusual ferocity broke out along the 'green line' dividing the western and eastern sectors of Beirut.[226] The hostilities were the most severe that the capital had experienced since the confrontation between Maronite militia and Syrian troops in 1978.

In southern Lebanon, beyond the reach of the Arab Deterrent Force, conditions remained tense. 1980 had ended with dogfights between Syrian and Israeli jets. The new year was punctuated by Israeli reprisals against Palestinian targets and by the shooting down of another Syrian aircraft by Israeli planes flying in Lebanese airspace.[227]

The troops of the UN Interim Force in the Lebanon found themselves under attack from Palestinians, seeking to cross UN lines into Israel, and from the right-wing militia controlled by Major Haddad. Attacks by the latter were prompted by concern at the proposed deployment of regular Lebanese army soldiers in southern Lebabon.[228]

Both Haddad and his Israeli backers believed that the Lebanese army lacked the ability, and also the motivation, to prevent Palestinian infiltration through its lines.[229] They also feared that Syria, which was unable to introduce its own forces in the area because of the 'red line' agreement with Israel, would exercise real control over any Lebanese troops sent to the south, and thus extend its authority over southern Lebanon.[230]

At the beginning of April, there were renewed clashes between Syrian troops and Phalange militiamen in Zahlé, in eastern Lebanon. The fighting in December had originated in attempts by the Phalange to extend its authority over this predominantly Greek Catholic city.[231]

The renewed violence was sparked off by an unprovoked attack on Syrian troops, and by the efforts of the Phalange to construct a road linking Zahlé with the Maronite heartland.[232]

For Syria, Zahlé was of considerable strategic and political significance. The city overlooked the Beirut – Damascus highway and was only ten miles from the Syrian border. An expansion of Phalangist power in this area posed a potential threat to Syrian security, and undermined Syrian influence, prestige and authority throughout the Lebanon.[233] These factors may explain the ferocity of Syria's reaction. Syrian artillery bombarded Zahlé for five days, injuring and killing scores of civilian inhabitants.[234] In Beirut, Syrian forces, using tanks, rockets and artillery, shelled the eastern sector of the city, causing substantial casualties.[235]

The Syrian assault on the Phalange, in Zahlé and in the East Beirut, was prompted by national political and strategic goals, rather than by the imperatives of the ADF's mandate in the Lebanon. The Syrian action was taken without reference to the Lebanese Commander of the Arab Deterrent Force, or the Lebanese President, to whom the Force was nominally accountable.

Following the rejection of Syrian peace proposals, which would have entailed the withdrawal of Phalange militiamen from Zahlé and the surrounding area, Syria resumed its shelling of the city. In addition, Syrian troops were despatched to occupy the mountain range connecting Zahlé with the Maronite heartland.[236] In desperation, Bashir Gemayel and Camille Chamoun turned to Israel for assistance.[237] Meeting on 28 April, the Israeli Cabinet, acting contrary to the advice of several ministers, authorized a limited action in support of the beleaguered Phalange. Two Syrian helicopters, ferrying troops to the battle around Zahlé, were destroyed by Israeli jets.[238] Unlike the deaths of several Syrian troops in an Israeli action in December 1980, this represented the first deliberate attack by Israel on Syrian soldiers of the ADF.

In a swift response, Syria installed SAM-6 ground-to-air missiles near Zahlé, while additional missile batteries were deployed just inside the Syrian border.[239] The Syrian initiative was denounced by Israel as a clear breach of the 1976 'red line' agreement, bringing Israeli threats that the Lebanese missile batteries would be destroyed.[240]

The conflict over Zahlé, which had led to the Syrian – Israeli confrontation, continued until the end of June, when Arab mediation resulted in an agreement between Syria and the Phalange. Under the terms of the agreement, negotiated with the assistance of the follow-up committee established by the Beiteddine Conference,[241] the Phalange were to withdraw from Zahlé, while a force of Lebanese gendarmes would take up positions in the city.[242] Syrian troops of the

Arab Deterrent Force were deployed around Zahlé to ensure that the agreement was fully implemented.

Earlier that month the Syrian authorities had tried, unsuccessfully, to achieve an overall settlement of the Lebanese conflict. The Syrian plan would have involved the formation of a government of 'national salvation', financial support by the Arab League for Lebanon's reconstruction, and continued Arab backing for the Deterrent Force.[243] However, the plan failed to secure general acceptance. The Phalange were determined to achieve the withdrawal of all Syrian troops from the Lebanon, while Syria remained deeply suspicious of Phalange links with Israel.[244]

In July, Syria established a militia known as the 'Arab Cavalry'. Units of the new force, which was commanded by General Rifaat Assad, brother of the Syrian President, were deployed in Beirut, and in the north Lebanese port of Tripoli.[245] The creation of the Arab Cavalry was seen as a means of preserving Syrian influence in the Lebanon, in the event of the withdrawal of the Arab Deterrent Force.[246]

On 28 May, Israeli jets had renewed their attacks on Palestinian targets in southern Lebanon.[247] In July, further Israeli assaults triggered an unexpectedly fierce Palestinian response. Katyusha rockets and artillery shells rained down on the Galilee, causing panic amongst local residents.[248] Israel countered with an aerial bombardment of Fatah headquarters in Beirut, resulting in substantial civilian casualties. The cycle of Palestinian – Israeli violence was finally arrested, at the end of July, when the US emissary, Philip Habib, negotiated a ceasefire.[249]

Although an uneasy calm was restored in the south following the conclusion of a ceasefire, there were numerous incidents elsewhere in the Lebanon. In August, fighting in Tripoli between rival pro-Syrian and pro-Iraqi militias led to the intervention of ADF troops, backed by tanks.[250] In a blatant display of partiality, the ADF soldiers took part in the fighting, aligning themselves with the pro-Syrian militiamen.[251]

In Beirut, supporters of the Shia Amal movement clashed with Lebanese leftists,[252] While a massive bomb explosion in Muslim west Beirut, on 1 October, left 100 dead and precipitated reprisals in the Christian east of the city.[253]

In an effort to arrest the mounting disorder, the ADF, in conjunction with the National Movement, the Palestinians and Amal, announced a new programme to re-establish security in Beirut and the surrounding areas. The programme involved the removal of barricades and checkpoints, the prohibition of the use of military vehicles by the militias, and a ban on wearing uniforms or carrying weapons in the street.[254]

The ADF made efforts to enforce the plan in Muslim West Beirut. However, the Christian Lebanese Forces who controlled the eastern sector of the city, following the ADF's redeployment in 1980, made no attempt to implement the new scheme.[255]

In early December, there was renewed fighting in Beirut between rival Muslim militias. Later that month, following a bomb explosion in West Beirut, there were heavy artillery duels across the 'green line' dividing the Muslim and Christian sectors of the city.[256]

A series of attacks on foreign diplomats in Beirut contributed to the growing sense of chaos and disorder, prompting the authorities to announce the formation of a new security force to protect diplomats and their missions.[257] In a telling demonstration of the ADF's diminished credibility, several governments insisted that Syrian troops should not participate in the security force.[258]

In the new year, the pattern of violence between Lebanon's diverse militias was repeated in Tripoli, Beirut and Sidon.[259] The Lebanese authorities no longer exerted any influence over ADF troops who had resumed the character of a Syrian occupation army serving the interests, and implementing the policies, of Damascus.

June 1982 – March 1983

On 3 June 1982, gunmen belonging to a Palestinian faction headed by Abu Nidal shot and critically wounded the Israeli Ambassador in London. The incident was to prove the catalyst for Israel's war in the Lebanon and led, inexorably, to the dissolution of the Arab Deterrent Force.

The Israeli Cabinet authorized the bombing of PLO targets in West Beirut, in retaliation for the attack on its ambassador.[260] Predictably, the PLO responded by shelling the Galilee. On 5 June the Israeli Cabinet sanctioned a limited operation to ensure the removal of PLO artillery from a 25-mile strip of territory in southern Lebanon.[261]

Initially, Syria tried to avoid any involvement in the Israeli action, which Damascus assumed was directed exclusively at Palestinian targets in the Lebanon. Thus, the southernmost Syrian units were instructed not to oppose the Israeli advance.[262] However, Syria's attitude changed when an Israeli armoured column thrust north through the Chouf towards the Beirut – Damascus highway. The Israeli manoeuvre threatened to encircle Syrian forces in the Bekaa, and to sever Syria's links with its troops in West Beirut.[263]

On Tuesday, 8 June, Israeli tanks engaged Syrian armour in Jezzine. Further north, a desperate battle developed as Syrian units tried to prevent the Israelis from reaching the highway connecting Beirut and Damascus.[264] On the following day, Defence Minister Sharon obtained Cabinet approval for an attack on Syrian missile batteries in the

Bekaa. In the ensuing strike, some fourteen batteries were destroyed together with 29 Syrian MiGs that had been sent up to defend the missiles.[265]

Alarmed by the scale of Israel's intervention in the Lebanon, and under mounting pressure from the Soviet government, President Reagan demanded Israeli acceptance of a ceasefire.[266] However, Israeli forces continued to press towards the Beirut – Damascus highway. A ceasefire between Syrian and Israeli forces finally went into effect at noon, on Friday 11 June.[267]

The Israeli Cabinet did not embark on a policy of deliberate confrontation with Syrian units in the Lebanon. However, this had been one of the tacit objectives of Defence Minister Sharon. Sharon's ultimate aim was to secure the removal of Syrian troops from the Lebanon, and the installation of a friendly regime under Bashir Gemayel.[268]

Although a ceasefire went into effect on Friday, 11 June, it only applied to the central and eastern zones of the Lebanon. Israeli columns continued to advance towards Beirut along the coast, and in the western sector. The Israeli forces were engaged south of the capital by Syrian troops of the 85th Brigade. Fighting continued until Sunday, 13 June, when Israeli units penetrated East Beirut, linking up with the Phalange.[269] In a bid to consolidate their access to the capital, Israeli troops clashed once again with the Syrians east of Beirut.[270]

During the next two months, Israeli forces besieging West Beirut used artillery and airpower in an effort to drive the PLO guerrillas out of the capital. The Israeli strategy proved increasingly costly to the beleaguered civilian population.[271]

An agreement concerning the withdrawal of PLO forces from Beirut was finally achieved on 18 August. This provided for the evacuation of the guerrillas by sea, under the supervision of a Multinational Force composed of US, French and Italian soldiers.[272] The evacuation began on Saturday 21 August and was completed by 1 September. In addition to over 14 000 Palestinian fighters who left by sea, some 6254 Syrian troops and members of the PLA left the capital, travelling overland towards the Bekaa.[273] The latter constituted the remnants of the ADF presence in Beirut.

On 24 July, at the height of the siege of Beirut, Bashir Gemayel declared his candidacy for the office of President. In the absence of other candidates, he was elected by the Lebanese Chamber of Deputies on 23 August.[274] However on 14 September, some days before his inauguration, Bashir Gemayel was killed in a bomb blast reputedly instigated by Syria.[275]

Syrian antagonism towards Lebanon's President-elect was well founded. Bashir had called, repeatedly, for the withdrawal of Syrian troops from the Lebanon. He was known to have had frequent contacts with Israeli leaders and military personnel and, although Bashir had conspicuously refrained from aiding the Israeli invasion, he was suspected of colluding with Israel. Following his election, Bashir Gemayel had held talks with Israel's Prime Minister, Menachem Begin, and with Defence Minister Ariel Sharon.[276] During these sessions the President-elect had been pressed to conclude a treaty of peace with Israel, which would have been anathema to the Ba'ath regime in Damascus. For his part, Bashir Gemayel had assured Israel's Prime Minister that his basic aim was 'to get the Palestinians and the Syrians out of the Bekaa and the north'.[277]

The out-going administration of President Sarkis had already taken a number of important steps towards achieving a Syrian withdrawal. On 27 July, while the Arab world was preoccupied with the Israeli siege of West Beirut, the mandate of the Arab Deterrent Force had expired.[278] The Lebanese government, which had previously requested successive renewals of the mandate decided, in August, to 'terminat[e] . . . the mission of the Arab Deterrent Force in Lebanon' and called for '[t]he withdrawal of all non-Lebanese armed forces from Lebanon'.[279]

President Sarkis continued to press for the withdrawal of Syrian troops at an Arab Summit Conference convened in Fez, on 6 September. The Arab Kings and Heads of State were notified of the Lebanese government's decision to terminate the mandate of the Arab Deterrent Force, and of its desire to secure the withdrawal of all non-Lebanese forces from its territory.[280] The Lebanese President received significant support from the Gulf states, who emphasized their reluctance to continue funding the Deterrent Force.[281]

After some initial prevarication, President Assad accepted the termination of the ADF's mandate. However, the Summit was extended beyond its scheduled closing date, because of a disagreement over the details of Syria's withdrawal.

President Sarkis was adamant that all non-Lebanese forces should withdraw unconditionally, while President Assad argued that this would place Syrian troops on a par with Israeli forces in the Lebanon.[282] He proposed, instead, that the modalities of the Syrian withdrawal should be resolved by negotiation between the states concerned.[283]

After prolonged discussion, the Heads of State agreed on a compromise formula which was incorporated in a resolution adopted by the Summit Conference.[284] With studied ambiguity, the text declared:[285]

> [t]he Conference has been informed of the decision of the Lebanese Government to terminate the functions of the Arab deterrent forces in Lebanon, on the condition that negotiations are to be conducted between the Lebanese Government and the

Syrian Government for the adoption of measures in the light of Israeli withdrawal from the Lebanon.

Thus, the Summit Conference recognized that the mission of the Arab Deterrent Force was terminated, while implying that the actual withdrawal of Syrian troops would be conditional on a prior Israeli evacuation. The text represented an ingenious, if only partially successful, attempt to satisfy both the Lebanese and Syrian authorities.[286]

On 21 September, Amin Gemayel, the elder brother of the murdered Bashir, was elected President of the Lebanon. In the wake of Bashir's death, Israeli troops had advanced briefly into West Beirut, permitting Christian militiamen to enter the camps of Sabra and Chatila in search of Palestinian guerrillas. The Phalangist forces responded with predictable brutality, killing hundreds of the civilian inhabitants.[287]

Amidst the international outcry following the Sabra and Chatila massacres, Israel withdrew its troops from West Beirut, while there was widespread agreement on the urgent need to introduce an international peacekeeping force. On 19 September, the Security Council unanimously adopted a resolution which envisaged the possible deployment of a UN force. Resolution 521 called on the Secretary-General, as a matter of urgency, 'to initiate appropriate consultations with the Government of Lebanon on additional steps which the Council might take, including the possible deployment of United Nations forces, to assist that Government in ensuring full protection for the civilian population in and around Beirut'.[288] However, it was the MNF, composed of US, French, Italian and British contingents, which was eventually introduced, in preference to a UN force. Ironically, the Multinational Force had left the Lebanon only days previously, having completed its mission of supervising the evacuation of Palestinian guerrillas from Beirut.[289]

Various explanations have been offered for the deployment of a non-UN force in Beirut. These include the apparent reluctance of many UN members to contribute troops and the alleged opposition of Israel, the United States and the Lebanon to the introduction of a potentially weak and unreliable UN force in Beirut.[290]

However, the deployment of an Arab force,. as an alternative to a UN or a Euro-American operation, was never even considered. This is all the more surprising when it is recollected that Palestine and the Lebanon are League members, and that the plight of the Palestinians has been one of the foremost concerns of the Arab League.[291] In addition, although the ADF's mandate had lapsed in July, the Syrian contingent of the Arab Deterrent Force had remained in the Lebanon.[292] Thus, the logistics of establishing an Arab presence in Beirut would have been relatively straightforward.

There are various explanations for the tacit consensus that an Arab peacekeeping force would have been inappropriate. As noted above, the Lebanese government had terminated the mission of the Arab Deterrent Force, and was trying to secure the withdrawal of Syrian troops from Lebanese territory. The Arab Summit Conference, which met in Fez from 6 to 9 September, had finally recognized the termination of the ADF's mandate after the Gulf states had indicated their reluctance to continue funding the Arab League Force. In these circumstances, there was little enthusiasm for the reintroduction of an Arab peacekeeping force in Beirut. Inevitably, such a force would have contained a sizeable Syrian element, thereby undermining Lebanese efforts to achieve the withdrawal of Syrian troops, and exposing the civilian population, once again, to the harsh realities of Syrian occupation.

In addition, the Lebanese authorities were acutely aware that an Israeli withdrawal from the Lebanon could only be achieved in the context of the departure of Syrian 'peacekeeping' forces.[293] The introduction of an Arab force in Beirut, containing a large Syrian contingent, would thus have retarded an Israeli withdrawal. Crucially also, the introduction of an Arab peacekeeping force in Beirut might have resulted in a confrontation with Israeli troops. The latter were not withdrawn from West Beirut until 29 September 1982.[294]

As US, French, Italian and, ultimately, British troops of the Multinational Force deployed in the western sector of the capital, the US tried to secure the removal of Israeli and Syrian forces from the Lebanon. US officials participated in talks between Lebanese and Israeli delegates. These talks culminated in the signing of a treaty in May 1983 providing, in part, for the withdrawal of Israeli troops.[295] On 31 March 1983, while the treaty negotiations were still in progress, President Gemayel issued a decree formally dissolving the Command of the Arab Deterrent Force.[296] The decree, which may have been intended to gratify Israeli – or possibly American – opinion had little practical significance. The Lebanese Commander of the ADF, General Sami al-Khatib, was reassigned to the Lebanese army, together with other Lebanese officers who had served in the Arab Deterrent Force. In addition, buildings which had been allocated to the ADF were restored to public use.[297]

Crucially, the decree had no impact on the continued presence of thousands of Syrian troops in the Lebanon. The decree was not even accompanied by an official request to Syria to recall her troops.[298] Whether this omission reflected a change of Lebanese policy since the Fez Summit Conference, at which Lebanon had pressed for the unconditional withdrawal of all foreign troops from her territory, is doubtful. Following the Fez Summit, the Lebanese government held talks with Syrian leaders at which 'Lebanon expressly requested the withdrawal of the Syrian troops'.[299]

However, during the course of 1983–4, Syria gradually restored its influence in the Lebanon, at the expense of the US and Israel. The MNF departed, and Israeli forces began a series of tactical withdrawals.[300] The Lebanese President, who had been compelled to abrogate the Israel – Lebanon Troop Withdrawal Agreement as part of the price of Syrian support for his regime, did not renew his demands for the withdrawal of Syrian troops.[301]

Notes

1   *Fiches du Monde Arabe*, 4 February 1981, No. 1812.
2   *Keesing's* (1976), p.28119.
3   Ibid.
4   *Fiches du Monde Arabe*, 4 February 1981, No. 1812.
5   Ibid.
6   See cable from President Frangieh of Lebanon to General-Secretary Riad of the Arab League, 30 June 1976, in *al-Nahar*, 1 July 1976. The text is available, in English, in *IDP* (1976), p.436.
7   Ibid.
8   Ibid.
9   For the text of the Prime Minister's statement, see *al-Nahar*, 2 July 1976. For an English-language translation see *IDP* (1976), p.438.
10 Bulloch, *Death of a Country*, p.156.
11 League Council Resolution No. 3456, 9 June 1976.
12 Ibid.
13 *Fiches du Monde Arabe*, 4 February 1981, No. 1812.
14 Ibid.
15 *Keesing's* (1976), p.28120.
16 See the interview with Dr Hassan Sabri al-Kholi, Envoy of the Arab League, in *al-Nahar*, 28 July 1976. The interview is reproduced, in English, in *JPS*. vol. 6 (1976/77), pp.187-8.
17 Bulloch, *Death of a Country*, p.156.
18 Ibid., pp.174-82.
19 Khalidi, *Conflict and Violence in Lebanon*, p.63.
20 *Keesing's* (1976), p.28122.
21 Khalidi, *Conflict and Violence in Lebanon*, p.63.
22 Dawisha, *Syria and the Lebanese Crisis*, p.161.
23 Ibid., p.162. On earlier attempts by Egypt and Saudi Arabia to secure a mini-summit, see e.g. Dawisha, *Syria and the Lebanese Crisis*, pp.159-60. As early as 14 August, the government of Saudi Arabia had issued a statement in which it 'call[ed] upon leaders of the Arab nation to come together and to meet at any level for the purpose of stopping Arab blood being shed on the soil of Lebanon'. See *al-Riyad*, 15 August 1976. For an English-language translation, see *IDP* (1976), p.463. For its part, the PLO was opposed to a mini-summit advocating, instead, a full Arab summit conference where '[a]ll the Arab rulers must meet and face up to the Lebanese crisis, so that they may put their signatures to the final solution of the crisis'. See *wafa*,

30 August 1976, p.3. For an English-language translation, see *IDP* (1976), p.470, at p.471.

24 Khalidi, *Conflict and Violence in Lebanon*, p.64.

25 Paras. 1, 5, Resolution adopted by the Six-Party Arab Summit Conference (Riyadh, 1976).

26 Ibid., para. 6.

27 Ibid., para. 2.

28 Ibid.

29 For additional discussion of this point see Chapter 5, notes 44-50, and the accompanying text.

30 Fourteen of the 21 member states (Djibouti was not admitted till September 1977; Palestine had been admitted as a full member in September 1976) were represented by their Heads of State. For details see *Keesing's* (1976), p.28123. On the legal and institutional significance of Arab Summit Conferences see Chapter 1, notes 86-9, and the accompanying text. The Cairo Summit Conference was the eighth Arab summit conference. See generally, *Le Monde*, 28 October 1976, p.5.

31 See Para. 1, Resolution I; Para. 1, Resolution III, Resolutions adopted by the Arab Summit Conference (Cairo, 1976).

32 Iraq and Libya were opposed to Syria's military intervention in the Lebanon, which had resulted in a series of debilitating clashes with Palestinian guerrillas. *International Herald Tribune*, 26 October 1976. Iraq tried, without success, to persuade the Summit to consider the politically sensitive question of Syria's military intervention. Ibid.

33 *Le Monde*, 6 November 1976, p.3.

34 Ibid.

35 Para. 2(b), Resolution adopted by the Six-Party Arab Summit Conference (Riyadh, 1976).

36 *Le Monde*, 9 November 1976, p.6.

37 *al-Nahar*, 10 November 1976. The statement is available, in English, in *IDP* (1976) p.506.

38 See, in particular, para. 2, Resolution adopted by the Six-Party Arab Summit Conference (Riyadh, 1976).

39 *Keesing's* (1976), p.28123.

40 *Kuwait Times*, 27 October 1976; *International Herald Tribune*, 27 October 1976.

41 *International Herald Tribune*, 27 October 1976.

42 *Kuwait Times*, 27 October 1976. Syria was anxious to limit the participation of troops from other Arab states. See, generally, Ben Amara, op. cit., p.ix, note 10, p.144.

43 *International Herald Tribune*, 27 October 1976.

44. Ibid.

45 *Fiches du Monde Arabe*, 2 August 1978, No. 1024. On the various factors which resulted in Syria forming the bulk of the force, see e.g., Ben Amara, op. cit., p.ix, note 10, p.144.

46 *The Times*, 26 October 1976, p.8.

47 *The Times*, 28 October 1976, p.10.

48 *Keesing's* (1976), p.28123.

49 *Fiches du Monde Arabe*, 2 August 1978, No. 1024.

50 Ibid. See also above p.110.

51 *Keesing's* (1976), p.28123.

52 *Fiches du Monde Arabe*, 9 August 1978, No. 1030.

53 Ibid.

54   *Keesing's* (1976), p.28123.
55   *Fiches du Monde Arabe,* 9 August 1978, No. 1030.
56   On the 'red line' in the Lebanon, see e.g. Cobban, *Lebanon,* pp.148-9.
57   See e.g. Khalidi, *Conflict and Violence in Lebanon,* p.108, note 144.
58   See para. 2(e), Resolution adopted by the Six-Party Arab Summit Conference (Riyadh, 1976).
59   *Keesing's* (1976), p.28733.
60   Khalidi, *Conflict and Violence in Lebanon,* p. 106. It has been suggested that, as a result of Syrian influence, the ADF was more zealous in collecting heavy weapons from Palestinian-Leftist forces, than from the various Maronite militias. Schiff and Ya'ari, *Lebanon War* p.22.
61   Khalidi, *Conflict and Violence in Lebanon,* p.106.
62   Ibid. The responsibilities of the Arab Deterrent Force included re-opening major roads, and the establishment of 'checkpoints and patrols' along 'unsafe routes'. See para. 4, Schedule adopted by the Six-Party Arab Summit Conference (Riyadh, 1976).
63   *Fiches du Monde Arabe,* 16 August 1978, No. 1035. The functions of the ADF included the supervision of 'the withdrawal of armed troops to positions . . . held prior to 13 April 1975'. See para. 2(d), Resolution adopted by the Six-Party Arab Summit Conference (Riyadh, 1976).
64   The interview is reproduced in *al-Thawra,* 11 May 1977. It is available, in English, in *IDP* (1977), p.369.
65   Ibid.
66   Cobban, *Lebanon,* pp.158-9.
67   *Keesing's* (1977), p.28734.
68   Ibid.
69   Ibid., p.28735.
70   Colonel al-Khatib assumed command of the Arab Deterrent Force on 11 April 1977. See *Keesing's* (1977), p.28735.
71   For details of the Chtaura Agreement, see e.g. *Keesing's* (1977), pp.28735-6. See also *Fiches du Monde Arabe,* 16 August 1978, No. 1035. The prohibition of guerrilla attacks into Israel, and of heavy weaponry in the refugee camps, were contained in the Melkart Understanding. See Chapter 5, notes 36-9, and the accompanying text.
72   See e.g. communiqué issued by the Command of the Arab Deterrent Force in Lebanon, July 1977, which stated that, as of 15 August, the Arab Deterrent Force 'will raid any illegal position, office or arms store inside or outside the camps'. Excerpts of the communiqué are reproduced in *al-Nahar,* 11 August 1977. The text is available, in English, in *IDP* (1977), p.387.
73   See communiqué issued by the Command of the Arab Deterrent Force in Lebanon, 30 July 1977. The text is reproduced in *al-Nahar,* 31 July 1977. It is available, in English, in *IDP* (1977), p.379. See also *Fiches du Monde Arabe,* 9 August 1978, No. 1030.
74   See communiqué issued by the Command of the Arab Deterrent Force in Lebanon, op. cit., note 72.
75   Some efforts were made to secure the implementation of the third stage of the Chtaura Agreement, before the resumption of fighting in the south rendered this impossible. For details see e.g. communiqué issued by the Arab Deterrent Forces, 31 August 1977. The text is reproduced in *al-Nahar,* 1 September 1977. It is available, in English, in *IDP* (1977), p.391. The PLO interpreted the resumption of fighting in the south, and Israel's artillery support for the Christian militias, as a deliberate attempt to prevent the implementation of the final stage of the Chtaura Agreement, and thereby to undermine efforts

to achieve national reconciliation in the Lebanon. See statement issued by the PLO Executive Committee, 21 October 1977. The text is reproduced in *Wafa*, 2 October 1977, p.5. It is available, in English, in *IDP* (1977), p.399.

76 *Keesing's* (1977), p.28735.
77 Khalidi, *Conflict and Violence in Lebanon*, p.107.
78 *Fiches du Monde Arabe*, 16 August 1978, No. 1035.
79 Ibid.
80 *Keesing's* (1977), p.28737.
81 Ibid.
82 *Fiches du Monde Arabe*, 16 August 1978, No. 1035.
83 *Keesing's* (1977), p.28738.
84 Ibid. The Syrians arrested four men who were believed to be responsible for the deaths. They were executed in Syria on the following day.
85 Ibid.
86 *Fiches du Monde Arabe*, 9 August 1978, No. 1030.
87 Ibid.
88 Ibid.
89 *Keesing's* (1977), p. 28739.
90 Ibid.
91 Khalidi, *Conflict and Violence in Lebanon*, pp.125, 127.
92 Ibid.
93 *Keesing's* (1978), p.29032.
94 Ibid., p.29031.
95 *Keesing's* (1978), p.29032.
96 *Fiches du Monde Arabe*, 16 August 1978, No. 1035.
97 *Keesing's* (1978), p.29033.
98 Ibid.
99 Khalidi, *Conflict and Violence in Lebanon*, p.116.
100 Ibid.
101 *Keesing's* (1978), p.29033.
102 Ibid.
103 *Fiches du Monde Arabe*, 16 August 1978, No. 1035.
104 Cobban, *Lebanon*, p.161.
105 For contrasting views of Israeli motives, see e.g. Rabinovich, *War for Lebanon*, p.107; Khalidi, *Conflict and Violence in Lebanon*, pp.123-9. The Israeli operation is difficult to reconcile with the requirements of international law. If the motive for the incursion into the Lebanon was essentially punitive, in retaliation for the Palestinian attack on Israeli civilians earlier in March, it must be classified as a forcible reprisal. As noted in Chapter 3, forcible self-help of this kind is contrary to Article 2(4) of the Charter. For a detailed analysis of this question see Chapter 3, note 178. If, however, the rationale of the Israeli intervention was primarily protective, it remains difficult to see how it can be reconciled with the requirements of the law relating to self-defence. As noted previously, there is broad support in state practice, and in the writing of jurists, for the view that if a state aids, or even acquiesces in, raids from its territory which are carried out by armed bands against another state, such measures constitute an 'armed attack' for the purposes of Article 51 of the Charter. See Chapter 3, notes 134-42, and the accompanying text. In such circumstances, a right of self-defence will arise for the injured state. However, it is important to recognize that, adopting a literal construction of the Charter, such an 'armed attack' must have occurred before a right of self-help will arise. At the very least, international law requires that the attack must be imminent. See generally on the question of when measures taken in self-defence

may be initiated, Pogany, *Security Council,* pp.6-7, 96-7. However, the Israeli intervention in the Lebanon, in March 1978, was not taken in response to an actual or imminent terrorist attack. The measures were therefore of doubtful legality. The right of self-defence is also subject to the requirements of necessity and proportionality. See e.g. Pogany, *Security Council,* p.7, and the authorities cited at ibid, notes 36-7; Higgins, *Development,* pp.204-5; Waldock, *Regulation of the Use of Force,* pp.463-4. The scale of the Israeli operation, involving 25 000 troops with extensive air and naval support, may well have exceeded the level of threat posed to Israel by Palestinian guerrillas in southern Lebanon. Moreover, in the absence of an actual or imminent armed attack by Palestinian guerrillas, it is difficult to accept that the Israeli measures were 'necessary'.

106   Cobban *Lebanon,* p.161.
107   Ibid.
108   SC Res. 425, 19 March 1978.
109   Ibid.
110   See e.g. Rikhye, *Peacekeeping,* p.103.
111   Cobban, *Lebanon,* p.162.
112   Khalidi, *Conflict and Violence in Lebanon,* pp.132-3.
113   See para. 2, Resolution adopted by the Six-Party Arab Summit Conference (Riyadh, 1976).
114   Ibid., paras. 4, 5.
115   See Chapter 5, notes 30-9, and the accompanying text. An excessively legalistic analysis of these texts would be inappropriate. It is doubtful whether the Arab leaders who met in Riyadh and Cairo, in 1976, were either aware of, or concerned about, these contradictions.
116   See notes 70-1 above, and the accompanying text.
117   SC Res. 426, 19 March 1978.
118   Schiff and Ya'ari, *Lebanon War,* p.24.
119   For the text of the Council's statement see BBC Monitoring Service, *Summary of World Broadcasts,* ME/5775/A/1-2. The text is reproduced in *IDP* (1978), p.448.
120   League Council Resolution No. 3689, 28 March 1978. See *Fiches du Monde Arabe,* 2 August 1978, No. 1024. The headquarters of the League were not transferred to Tunis until March 1979. See Chapter 1, notes 65-6, and the accompanying text.
121   The expiry dates of the ADF's mandate were 28 October and 28 April of each year. The mandate was renewed on 29 March 1977 (Iraq opposing), 6 September 1977 (Iraq and Libya opposing) and 28 March 1978. See League Council Resolution Nos. 3541, 3626, 3689. See generally *Fiches du Monde Arabe,* 2 August 1978, No. 1024.
122   Para 4, Resolution III, Resolutions adopted at the Arab Summit Conference (Cairo, 1976).
123   *Fiches du Monde Arabe,* 2 August 1978, No. 1024. However, the states participating in the Council session voted unanimously to extend the ADF's mandate. Ibid.
124   Ibid.
125   *Monday Morning* (Beirut), 20–26 February, 1978, pp.20-1. The interview is reproduced in *IDP* (1978), p.428.
126   *Fiches du Monde Arabe,* 2 August 1978, No. 1024.
127   *Keesing's* (1979), p.30005.
128   Ibid.
129   Ibid. Another factor contributing to the Saudi decision to withdraw its contingent from the ADF may have been the realization that the civil conflict

in the Lebanon showed few signs of abating. Publicly, the Saudis explained that the withdrawal was prompted by concern at the security implications of an invasion of North Yemen by the armed forces of South Yemen. See e.g. *Middle East Economic Digest Arab Report,* 14 March 1979, p.2. See also, *The Daily Telegraph,* 2 March 1979, p.36.

130 *The Times,* 11 April 1978, p.7.
131 *Fiches du Monde Arabe,* 9 August 1978, No. 1030.
132 *Fiches du Monde Arabe,* 4 October 1978, No. 1079.
133 Ibid.
134 Ibid.
135 *Keesing's* (1979), p.30007.
136 *Le Monde,* 28 November 1978, p.10.
137 Ibid.
138 Schiff and Ya'ari, *Lebanon War,* p.26.
139 Ibid.
140 *Fiches du Monde Arabe,* 4 October 1978, No. 1079.
141 *Keesing's* (1979), p.30007.
142 Ibid.
143 *Fiches du Monde Arabe,* 4 October 1978, No. 1079.
144 Schiff and Ya'ari, *Lebanon War,* p.27.
145 *Fiches du Monde Arabe,* 25 October 1978, No. 1098.
146 Ibid.
147 Ibid.
148 Ibid.
149 *Fiches du Monde Arabe,* 7 January 1981, No. 1786.
150 Ibid.
151 *Keesing's* (1979), p.30007.
152 *Fiches du Monde Arabe,* 1 November 1978, No. 1103.
153 *Fiches du Monde Arabe,* 25 October 1978, No. 1098.
154 SC Res. 436, 6 October 1978.
155 *Fiches du Monde Arabe,* 25 October 1978, No. 1098.
156 *Fiches du Monde Arabe,* 1 November 1978, No. 1103.
157 *Fiches du Monde Arabe,* 8 November 1978, No. 1107.
158 The text of the statement adopted by the Beiteddine conference is reproduced in *al-Nahar,* 18 October 1978. It is available, in English, in *IDP* (1978),p.561.
159 Ibid.
160 Ibid.
161 Ibid.
162 Ibid.
163 Ibid.
164 Ibid.
165 *Fiches du Monde Arabe,* 8 November 1978, No. 1107.
166 Ibid.
167 For evidence of this tacit understanding, see e.g. Cobban, *Lebanon,* p.166.
168 *Keesing's* (1979), p.30005. The reference number, and other details, concerning this resolution are unavailable.
169 *Fiches du Monde Arabe,* 8 November 1978, No. 1107.
170 *Fiches du Monde Arabe,* 7 January 1981, No. 1786.
171 *Keesing's* (1979), pp.30008-9.
172 *Fiches du Monde Arabe,* 1 April 1981, No. 1862.
173 Ibid.
174 Ibid. See also Randal, *Tragedy of Lebanon,* p.217.
175 League Council Resolution No. 3799, 25 March 1979. See generally *Fiches*

du Monde Arabe, 1 April 1981, No. 1862.
176   *Le Monde,* 29 March 1979, p.6. On the various factors that may have persuaded the Saudis that there was little point in maintaining the ADF see note 129 above, and the accompanying text.
177   *Le Monde,* 29 March 1979, p.6.
178   *Fiches du Monde Arabe,* 1 April 1981, No.1862.
179   League Council Resolution No. 3845, 28 June 1979; League Council Resolution No. 3902, 23 January 1980.
180   League Council Resolution No. 3947, 26 July 1980.
181   *Keesing's* (1983), p.31924.
182   On 18 April, 1979, Major Haddad proclaimed the establishment of an independent 'free Lebanon' in his border enclave. See e.g. *Keesing's* (1980), p.30094.
183   Ibid., p.30093.
184   Ibid., p.30095.
185   Randal, *Tragedy of Lebanon,* pp.195-6.
186   *Keesing's* (1980), p.30096; *The Times,* 16 March 1978, p.8. The Syrian aircraft remained under exclusive Syrian control and were never integrated into the ADF.
187   *Keesing's* (1980), p.30095.
188   Ibid., p.30096.
189   Ibid., p.30098.
190   Randal, *Tragedy of Lebanon,* p.204.
191   *Keesing's* (1981), p.30917.
192   The interview was published in *al-Ba'ath,* 10 March 1980. Excerpts are available, in English, in IDP (1980), p.73.
193   *Fiches du Monde Arabe,* 15 April 1981, No. 1873.
194   Ibid.
195   Ibid.
196   *Keesing's* (1981), p.30918.
197   Ibid.
198   *Fiches du Monde Arabe,* 15 April 1981, No. 1873.
199   Ibid.
200   Rabinovich, *War for Lebanon,* p.113.
201   The text of the broadcast is reproduced in *Keesing's* (1981), p.30918.
202   See note 192 above.
203   Ibid.
204   Rabinovich, *War for Lebanon,* p.113.
205   Randal, *Tragedy of Lebanon,* p.196.
206   *Fiches du Monde Arabe,* 15 April 1981, No. 1873.
207   Ibid.
208   Ibid.
209   *Keesing's* (1981), p.30919.
210   *Fiches du Monde Arabe,* 15 April 1981, No. 1873.
211   C. Brière, *Liban, guerres ouvertes,* (1985), p.180.
212   Radal, *Tragedy of Lebanon,* p.221.
213   *Keesing's* (1981), pp.30920-2.
214   Ibid., p.30922.
215   Ibid.
216   Randal, *Tragedy of Lebanon,* pp.221-2.
217   Ibid., p.221.
218   Ibid., p.222.
219   Cobban, *Lebanon* pp.168-9.

220 L.W. Snider, 'The Lebanese Forces: Their Origins and Role in Lebanon's Politics', *MEJ,* vol. 38 (1984), p.1, at pp.8-9.
221 Randal, *Tragedy of Lebanon,* p.139.
222 *Keesing's* (1981), p.30925.
223 Cobban, *Lebanon,* p.176. On the increasing radicalization of the Shia, the formation of AM AL and the rift with the PLO, see ibid., pp.172-6.
224 *Keesing's* (1981), p.30925.
225 Ibid., p.30926.
226 Ibid.
227 Ibid., p.30924.
228 Ibid., p.30923.
229 Rabinovich, *War for Lebanon,* p.112.
230 Ibid.
231 Randal, *Tragedy of Lebanon,* p.224.
232 Schiff and Ya'ari, *Lebanon War,* p.32.
233 Rabinovich, *War for Lebanon,* pp.115-16.
234 Cobban, *Lebanon,* p.170.
235 Randal, *Tragedy of Lebanon,* p.225.
236 Ibid., p.230.
237 Schiff and Ya'ari, *Lebanon War,* p.33.
238 Ibid., p.34.
239 Ibid.
240 On the 'red line' agreement, see e.g. Randal, *Tragedy of Lebanon,* pp.195-6.
241 On the formation of the committee, see e.g. *Keesing's* (1979), p.30008.
242 *Keesing's* (1983), p.31921.
243 Ibid., p.31922.
244 Ibid.
245 Ibid.
246 Ibid.
247 Randal, *Tragedy of Lebanon,* p.234.
248 Ibid., pp.236-7.
249 Rabinovich, *War for Lebanon,* p.120. The US had previously sent Special Envoy Phillip Habib to the Middle East in an attempt to solve the Lebanese missile crisis. See ibid., p.119.
250 *Keesing's* (1983) p.3123.
251 Ibid.
252 Ibid.
253 Ibid.
254 Ibid.
255 On the redeployment of the Syrian troops see notes 191-205 above, and the accompanying text.
256 *Keesing's* (1983), p.31924.
257 Ibid.
258 There were estimated to be 43 private militias active in the Lebanon by July 1981, *prior* to the formation of the Syrian-controlled Arab cavalry. See e.g. *Keesing's* (1983), p.31922.
259 *Keesing's* (1983), p.31925.
260 Rabinovich, *War for Lebanon,* p.134.
261 Schiff and Ya'ari, *Lebanon War,* pp.102-5. Israel's Ambassador to the United Nations argued that the Israeli intervention was justified by international law: '[f]aced with intolerable provocations, repe atedaggression and harassment, Israel has now been forced to exercise its right of self-defence, to arrest the never-ending cycle of attacks against Israel's northern border, to deter continued

terrorism against Israel's citizens in Israel and abroad, and to instill the basic concept in the minds of the PLO assassins that Jewish life will never again be taken with impunity'. S/PV. 2375th meeting, p.33. However, it is doubtful whether the Israeli measures were consistent with the doctrine of self-defence as understood by international law. In particular, there was no actual or imminent threat to the Galilee from PLO concentrations in southern Lebanon. There had been a ceasefire along the Lebanese border from July 1981 until May 1982, when the PLO briefly resumed its rocket attacks against the Galilee in retaliation for an Israeli air-strike on Beirut. Without evidence of an actual or imminent threat to Israel, the claim of self-defence cannot succeed. As noted previously, a literal construction of Article 51 of the UN Charter suggests that a state resorting to self-defence may do so only in response to an 'armed attack'. See Chapter 3, notes 134-6, and the accompanying text. Arguments founded on a right of anticipatory self-defence, in accordance with alleged rules of customary international law, are complicated by the lack of consensus concerning the permissibility of preventive measures, and by the general recognition that, if such a right exists, it may only be exercised in response to a threat which is 'instant, overwhelming, leaving no choice of means and no moment for deliberation'. See the *Caroline* incident (1841), 29 *British and Foreign State Papers,* pp.1129, 1138. For a detailed analysis of the law relating to anticipatory self-defence see my 'Nuclear Weapons and Self Defence in International Law', in I. Pogany (ed), *Nuclear Weapons and International Law* (1987). There is, moreover, a requirement of necessity. See note 105 above. Thus, a state may only resort to force in self-defence if there are no satisfactory non-forcible means by which it can respond to the attack on its territory. In the absence of even an actual, or imminent, armed attack, it is clear that there can be no 'necessity' of self-defence as understood by international law. In addition, the extent of the Israeli operation was, without doubt, disproportionate to the threat posed by the guerrillas. Thus, even if the Israeli action had been initiated in conformity with the doctrine of self-defence, the scale of the Israeli measures would have rendered them unlawful. It may even be doubted whether the Israeli operation was actually motivated by considerations of self-defence. Ze'ev Schiff and Ehud Ya'ari argue, persuasively, that Defence Minister Sharon's ultimate goals, of which the Israeli Ceabint remained largely ignorant, were the installation of a friendly regime in Beirut, the expulsion of Syrian forces from the Lebanon, and the destruction of the PLO's political and military infrastructure. Such far-reaching aims cannot be reconciled with the concept of self-defence as understood by international law. See Schiff and Ya'ari, *Lebanon War,* esp. Chapters 2 and 3. For a more detailed analysis of the legality of the Israeli intervention, see e.g. Pogany, *Security Council,* pp.155-9; Report of the International Commission to Enquire into Reported Violations of International Law by Israel during its Invasion of the Lebanon, *Israel in Lebanon,* 1983, Chapter 3.

262   Schiff and Ya'ari, *Lebanon War,* p.118.
263   Ibid., p.157.
264   Ibid., pp.158-63.
265   Ibid., pp.166-7.
266   Rabinovich, *War for Lebanon,* p.138.
267   Ibid.
268   Schiff and Ya'ari, *Lebanon War,* pp.41-3.
269   Ibid., pp.185-93.
270   Ibid., pp.203-4.

271 For a somewhat impassioned account, see e.g. M. Jansen, *The Battle of Beirut* (1982), Chapter 3. On the legality of the Israeli measures in terms of international humanitarian law, see e.g. Pogany, *Security Council*, pp.164-8; Report of the International Commission, op. cit., note 261, Chapter 14.

272 See e.g. Rikhye, *Peacekeeping*, pp.74-5.

273 Schiff and Ya'ari, *Lebanon War*, p.228.

274 Cobban, *Lebanon*, pp.186-7.

275 Ibid., p.187. See also Schiff and Ya'ari, *Lebanon War*, pp.246-7.

276 Schiff and Ya'ari, *Lebanon War*, pp.233-6, 246.

277 Ibid., p.234.

278 *Keesing's* (1983), p.32037. For previous extensions of the ADF's mandate since July 1980, see League Council Resolution No. 4011, 20 January 1981; No. 4065, 22 July 1981 (Iraq opposing); No. 4125, 19 January 1982 (Jordan, Sudan and Iraq opposing. Somalia, Saudi Arabia, Kuwait and Oman did not participate in the vote as their delegates had not received any instructions). The resolution of 20 January 1981, while extending the mandate of the Force, had noted that the states previously funding the ADF would cease their financial assistance. According to reports in the press, the states concerned resumed their financial support in May. See Chapter 7.

279 For details see letter from Lebanon's Minister of Foreign Affairs to the Secretary-General of the Arab League, 2 September 1983. The letter is reproduced in UN Doc. S/15953, 2 September 1983.

280 Ibid. In purely legal terms, the decision of the Lebanese President to terminate the mission of the Arab Deterrent Force was conclusive. The Council resolution establishing the Arab League Force, in June 1976, had stated '[t]he task of this Arab security force should be brought to an end if the president . . . of the republic of Lebanon so requests'. Para. 3, League Council Resolution No. 3456, 9 June 1976. Moreover, the Mandate of the Force had expired.

281 *Le Monde*, 11 September 1982, p.3.

282 Ibid.

283 Ibid.

284 The resolutions adopted at the Fez Summit Conference are reproduced in *Le Monde*, 11 September 1982, p.3. They are also available in UN Doc. S/15510, 15 December 1982.

285 Resolution II, para. 3, Resolutions adopted by the Arab Summit Conference (Fez, 1982). See S/15510, 15 December 1982.

286 The Lebanese remained dissatisfied with the resolution because it did not call for the unconditional withdrawal of Syrian troops. See e.g. letter from Lebanon's Minister of Foreign Affairs etc., op.cit., note 279, p.3.

287 See e.g. Schiff and Ya'ari, *Lebanon War*, Chapter 13. On the question of Israel's responsibility, under international law, for the deaths of the Palestinian civilians, see e.g. I. Pogany, 'International Law and the Beirut Massacre', *Bracton Law Journal*, vol. 16 (1983), p.32.

288 SC Res. 521, 19 September 1982.

289 MNF I, constituted in late August 1982, had left the Lebanon by 10 September, following the successful completion of its mission. See e.g. Rikhye, *Peacekeeping*, p.75. The mandate of MNF II was the following: 'to provide an interposition force at agreed locations and thereby provide the multinational presence requested by the Lebanese Government to assist it and the Lebanese Armed Forces . . . in the Beirut area. This presence will facilitate the restoration of Lebanese Government sovereignty and authority over the Beirut area'. For the text of the mandate of the ADF, and for other related documents, see e.g. N. Pelcovits, *Peacekeeping on Arab-Israeli Fronts* (1984), pp.139-68.

290 These explanations, which are partially conflicting are based on interviews conducted with senior Lebanèse, UK, US and UN officials.

291 The Pact of the Arab League, drafted in 1945, contains an 'Annex Regarding Palestine'. This notes, *inter alia,* that Palestine's 'international existence and independence in the legal sense cannot . . . be questioned any more than could the independence of the other Arab countries'. The cause of Palestinian self-determination has remained one of the principal concerns of the Arab League. See, generally, Hassouna, *Arab League,* Chapter XI.

292 At the Arab Summit Conference in Fez, in early September 1982, President Assad offered to withdraw Syrian troops from the Lebanon in the context of an Israeli withdrawal. The resolution adopted by the Summit Conference noted, with deliberate ambiguity, that 'the Lebanese and Syrian Governments will start negotiations on measures to be taken in the light of the Israeli withdrawal from Lebanon'. *Keesing's* (1983), p.32037. As no Israeli withdrawal had materialized, President Assad had not been confronted with the necessity of removing his own troops.

293 The Israeli government had asserted, repeatedly, that it would not withdraw its troops from the Lebanon while Syrian and Palestinian forces remained in place. *Keesing's* (1983), p. 32037.

294 Cobban, *Lebanon,* p.190.

295 For the text of the Israel – Lebanon Agreement on Withdrawal of Troops, see e.g. Pelcovits, op. cit., note 289, p.142; *ILM,* vol. XXII (1983), p.708. The text of the Agreement, together with numerous related documents and a detailed chronology, are available in Lebanese Centre for Documentation and Research, *Lebanese – Israeli Negotiations* (1984). The treaty was signed by Israeli and Lebanese delegates on 17 May 1983. However, it was subsequently repudiated by President Gemayel.

296 *Le Monde,* 2 April 1983, p.3.

297 Ibid.

298 Ibid.

299 See letter from the Minister for Foreign Affairs of Lebanon etc., op. cit., note 279, p.3.

300 See e.g. Rabinovich, *War for Lebanon,* pp.183-99.

301 Ibid., pp.178-80.

9 Conclusion

The Arab League Force in the Lebanon: a political assessment

The achievements of the Arab League Force in the Lebanon clearly fell short of its declared objectives. The mandate of the Force, between June and October 1976, was to 'maintain security and stability in Lebanon'.[1] In the absence of a general climate of national reconciliation, and in the face of a resumption of armed clashes, the 2500 strong Symbolic Arab Security Force was incapable of fulfilling its mandate.[2]

Following the transformation of the Symbolic Arab Security Force into the Arab Deterrent Force the functions of the Force were greatly expanded. These included a duty to ensure 'observance of the ceasefire and termination of hostilities' and detailed responsibilities for the collection of heavy weapons, the implementation of the Cairo Agreement and its Annexes, and for re-opening the major roads.[3]

In the first months of its existence, the Arab Deterrent Force made a genuine contribution to the restoration of peace and security in the Lebanon. As noted in Chapter 8, the ADF collected a quantity of heavy weapons from the militias, re-opened the principal roads, established its presence in the cities, and supervised the withdrawal of PLA units from the Lebanon.[4] Armed militiamen disappeared from public view, Beirut airport was restored to use, and commercial activity was gradually resumed.

There are various reasons why these encouraging developments were first arrested, then reversed. Israeli obduracy, in refusing to allow units of the ADF to enter southern Lebanon, was undoubtedly a factor. So also was Israel's policy of creating and supporting local Christian militias in the south. In the absence of Syrian troops, who alone could have established firm control over the border area, southern Lebanon became a focal point of Palestinian activity once again. Clashes between PLO guerrillas and rightist militias, Palestinian raids into Israel and massive Israeli reprisals, became almost commonplace.[5]

The chronic turmoil in southern Lebanon undermined efforts to restore peace and security elsewhere in the country and aggravated the persistent tensions between the Palestinians, their Muslim-Leftist allies, and the Maronite community. The Chtaura Agreement of July 1977, which envisaged the withdrawal of Palestinian guerrillas from the south, was intended to resolve these differences. However, the Palestinians failed to implement the crucial third stage of the Agreement, concerning their withdrawal from the border regions, because of a resumption of Christian–Palestinian fighting in southern Lebanon instigated, it was alleged, by Israel.[6]

Israel's expanding links with a number of prominent Maronite leaders, especially Bashir Gemayel and Camille Chamoun, also had a destabilizing effect on the Lebanon. In particular, Syria became increasingly suspicious of Maronite politicians enjoying regular contacts with Israeli officials. In addition, the 'Israeli connection' encouraged Bashir Gemayel and Camille Chamoun to believe that the Maronites could achieve supremacy in the Lebanon.[7] In the absence of an Israeli 'option', which was largely fostered and cultivated by the Maronites themselves,[8] it is at least conceivable that the Christian leaders would have pursued more conciliatory policies towards Syria, towards the Palestinians, and towards Lebanon's Sunni, Shia and Druze communities.

However, it is difficult to accept the thesis that Israel was exclusively, or even primarily, responsible for the collapse of efforts to achieve national reconciliation, and thus for the inevitable failure of the Arab League Force. While Israel undoubtedly exacerbated Lebanon's internal difficulties, it is all too probable that, even in her absence, the outcome would have been much the same.

The establishment of the Arab Deterrent Force, in October 1976, failed to resolve the grievances that had led to Lebanon's civil war. The Riyadh and Cairo Summit Conferences undoubtedly hoped to restore Lebanon's national unity, sovereignty and independence. However, they were conferences of Arab Kings and Heads of State. Lebanon's confessional leaders, whose agreement was essential for ending the civil war, were not involved.

The resolutions adopted by the Riyadh and Cairo summit conferences dealt, very largely, with the symptoms rather than the causes of the civil war. Thus, the texts were concerned with collecting heavy weapons from the militias, re-opening major roads, and 'deterring' violations of the ceasefire. Only in their emphasis on the implementation of the Cairo Agreement and its Annexes did they address themselves to one of the causes of the civil war. However, as noted previously, the Cairo Agreement and its Annexes gave rise to numerous difficulties of interpretation, particularly concerning the permissibility of launching guerrilla operations from southern Lebanon into Israel.[9] The Riyadh and Cairo texts did not clarify these ambiguities. Indeed, it is doubtful whether the Arab leaders participating in the Summits were even aware of the contradictions.

Ultimately, the Lebanese civil war had its roots in the growing resentment of the Muslim community at their exclusion from an equitable share of political and economic power. The Palestinian issue inflamed these tensions, accentuating the cleavage between Maronites and Muslims. For the largely western-oriented Maronite population, the Palestinian presence was a threat to Lebanese sovereignty and a source of unnecessary friction with Israel. For Lebanese Muslims, whose cultural and political identity was essentially Arab, support for the Palestinians in their struggle against Israel was an individual and a national responsibility.

With the proliferation of militias, the wide availability of arms of every calibre, and the gradual habituation of many Lebanese to the endless cycle of violence, the civil war acquired a momentum of its own. The Riyadh and Cairo Summit Conferences, and the establishment of the ADF, achieved a temporary respite. However, they were incapable of effecting a permanent end to the conflict without tackling the political, cultural and economic roots of the civil war.

The inherent limits of peacekeeping must also be recognized and understood. Peacekeeping forces can contribute to the maintenance or restoration of peace. They cannot *impose* peace on unwilling states or on entire peoples.[10] Even the 'deterrent' powers exercised by the ADF failed to enforce peace. On the contrary, the repeated lapse into excessive and sometimes indiscriminate violence by Syrian troops in the Lebanon fuelled the resentment of large sections of the Maronite community.

Peacekeeping forces function best where there is a clear line of demarcation separating the belligerents, and where both parties share a genuine desire for peace.[11] Peacekeeping forces are at a grave disadvantage, inevitably, in civil war situations where opposing sides are hopelessly intermingled, and where there is a lack of discipline and effective central authority.[12]

The failure of the ADF was due, ultimately, to the lack of a credible alternative to the largely discredited National Pact, negotiated before Lebanon's independence.[13] Without genuine agreement amongst Lebanon's confessional leaders concerning the distribution of political and economic power, the efforts of the Arab League Force were of marginal importance.

However, there were also serious deficiencies in the Arab League Force which contributed to the failure of its mission. In particular, the inclusion of a massive Syrian contingent, accounting for more than 80 per cent of all Arab Deterrent Force troops, was bound to cause difficulties. In view of Syria's strategic and historical interests in the Lebanon, the *exclusion* of Syrian troops was inconceivable.[14] However, the very depth of Syrian interests made it likely that Syrian troops would deviate from the standards of restraint and neutrality normally associated with peacekeeping forces.

The Syrian contingent frequently ignored the Lebanese Commander of the ADF, and President Sarkis, to whom they were technically accountable. They received their instructions from the Commander of Syrian forces in the Lebanon and from the government in Damascus.

As chronicled in Chapter 8, Syrian troops repeatedly reacted to breaches of the ceasefire with disproportionate, and even indiscriminate, violence. The shelling of residential areas in East Beirut alienated the Maronite community, and contributed to the decision of the Saudi, Sudanese and UAE authorities to withdraw their contingents.

The Arab League Force in the Lebanon: a legal assessment

As noted in Chapter 6 the concept of 'peacekeeping', as understood by international law, permits the use of force in self-defence or, within limits, for the maintenance of law and order. These conclusions are warranted by the UN's peacekeeping practice, particularly in the Congo (ONUC), and by the Advisory Opinion of the International Court of Justice in the *Certain Expenses Case*.[15]

Thus, the Arab League Force in the Lebanon was, at least in conception, a genuine peacekeeping operation. This conclusion remains valid even after the operation was transformed into the Arab Deterrent Force, by the Riyadh and Cairo Summit Conferences, with authority to use 'deterrent force whenever security so requires'.[16] Crucially, the Arab League Force never amounted to 'enforcement action' within the meaning of Article 53(1) of the Charter, which would have required Security Council 'authorization'.[17] The creation of the Arab League Force may thus be regarded as consistent with Chapter VIII of the Charter, which is concerned with 'regional arrangements' and, in particular, with Article 52(1). This recognizes the authority of regional organizations to deal 'with such matters relating to the maintenance of international peace and security as are appropriate for regional action'.

The establishment of the Force was also consistent with the Pact of the League of Arab States. Neither the Pact, nor the Treaty of Joint Defence, *expressly* authorizes peacekeeping operations. Nevertheless, as discussed in Chapter 6, the power to establish peacekeeping forces may be inferred from certain provisions of the Pact and of the Treaty of Joint Defence.[18]

An international peacekeeping force, in common with other third parties, must refrain from unlawful intervention in civil conflicts.[19] However, it is doubtful whether, in conception, the Arab League Force constituted 'intervention' in any meaningful sense.[20] The functions of the Arab League Force in the Lebanon were strictly neutral in character. The Force was not authorized to lend assistance to either the government, or to the insurgents, in waging an armed conflict.

In addition, the internationalization of the Lebanese situation calls into question its designation as a 'civil war'. As noted in Chapters 4 and 8, the conflict was not confined to Lebanese militias. Thousands of Palestinian guerrillas and substantial numbers of regular Syrian troops took an active part in the fighting. Thus, it is by no means clear that the normal rules relating to intervention in civil wars are applicable to the Lebanese conflict.

Nevertheless, while the Arab League Force may have been lawful in conception, its actual behaviour requires further comment. As noted above, Syrian units regularly flouted the instructions of the Lebanese Commander of the ADF and the wishes of the Lebanese President, to whom they were nominally accountable.[21] In addition, Syrian troops frequently resorted to excessive, and sometimes indiscriminate, violence.[22] Thus, the level of coercion used by Syrian troops was often disproportionate to actual violations of the ceasefire, and was sometimes directed at civilians and non-combatants who were not the source of the disturbances.

From the perspective of international law the *actual* conduct of ADF troops, as distinct from their theoretical powers and functions, is of considerable significance. The principle of proportionality is of fundamental importance in many areas of international law. It has been a vital criterion, for example, in measuring the legitimacy of forcible measures taken in self-defence or by way of reprisal.[23] In the opinion of the present writer, the repeated use of disproportionate force by Syrian units of the ADF, albeit in order to maintain the ceasefire and to prevent the resumption of fighting by the militias, cannot be reconciled with the concept of peacekeeping as understood by international law.

Thus, the *actual* behaviour of ADF troops cannot be characterized as 'regional action' within the meaning of Article 52(1) of the Charter, or as legitimate peacekeeping in accordance with the Pact of the League of Arab States.

In addition, as noted above, Syrian troops in the Lebanon frequently ignored the pan-Arab framework, within which they were supposed to operate, acting instead in accordance with instructions from the Damascus government. Such behaviour was comprehensible. As emphasized in previous chapters, Syria had genuine strategic, political and historical interests in the Lebanon which it could not ignore. Moreover, the anarchy and hopeless political divisions in the Lebanon must have acutely exasperated President Assad. Nevertheless, the quasi-autonomous behaviour of the Syrian troops calls into question their designation as simply a contingent of the ADF. In so far as the Syrian troops did not *actually* conduct themselves as part of the Arab League Force it is at least questionable whether they should benefit from any legitimacy which the Force possessed under international law. In such circumstances, the propriety of the Syrian presence, and of its actions, should perhaps be assessed independently of the legality of the Arab League Force.

Notes

1　League Council Resolution No. 3456, 9 June 1976.
2　See, Chapter 8, notes 17-22, and the accompanying text.
3　Para. 2, Resolution Adopted by the Six-Party Summit Conference (Riyadh, 1976).
4　See, Chapter 8, notes 53-63, and the accompanying text.
5　See, generally Chapter 8.
6　Ibid, notes 70-5, and the accompanying text.
7　See, generally Schiff and Ya'ari, *Lebanon War*, Chapters 1, 2.
8　Ibid.
9　See Chapter 8, notes 114-15, and the accompanying text.
10　See e.g. B. Urquhart, 'Peacekeeping: a View from the Operational Center', in H. Wiseman (ed.), *Peacekeeping: Appraisals and Proposals* (1983), p.163, at p.164. Urquhart, who until recently was UN Under-Secretary-General for Special Political Affairs, observes that: '[p]eacekeeping can only function under certain conditions. If these are not present, it will either function ineffectively or will cease to function at all. The most important of these conditions is acceptance . . . by the countries or parties principally concerned in the conflict'. Ibid. However, a reasonable and proportionate use of force, in order to promote 'law and order' is not inconsistent with the concept of peacekeeping. See above, Chapter 5, notes 6-26.
11　Some of the most successful recent peacekeeping operations have benefited from such conditions. These include UNEF II, which was deployed in the Sinai from October 1973 until July 1979, separating Egyptian and Israeli forces. They include, in addition, the United Nations Disengagement Observer Force

(UNDOF), which was established in 1974 to serve as a buffer between Syrian and Israeli troops in the Golan. See generally Rikhye, *Peacekeeping*, pp.49-69. See also A. Verrier, *International Peacekeeping* (1981), Chapter 6.

12 This may explain, in part, the serious difficulties encountered by the UN Operation in the Congo (ONUC) and by the Multinational Force which was introduced in the Lebanon in September 1982. On ONUC see e.g. Abi-Saab, *Congo*. On the MNF see e.g. Rikhye, *Peacekeeping*, pp.75-9.

13 On the National Pact see Chapter 3, notes 72-5, and the accompanying text.

14 In June 1976, the League Council had envisaged the withdrawal of the bulk of Syrian forces from the Lebanon. Thus, the Council resolution of 9 June had referred to the 'replacement' of Syrian troops. See League Council Resolution No. 3456, 9 June 1976. However, by October 1976, Syria had deployed over 20 000 regular troops in the Lebanon and had secured a decisive military advantage over the Palestinian-Leftist forces. Against this background, and in the light of Syria's traditional interests in the Lebanon, the debate at the Cairo summit was confined to the size of the Syrian contingent, not to whether it should be included at all. On the discussions at the Cairo Summit see Chapter 8, notes 38-47, and the accompanying text.

15 See, generally Chapter 6, notes 1-26, and the accompanying text.

16 See statement issued by Colonel al-Hajj, Commander of the ADF, on 9 November 1976, in *IDP* (1976), p.506. On the transformation of the Symbolic Arab Security Force into the Arab Deterrent Force see Chapter 8, notes 23-50, and the accompanying text.

17 Article 53(1) states: 'The Security Council shall, where appropriate, utilize such regional arrangements or agencies for enforcement action under its authority. But no enforcement action shall be taken under regional arrangements or by regional agencies without the authorization of the Security Council'. The reasoning of the International Court, in the *Certain Expenses Case*, suggests that a measure may constitute 'enforcement action' *either* because it is mandatory *or* because it is coercive. See Chapter 6, note 53, and the accompanying text. The Arab League Force in the Lebanon did not impose binding obligations on any state. Participation in the Force, and contributions to its upkeep, were purely voluntary. The deployment of the Force on Lebanese territory was in accordance with the wishes of the Lebanese President. Moreover, the Arab League Force did not amount to a sanction against the Lebanon. Thus, it was not 'coercive' as understood by the International Court in the *Certain Expenses Case*. For an analysis of the concept of 'enforcement action' see Chapter 6, notes 51-7, and the accompanying text.

18 See Chapter 6, notes 39-45, and the accompanying text.

19 There is, however, a lack of consensus amongst jurists concerning the character of impermissible intervention. See supra, Chapter 6, notes 28-30, and the accompanying text.

20 Ibid., notes 31-4, and the accompanying text.

21 See, generally Chapter 8.

22 Ibid.

23 In 1841, following the *Caroline* incident, US Secretary of State Webster expounded the requirements of self-defence as understood by international law. Having noted that a state may only resort to self-defence where it can demonstrate a necessity 'instant, overwhelming, leaving no choice of means and no moment for deliberation', he emphasized that 'the act, justified by the necessity of self-defence, must be limited by that necessity, and kept clearly within it'. (1841) 29 *British and Foreign State Papers*, pp.1129, 1138. The overwhelming majority of jurists continue to recognize that proportionality is

an essential requirement of lawful self-defence. See e.g. Brownlie, *Use of Force*, pp.261-4; Bowett, *Self-Defence*, pp.11, 25, 269; McDougal and Feliciano, *World Public Order*, pp.217-18, 241-4. Forcible reprisals are generally considered to be unlawful, following the conclusion of the UN Charter. See, generally Chapter 3, note 178. However, in the pre-Charter period, reasonable proportionality was regarded as a condition of a forcible reprisal. Thus, in the celebrated *Naulilaa* Case, the Mixed Arbitral Tribunal held: '[e]ven if one admitted that international law does not require that a reprisal should be approximately in proportion to the offense, one should certainly consider as excessive and illegal, a reprisal out of all proportion to the act justifying it.' See *United Nations Reports of International Arbitral Awards*, vol. 2 (1928), p.1012.

Postscript

The International Court of Justice delivered its Judgment on the merits in the *Military and Paramilitary Activities in and against Nicaragua Case* on 27 June 1986, some weeks after this book was completed. Accordingly, the arguments advanced in the book concerning, *inter alia,* the scope of individual and collective self-defence, the prohibition of the use of force etc. were formulated before the Judgment was available. In view of the extraordinary importance of the *Nicaragua Case* a brief comment is warranted.[1] However, this analysis is confined to those aspects of the case that are relevant to the legal issues that have featured prominently in the book.

The background

The *Military and Paramilitary Activities in and against Nicaragua Case* was brought by Nicaragua in April 1984. Nicaragua alleged, *inter alia,* that the United States had carried out 'armed attacks against Nicaragua by air, land and sea' and that the United States was responsible for 'recruiting, training, arming, equipping, financing ... and directing military and paramilitary actions in and against Nicaragua'.[2]

In view of the terms of the US acceptance of the Court's compulsory jurisdiction, the International Court ruled that it was unable to examine the dispute under either the United Nations Charter or the Charter of the Organization of American States.[3] Accordingly, the findings of the Court are confined to the relevant rules of customary international law, and to the 1956 US–Nicaragua Treaty of Friendship, Commerce and Navigation. However, the Court emphasized that '[t]he differences which may exist between the specific content' of the UN and OAS Charters and customary international law 'are not, in the Court's view, such as to cause a judgment confined to the field of customary international law to be ineffective or inappropriate, or a judgment not susceptible of compliance or execution'.[4] Thus, the Judgment should not be dismissed as of limited interest. While the relevant rules of customary and conventional law are not identical throughout, they coincide on the prohibition of the use of force, on the principle of non-intervention, and on the meaning of an 'armed attack' for the purposes of self-defence.[5]

Self-defence

The United States characterized its support for the *contras* in Nicaragua as collective self-defence on behalf of El Salvador, Honduras and Costa Rica.[6] Accordingly, the Court examined various aspects of the law relating to self-defence, including the requirements of necessity and proportionality, the nature of an 'armed attack' and the doctrine of collective self-defence.

The permissibility of preventive measures

The Court noted that '[i]n view of the circumstances in which the dispute has arisen, reliance is placed by the parties only on the right of self-defence in the case of an armed attack which has already occurred, and the issue of the lawfulness of a response to the imminent threat of armed attack has not been raised. Accordingly the Court expresses no view on that issue'.[7] Nevertheless, the Court went on to observe '[i]n the case of individual self defence, the exercise of this right is subject to the State concerned having been the victim of an armed attack'.[8]

It is unclear whether the latter statement represents a deliberate attempt by the Court to confine the right of self-defence to circumstances in which there has been an antecedent 'armed attack'. If so, it is difficult to reconcile with the Court's earlier disavowal of any intention to express a view on the permissibility of preventive measures.

In his Dissenting Opinion, Judge Schwebel drew attention to the ambivalence of the Judgment on this matter, declaring that it 'may be open to the interpretation of inferring that a State may react in self-defence, that supportive States may react in collective self-defence, only if an armed attack occurs'.[9] Judge Schwebel declared that if his interpretation of the Judgment were correct 'such an inference is *obiter dictum*. The question of whether a State may react in self-defence to actions other than armed attack was not in issue in this case'.[10] Judge Schwebel went on to quote, approvingly, from Sir Humphrey Waldock's celebrated commentary on self-defence and to affirm:[11]

> for my part, I do not agree with a construction of the United Nations Charter which would read Article 51 as if it were worded: 'Nothing in the Present Charter shall impair the inherent right of individual or collective self-defence if, and only if, an armed attack occurs . . .' I do not agree that the terms or intent of Article 51 eliminate the right of self-defence under customary international law, or confine its entire scope to the express terms of Article 51.

While neither this passage, nor Judge Schwebel's quotation from Sir Humphrey Waldock, expressly affirms a right of anticipatory self-defence, they constitute an implicit rejection of the view that preventive measures are impermissible under international law.

In view of the uncertainty as to whether the Judgment even purported to proscribe resort to anticipatory self-defence, and the failure of the Court to cite any authority for such a proposition, it is by no means clear that anticipatory self-defence should be viewed as unlawful. This conclusion is strengthened by Judge Schwebel's Dissenting Opinion. Thus, the present writer does not feel it necessary to revise or amend his comments on anticipatory self-defence as stated in Chapter Eight.[12]

The requirements of necessity and proportionality

The Court noted the agreement of the Parties that a lawful response to an armed attack 'depends on observance of the criteria of the necessity and the proportionality of the measures taken in self-defence'.[13] The Court went on to find that US measures against Nicaragua were neither necessary nor proportionate.[14]

These criteria have long been recognized under customary international law. Their reaffirmation by the World Court constitutes additional support for the arguments advanced in this book. Thus, as emphasized in Chapter 8, the Israeli incursions into the Lebanon in March 1978 and June 1982 can be criticized, *inter alia*, for having been both unnecessary and disproportionate.[15]

The existence of an armed attack

Both the UN Charter and general international law recognize that a state may resort to force in self-defence in the event of an 'armed attack', provided that the criteria of necessity and proportionality are satisfied. In view of US claims to have responded in collective self-defence to an armed attack on El Salvador, Honduras and Costa Rica, the International Court considered the requirements of an 'armed attack' in some detail:[16]

> the prohibition of armed attacks may apply to the sending by a State of armed bands to the territory of another State, if such an operation, because of its scale and effects, would have been classified as an armed attack rather than as a mere frontier incident had it been carried out by regular armed forces. But the Court does not believe that the concept of 'armed attack' includes not only acts of armed bands where such acts occur on a significant scale but also assistance to rebels in the form of the provision of weapons or logistical or other support. Such assistance may be regarded as a threat or use of force, or amount to intervention in the internal or external affairs of other States.

The finding of the Court that an 'armed attack' may encompass 'the sending by a State of armed bands to the territory of another State etc.' was based on Article 3(g) of the General Assembly's Definition of Aggression,[17] which the Court recognized as 'reflect[ing] customary international law'.[18] The Court held that the facts disclosed did not suggest that Nicaragua was responsible for an 'armed attack' against El Salvador, Honduras or Costa Rica.[19] Accordingly, the United States had not been justified in invoking a right of collective self-defence on behalf of the three states in question.

A number of the incidents discussed in this book require further comment in the light of the World Court's construction of an 'armed attack'. As noted in Chapter 3, the Lebanese government alleged, in the spring of 1958, that the United Arab Republic was infiltrating substantial numbers of guerrillas into the Lebanon. While there has been some dispute as to whether the Lebanese allegations were well-founded, there can be little doubt that such facts would, if accurate, amount to an 'armed attack' as understood by the International Court. Crucially, the Lebanese government alleged that the UAR was actively responsible for the infiltration of armed bands into the Lebanon, and not merely for supplying the insurgents with material or other support. In these circumstances, there can be little doubt that the alleged measures amounted to the 'sending by a State of armed bands into the territory of another State' where they engaged in operations whose 'scale and effects' could have been characterized 'as an armed attack . . . had it been carried out by regular armed forces'.[20] It is more doubtful whether Lebanese support, since 1967, for Palestinian guerrillas mounting operations against Israel would constitute an 'armed attack' as understood by the International Court. It is unclear whether Lebanese aid could be characterized as the 'sending by a State of armed bands into the territory of another State' or even 'its substantial involvement therein'.

However, the present writer has difficulty in accepting the restrictive interpretation of an 'armed attack' advanced by the International Court. As noted in Chapter 3, there is substantial support in state practice, and in the writing of jurists, for the view that an 'armed attack' should be interpreted broadly so as to encompass 'support for, or even acquiescence towards, armed bands which infiltrate across the borders of a state and engage in subversion'.[21] Thus, the present writer cannot accept the distinction introduced by the Court between 'assistance to rebels in the form of the provision of weapons or logistical or other support', which is deemed to constitute intervention or an unlawful use of force, and the 'sending by a State of armed bands into the territory of another State etc.',[22] which is acknowledged to constitute an 'armed attack'.

In his Dissenting Opinion, Judge Schwebel also rejected the Court's restrictive interpretation of an 'armed attack'. Judge Schwebel declared '[i]n my view, the Judgment of the Court on the critical question of whether aid to irregulars may be tantamount to an armed attack departs from accepted – and desirable – law'.[23] Judge Schwebel continued:[24]

> The Court's conclusion is inconsonant with generally accepted doctrine, law and practice . . . the Court's conclusion is inconsistent with the views of Professor Brownlie . . . that a general campaign by irregulars with the complicity of the government of the State from which they operate may constitute an 'armed attack' . . . It is inconsistent with the position which the United States has maintained since 1947 that one State's support of guerrillas operating against another is tantamount to an armed attack against the latter's territorial integrity and political independence. It is inconsistent with what Nicaragua rightly observes is a consistent practice of the United Nations holding that 'substantial involvement' in the activities of armed insurgent groups is a violation of 'the prohibition on the use of force in Article 2(4).' It is inconsistent with repeated declarations of the United Nations expressive of the international legal duty of States to refrain from

fomenting civil strife – a form of aggression which the General Assembly has denominated as among 'the gravest of all crimes against peace and security . . .' It is inconsistent with the terms of the 'Friendly Relations' Declaration, which the Court treats as an authoritative expression of customary international law – a declaration which, in its interpretation of Article 2, paragraph 4 of the Charter, holds that, 'Every State has the duty to refrain from organizing, instigating, assisting or participating in acts of civil strife or terrorist acts in another State . . . when the acts . . . involve a threat or use of force' . . . And the Court's conclusion is inconsistent with the terms and intent of the United Nations Definition of Aggression . . .

Judge Schwebel argued, further, that the weight of UN practice indicated that 'substantial involvement' in the sending of armed bands into the territory of another state constituted an 'armed attack'.[25]

The present writer remains of the opinion that an 'armed attack' should be interpreted broadly to encompass, at the very least, 'a co-ordinated and general campaign by powerful bands of irregulars, with obvious or easily proven complicity of the government of a State from which they operate'.[26] To conclude otherwise, would be to deprive states which are the target of guerrilla campaigns, funded, trained and supported by foreign powers, of the right to resort to force in self-defence or to seek military assistance from third parties in accordance with the doctrine of collective self-defence.[27]

Collective self-defence

As noted in Chapter 3, the concept of collective self-defence has given rise to considerable difficulties of interpretation.[28] In reviewing US claims to have acted in collective self-defence of El Salvador, Honduras and Costa Rica, the International Court held:[29]

It is . . . clear that it is the State which is the victim of an armed attack which must form and declare the view that it has been so attacked. There is no rule in customary international law permitting another State to exercise the right of collective self-defence on the basis of its own assessment of the situation. Where collective self-defence is invoked, it is to be expected that the State for whose benefit this right is used will have declared itself to be the victim of an armed attack.

In addition, the Court found that 'in customary international law, whether of a general kind or that particular to the inter-American legal system, there is no rule permitting the exercise of collective self-defence in the absence of a request by the State which regards itself as the victim of an armed attack'.[30] Thus, the International Court held that there are two requirements of collective self-defence. These are the determination by a state that it is the victim of an armed attack, and a request for assistance from the victim to a third party.

The Court did not state that these are the *only* prerequisites of collective self-defence. However, that would be a reasonable inference. Accordingly, the Judgment supports the 'broad' view of collective self-defence favoured by Brownlie, Kelsen, Stone and others,[31] and confirms the argument advanced in this book that the US intervention on behalf of the Lebanon, in July 1958, was consistent with the doctrine of collective self-defence as understood by international law.[32]

The prohibition of the use of force and of intervention

As noted previously, the Court adopted a restrictive interpretation of the term 'armed attack', thus limiting the circumstances in which a state may resort to force in self-defence, or receive military support from other states in collective self-defence.[33] The Court held that 'assistance to rebels in the form of the provision of weapons or logistical or other support' does not amount to an 'armed attack', although it may be regarded 'as a threat or use of force, or amount to intervention in the internal or external affairs of other states'.[34]

Accordingly, the Court found that 'the support given by the United States, up to the end of September 1984, to the military and paramilitary activities of the *contras* in Nicaragua, by financial support, training, supply of weapons, intelligence and logistic support, constituted a clear breach of the principle of non-intervention.[35] Similarly, the Court held that the alleged activities of Nicaragua, such as the supply of arms to rebels in El Salvador, could not amount to an 'armed attack', although 'such activities may well constitute a breach of the principle of the non-use of force and an intervention in the internal affairs of a State, that is, a form of conduct which is certainly wrongful, but is of lesser gravity than an armed attack'.[36]

However, the Court emphasized that the alleged intervention by Nicaragua in the internal affairs of neighbouring states could not justify US counter-measures against Nicaragua involving the use of armed force:[37]

> While an armed attack would give rise to an entitlement to collective self-defence, use of force of a lesser degree of gravity cannot

... produce any entitlement to take collective counter-measures involving the use of force. The acts of which Nicaragua is accused, even assuming them to have been established and imputable to that State, could only have justified proportionate counter-measures on the part of the State which has been the victim of these acts ... They could not justify counter-measures taken by a third State, the United States, and particularly could not justify intervention involving the use of force.

The reasoning of the Court has a bearing on a number of the arguments advanced in this book. In particular, it suggests that Lebanese support for, or acquiescence towards, Palestinian guerrilla operations against Israel did not amount to an 'armed attack' but constituted, at most, a use of force against Israel and an intervention in its internal affairs.[38] Accordingly, Israel's incursions into the Lebanon, in 1978 and 1982, could not be viewed as legitimate self-defence.[39]

However, as noted above, the present writer cannot accept the Court's severely restrictive interpretation of an 'armed attack'. Moreover, the Court's distinction between an 'armed attack' and a 'use of force of a lesser degree of gravity' is unhelpful. While the former gives rise to a right of self-defence the latter, apparently, can only justify 'proportionate counter-measures' on the part of the victim.[40] However, it is unclear from the Judgment what 'proportionate counter-measures' may actually involve, and how such measures should be distinguished from action permitted in legitimate self-defence. Nor does the Court explain why an 'armed attack' entitles the target state to receive aid in collective self-defence, while 'a use of force of a lesser degree of gravity' does not permit the victim to benefit from collective counter-measures involving the use of force. As Judge Schwebel emphasized, in his Dissenting Opinion, 'the Court appears to offer ... a prescription for overthrow of weaker governments by predatory governments, while denying potential victims what in some cases may be their only hope of survival'.[41]

Intervention in civil wars

In examining possible legal bases for the US intervention in Nicaragua, the International Court observed:[42]

it is difficult to see what would remain of the principle of non-intervention in international law if intervention, which is already allowable at the request of the government of a State, were also to be allowed at the request of the opposition.

This would permit any state to intervene at any moment in the internal affairs of another State, whether at the request of the government or at the request of its opposition. Such a situation does not in the Court's view correspond to the present state of international law.

It is clear from this passage that the Court was addressing itself to the doctrine of non-intervention in its widest sense, and not simply to the question of intervention in civil wars. In rejecting the right of third parties to intervene in the internal affairs of states at the request of 'the opposition', the Court was reaffirming a well-established legal rule.[43] However, the Court's finding that intervention 'is already allowable at the request of the government of a State' is more controversial, at least with reference to intervention in civil wars. There has been some support amongst jurists for the view that intervention in civil conflicts is no longer permissible *even at the request of the government.*[44] Nevertheless, the Court's finding, although *obiter,* is consistent with the view set forth in this book – that the introduction of US troops in the Lebanon in 1958, at the request of the Lebanese government, did not amount to unlawful intervention as generally understood.[45]

Humanitarian intervention

As noted in Chapter 2, the concept of 'humanitarian intervention' is viewed by its protagonists as an exception to the general prohibition of intervention in permitting a state to intervene forcibly on the territory of another state to protect the local population from gross and persistent human rights violations.[46] In *Nicaragua* vs. *USA,* the International Court was not concerned with 'humanitarian intervention' *per se.* Nevertheless, the Court drew attention to the fact that American aid to the *contras* was motivated, in part, by the belief that the Nicaraguan government would be forced to secure 'political pluralism, human rights, free elections, non-alignment and a mixed economy'.[47] However, the Court was emphatic in its rejection of the validity of intervention for such purposes. While declining to evaluate the extent to which civil liberties were endangered in Nicaragua, the Court emphasized:[48]

the use of force could not be the appropriate method to monitor or ensure such respect . . . the protection of human rights, a strictly humanitarian objective, cannot be compatible with the mining of ports, the destruction of oil installations, or again with the training, arming and equipping of the *contras.* The Court concludes that the argument derived from the preservation of human rights in Nicaragua cannot afford a legal justification for the conduct of the United States. . .

As noted above, the doctrine of humanitarian intervention was never in issue as such. Nevertheless, the reasoning of the Court suggests an outlook that would be unsympathetic to the concept. This conclusion is strengthened by the observation of the Court that 'where human rights are protected by international conventions, that protection takes the form of such arrangements for monitoring or ensuring respect for human rights as are provided for in the conventions themselves'.[49] Such 'arrangements' scarcely encompass resort to humanitarian intervention.

Notes

1   It should perhaps be emphasized that this is the first case since the *Corfu Channel* decision of 1949 in which the World Court has considered the law governing the use of force by states in any detail.
2   *ICJ Rep* 1986, p.14, para.15.
3   On the effects of the US multilateral treaties reservation, see ibid., paras 42-56.
4   Ibid., para. 181.
5   See generally ibid., paras. 175-81.
6   Ibid., para. 229.
7   Ibid., para.194.
8   Ibid., para.195.
9   Ibid., para.172.
10   Ibid.
11   Ibid., para. 173. For Sir Humphrey Waldock's commentary, see Waldock, *Regulation of the Use of Force*, pp.495-9.
12   See, in particular, Chapter 8, notes 105 and 261. For a more detailed analysis of the permissibility of anticipatory self-defence, see I. Pogany, 'Nuclear Weapons and Self-Defence in International Law', in I. Pogany (ed), *Nuclear Weapons and International Law* (1987), Chapter 4.
13   *ICJ Rep.* (1986), p.14, para. 194.
14   Ibid., para. 237.
15   See Chapter 8, notes 105 and 261.
16   *ICJ Rep.* (1986), p.14, para. 195.
17   See GA Res. 3314 (XXIX), 14 December 1974. Art. 3(g) provides that aggression is established by, *inter alia,*'[t]he sending by or on behalf of a State of armed bands, groups, irregulars or mercenaries, which carry out acts of armed force against another State of such gravity as to amount to the acts listed above, or its substantial involvement therein'.
18   *ICJ Rep.* (1986), p.14, para. 195. However, the Court effectively ignored the term 'or its substantial involvement therein', thereby significantly limiting the scope of an 'armed attack'.
19   *ICJ Rep.* (1986), p.14, paras. 229-36.
20   Ibid., para. 195.

21 See Chapter 3, notes 134-42, and the accompanying text.
22 *ICJ Rep.* (1986), p.14, para. 195.
23 Ibid., para. 155.
24 Ibid., para. 161. See generally ibid., paras. 155-77.
25 See generally ibid., paras. 154-70. Judge Schwebel's reasoning is based, in part, on Article 3(g) of the Definition of Aggression adopted by the UN General Assembly in 1974. As noted above, the Court effectively ignored the term 'or its substantial involvement therein', contained in Article 3[g] in its formulation of an 'armed attack'. See notes 16-17 above and the accompanying text.
26 Brownlie, *Use of Force*, p.279.
27 As noted previously, the Judgment of the ICJ in *Nicaragua vs USA* is open to the interpretation that force may only be used in individual or collective self-defence in the event of an 'armed attack'. See notes 8-9 above and the accompanying text.
28 See Chapter 3, notes 149-57, and the accompanying text.
29 *ICJ Rep.* (1986), p.14, para. 195.
30 Ibid., para. 199.
31 On the doctrine of collective self-defence see Chapter 3, notes 149-57, and the accompanying text.
32 It may be recollected that the Lebanese government claimed that the UAR was carrying out an 'armed attack' against the Lebanon by infiltrating guerrillas across its border. The Lebanon requested the assistance of US troops in accordance with the doctrine of collective self-defence, as recognized by Article 51 of the UN Charter. See Chapter 3, notes 115-18, and the accompanying text. As noted above, the degree of UAR involvement in the infiltration of guerrillas into the Lebanon amounted to an 'armed attack' even within the strict definition adopted by the World Court in *Nicaragua* vs *USA*.
33 This presupposes, of course, that the use of force in individual or collective self-defence is conditional upon an 'armed attack'. However, this appears to have been the assumption of the International Court. See notes 8-9 above, and the accompanying text.
34 *ICJ Rep.* (1986), p.14, para. 195.
35 Ibid., para. 242.
36 Ibid.,para. 247.
37 Ibid., para. 249.
38 For details concerning Lebanese support for Palestinian guerrilla operations against Israel, see Chapters 3, 5 and 8.
39 There are, of course, other serious obstacles to the acceptance of Israel's incursions into the Lebanon, in 1978 and 1982, as legitimate self-defence. See Chapter 8, notes 105 and 261.
40 See note 37 above and the accompanying text.
41 Ibid., para. 177.
42 Ibid., para. 246.
43 The principle of non-intervention has been affirmed, for example, in the 1970 Declaration on Principles of International Law adopted by the UN General Assembly: 'No State or group of States has the right to intervene, directly or indirectly, for any reason whatever, in the internal or external affairs of any other State'. GA Res. 2625 (XXV), 24 October 1970. In general, 'intervention' is identified with the *absence* of consent on the part of the government. See e.g. I. Pogany, 'Humanitarian Intervention in International Law: the French Intervention in Syria Re-Examined,' *ICLQ*, vol. 35 (1986), p.182, at pp.188-9. By contrast, the consent of opposition groups is immaterial to the question of intervention.

44   See Chapter 6, notes 28-30, and the accompanying text.
45   See Chapter 3, notes 159-62, and the accompanying text.
46   See generally Chapter 2, note 73.
47   *ICJ Rep.* (1986), p.14, para. 169. It should be emphasized, however, that the US did not assert a right to intervene in order to protect human rights etc. Instead, the US relied on the doctrine of collective self-defence.
48   Ibid., para. 268.
49   Ibid., para. 267.

Appendix I
The Pact of the League of Arab States*

HIS EXCELLENCY THE PRESIDENT OF THE SYRIAN REPUBLIC;
HIS ROYAL HIGHNESS THE AMIR OF TRANS-JORDAN;
HIS MAJESTY THE KING OF IRAQ;
HIS MAJESTY THE KING OF SAUDI ARABIA;
HIS EXCELLENCY THE PRESIDENT OF THE LEBANESE REPUBLIC;
HIS MAJESTY THE KING OF EGYPT;
HIS MAJESTY THE KING OF YEMEN;

Desirous of strengthening the close relations and numerous ties which link the Arab States;

And anxious to support and stabilize these ties upon a basis of respect for the independence and sovereignty of these states, and to direct their efforts towards the common good of all the Arab countries, the improvement of their status, the security of their future, the realisation of their aspirations and hopes;

And responding to the wishes of Arab public opinion in all Arab lands;

Have agreed to conclude a Pact to that end and have appointed as their representatives the persons whose names are listed hereinafter, have agreed upon the following provisions:

Article 1   The League of Arab States is composed of the independent Arab states which have signed this Pact.

* H.A. Hassouna, *The League of Arab States and Regional Disputes*, (1975), p.403.

179

Any independent Arab state has the right to become a member of the League. If it desires to do so, it shall submit a request which will be deposited with the Permanent Secretariat-General and submitted to the Council at the first meeting held after submission of the request.

Article 2   The League has as its purpose the strengthening of the relations between the member states; the co-ordination of their policies in order to achieve cooperation between them and to safeguard their independence and sovereignty; and a general concern with the affairs and interests of the Arab countries. It has also as its purpose the close cooperation of the member states, with due regard to the organisation and circumstances of each state, on the following matters:

A. Economic and financial affairs, including commercial relations, customs, currency, and questions of agriculture and industry.
B. Communications, this includes railroads, roads, aviation, navigation, telegraphs, and posts.
C. Cultural affairs.
D. Nationality, passports, visas, execution of judgements, and extradition of criminals.
E. Social affairs.
F. Health problems.

Article 3   The League shall possess a Council composed of the representatives of the member states of the League; each state shall have a single vote, irrespective of the number of its representatives.

It shall be the task of the Council to achieve the realisation of the objectives of the League and to supervise the execution of agreements which the member states have concluded on the questions enumerated in the preceding article, or on any other questions.

It likewise shall be the Council's task to decide upon the means by which the League is to cooperate with the international bodies to be created in the future in order to guarantee security and peace and regulate economic and social relations.

Article 4   For each of the questions listed in Article 2 there shall be set up a special committee in which the member states of the League shall be represented. These committees shall be charged with the task of laying down the principles and extent of cooperation. Such principles shall be formulated as draft agreements, to be presented to the Council for examination preparatory to their submission to the aforesaid states.

Representatives of the other Arab countries may take part in the work of the aforesaid committees. The Council shall determine the conditions under which these representatives may be permitted to participate and the rules governing such representation.

Article 5 Any resort to force in order to resolve disputes arising between two or more member states of the League is prohibited. If there should arise among them a difference which does not concern a state's independence, sovereignty, or territorial integrity, and if the parties to the dispute have recourse to the Council for the settlement of this difference, the decision of the Council shall then be enforceable and obligatory.

In such a case, the states between whom the difference has arisen shall not participate in the deliberations and decisions of the Council.

The Council shall mediate in all differences which threaten to lead to war between two member states, or a member state and a third state, with a view to bringing about their reconciliation.

Decisions of arbitration and mediation shall be taken by majority vote.

Article 6 In case of aggression or threat of aggression by one state against a member state, the state which has been attacked or threatened with aggression may demand the immediate convocation of the Council.

The Council shall by unanimous decision determine the measures necessary to repulse the aggression. If the aggressor is a member state, his vote shall not be counted in determining unanimity.

If, as a result of the attack, the government of the state attacked finds itself unable to communicate with the Council, that state's representative in the Council shall have the right to request the convocation of the Council for the purpose indicated in the foregoing paragraph. In the event that this representative is unable to communicate with the Council, any member state of the League shall have the right to request the convocation of the Council.

Article 7 Unanimous decisions of the Council shall be binding upon all member states of the League; majority decisions shall be binding only upon those states which have accepted them.

In either case the decisions of the Council shall be enforced in each member state according to its respective basic laws.

Article 8 Each member state shall respect the systems of government established in the other member states and regard them as exclusive concerns of those states. Each shall pledge to abstain from any action calculated to change established systems of government.

Article 9 States of the League which desire to establish closer cooperation and stronger bonds than are provided by this Pact may conclude agreements to that end.

Treaties and agreements already concluded or to be concluded in the future between a member state and another state shall not be binding or restrictive upon other members.

Article 10 The permanent seat of the League of Arab States is established in Cairo. The Council may, however, assemble at any other place it may designate.

Article 11 The Council of the League shall convene in ordinary session twice a year, in March and in September. It shall convene in extraordinary session upon the request of two member states of the League whenever the need arises.

Article 12 The League shall have a permanent Secretariat-General which shall consist of a Secretary-General, Assistant Secretaries, and an appropriate number of officials.

The Council of the League shall appoint the Secretary-General by a majority of two-thirds of the states of the League. The Secretary-General, with the approval of the Council shall appoint the Assistant Secretaries and the principal officials of the League.

The Council of the League shall establish an administrative regulation for the functions of the Secretariat-General and matters relating to the Staff.

The Secretary-General shall have the rank of Ambassador and the Assistant Secretaries that of Ministers Plenipotentiary. The first Secretary-General of the League is named in an Annex to this Pact.

Article 13 The Secretary-General shall prepare the draft of the budget of the League and shall submit it to the Council for approval before the beginning of each fiscal year. The Council shall fix the share of the expenses to be borne by each state of the League. This share may be reconsidered if necessary.

Article 14 The members of the Council of the League as well as the members of the committees and the officials who are to be designated in the administrative regulation shall enjoy diplomatic privileges and immunity when engaged in the exercise of their functions.

The buildings occupied by the organs of the League shall be inviolable.

Article 15 The first meeting of the Council shall be convened at the invitation of the Head of the Egyptian Government. Thereafter, it shall be convened at the invitation of the Secretary-General.

The representatives of the member states of the League shall alternatively assume the presidency of the Council at each of its ordinary sessions.

Article 16 Except in cases specifically indicated in this Pact, a majority vote of the Council shall be sufficient to make enforceable decisions on the following matters:
A. Matters relating to personnel;
B. Adoption of the budget of the League;
C. Establishment of the administrative regulations for the Council, the committees, and the Secretariat-General;
D. Decisions to adjourn the sessions.

Article 17 Each member state of the League shall deposit with the Secretariat-General one copy of every treaty or agreement concluded or to be concluded in the future between itself and another member state of the League or a third state.

Article 18 If a member state contemplates withdrawal from the League, it shall inform the Council of its intention one year before such withdrawal is to go into effect.

The Council of the League may consider any state which fails to fulfil its obligations under this Pact as having become separated from the League, this to go into effect upon a unanimous decision of the states, not counting the state concerned.

Article 19 This Pact may be amended with the consent of two-thirds of the states belonging to the League, especially in order to make firmer and stronger the ties between the member states, to create an Arab Tribunal of Arbitration, and to regulate the relations of the League with any international bodies to be created in the future to guarantee security and peace.

Final action on an amendment cannot be taken prior to the session following the session in which the motion was initiated.

If a state does not accept such an amendment it may withdraw at such time as the amendment goes into effect, without being bound by the provisions of the preceding article.

Article 20 This Pact and its Annexes shall be ratified according to the basic laws in force among the High Contracting Parties.

The instruments of ratification shall be deposited with the Secretariat-General of the Council and the Pact shall become operative as regards each ratifying state fifteen days after the Secretary-General has received the instruments of ratification from four states.

This Pact has been drawn up in Cairo in the Arabic language on this 8th day of Rabi' II, thirteen hundred and sixty-four, [22 March, 1945], in one copy which shall be deposited in the safekeeping of the Secretariat-General.

An identical copy shall be delivered to each state of the League.
(Here follow the signatures.)

(1) Annex regarding Palestine

Since the termination of the last great war, the rule of the Ottoman Empire over the Arab countries, among them Palestine, which had become detached from that Empire, has come to an end. She has come to be autonomous, not subordinate to any other state.

The Treaty of Lausanne proclaimed that her future was to be settled by the parties concerned.

However, even though she was as yet unable to control her own affairs, the Covenant of the League [of Nations] in 1919 made provision for a regime based upon recognition of her independence.

Her international existence and independence in the legal sense cannot, therefore, be questioned, any more than could the independence of the other Arab countries.

Although the outward manifestations of this independence have remained obscured for reasons beyond her control, this should not be allowed to interfere with her participation in the work of the Council of the League.

The states signatory to the Pact of the Arab League are therefore of the opinion that, considering the special circumstances of Palestine and until that country can effectively exercise its independence, the Council of the League should take charge of the selection of an Arab representative from Palestine to take part in its work.

(2) Annex regarding cooperation with countries which are not members of the Council of the League

Whereas the member states of the League will have to deal in the Council as well as in the committees with matters which will benefit and affect the Arab world at large;

And whereas the Council has to take into account the aspirations of the Arab countries which are not members of the Council and has to work toward their realisation;

Now, therefore, it particularly behoves the states signatory to the Pact of the Arab League to enjoin the Council of the League, when considering the admission of those countries to participation in the committees referred to in the Pact, that it should do its utmost to cooperate with them and furthermore, that it should spare no effort to learn their needs and understand their aspirations and hopes; and that it should work thenceforth for their best interests and the safeguarding of their future with all the political means at its disposal.

(3) Annex regarding the appointment of a Secretary-General of the League

The states signatory to this Pact have agreed to appoint His Excellency Abdul-Rahman 'Azzam Bey, to be the Secretary-General of the League of Arab States.

This appointment is made for two years. The Council of the League shall hereafter determine the new regulations for the Secretariat-General.

Appendix II
Resolutions of the Arab League Council Regarding the War in Lebanon*

Cairo, 9 June 1976

In the course of its session, the Arab League Council considered the deteriorating situation in Lebanon and the bloody incidents that are taking place there and, in the light of its responsibility to the Arab nation, resolves the following:

1 To thank the Secretary-General of the Arab League for his initiative in calling this extraordinary session to discuss this fateful issue.

2 To call on all parties to cease fighting immediately and to consolidate such a ceasefire.

3 To form a symbolic Arab security force under the supervision of the General Secretary of the Arab League to maintain security and stability in Lebanon, which force should start to perform its task immediately, replacing the Syrian forces. The task of this Arab Security force should be brought to an end if the President-elect of the Republic of Lebanon so requests.

4 That a commission representing the League Council and consisting of the Foreign Minister of Bahrein, chairman of the session, the Secretary of the Arab League and the heads of the Algerian and Libyan delegations, should be despatched immediately to cooperate with the parties concerned in following up the situation and ensuring security and stability in Lebanon.

* *International Documents on Palestine* (1976), p.431.

5 The Council calls on all the Lebanese parties to bring about comprehensive national conciliation under the auspices of the Lebanese President-elect, to ensure the maintenance of the unity of the Lebanese people and the unity of their territory and the country's sovereignty, security and stability.

6 To affirm Arab commitment to support the Palestine revolution and to protect it from all dangers, and to ensure that it is provided with everything that can increase its strength and effectiveness.

7 The Council will remain in session to follow up the situation.

Appendix III
Statement Issued by Six-Party Arab Summit Conference Held in Riyadh and Related Documents*

Statement issued by Six-Party Arab Summit Conference held in Riyadh

On the initiative of the Kingdom of Saudi Arabia and the State of Kuwait, a six-party conference, attended by President Mohammed Anwar El Sadat of the Arab Republic of Egypt, President Hafez El Assad of the Syrian Arab Republic, President Elias Sarkis of the Lebanese Republic, Mr. Yasser Arafat, Chairman of the Palestine Liberation Organization, His Highness Sheikh Sabah Al Salem Al Sabah, Ruler of the State of Kuwait, and His Majesty King Khaled bin Abdel Aziz Al Saud of the Kingdom of Saudi Arabia was held in Riyadh from 16 to 18 October 1976 to discuss the crisis in Lebanon, to consider ways of solving that crisis, and to agree on the steps necessary to halt the bloodshed in the country; it was agreed to resort to dialogue rather than fighting, to preserve the security, safety, independence and sovereignty of Lebanon, and further to safeguard Palestinian resistance as represented by the Palestine Liberation Organization.

The Conference recognized the national and historical commitment to enhancing the collective Arab role in such a way as to ensure the settlement of the situation in Lebanon and prevent any further outbreak of hostilities.

* Translated from the Arabic. Mineographed UN document, Job. No. 77-06459 mmb (SC/GA classification unknown).

The Conference also recognized the need to transcend the attitudes and negativism of the past, to move towards the future in a spirit of conciliation, peace and construction, to provide the guarantees necessary to ensure stability and normalcy in Lebanon, to preserve Lebanese political, economic and other institutions, to maintain Lebanese sovereignty, and to ensure the continuation of Palestinian determination.

The Conference examined the situation in Lebanon and considered the measures and steps necessary to restore normalcy in that country within the context of the preservation of the country's sovereignty and independence, the solidarity of the Lebanese and Palestinian peoples, and the collective Arab guarantee of the foregoing. The Conference decided to declare a ceasefire and an end to the fighting, and pledged the full commitment of all parties to this agreement.

The Conference further decided to reinforce existing Arab security forces, so that they might act as a deterrent force within Lebanon under the command of the President of Lebanon himself.

The Conference requested all Lebanese parties to engage in a political dialogue with the aim of achieving national reconciliation and establishing unity among the Lebanese people.

Agreement was also reached on the implementation of the Cairo Agreement and its annexes, and the Chairman of the Palestine Liberation Organization announced his full commitment to that Agreement. In that connexion, the Conference decided to establish a committee consisting of representatives of the Kingdom of Saudi Arabia, the Arab Republic of Egypt, the Syrian Arab Republic and the State of Kuwait to ensure coordination with the President of Lebanon in respect of the implementation of the Cairo Agreement. The Committee's mandate will cover a period of 90 days, beginning on the date of the announcement of the ceasefire.

The Conference affirmed its commitment to the decisions of the Seventh Arab Summit Conference held in Rabat declaring the Palestine Liberation Organization the sole legitimate representative of the Palestine people, pledging the full support of all member States of the Arab League to the Palestine Liberation Organization, as well as their non-interference in its affairs, and confirming the Organization's policy of non-interference in the internal affairs of any Arab country.

In that connexion, the Conference affirmed that participating States would guarantee the security, unity, sovereignty and independence of Lebanon.

The Conference also discussed the question of reconstruction in Lebanon and the cost of removing the traces of the armed conflict and making good damage affecting both the Lebanese and the Palestinian peoples.

Resolutions adopted by this Conference will be submitted to the full Arab Summit.

Annex

Resolutions of the Six-Party Arab Summit Conference held in Riyadh

The limited Arab Summit Conference, held in Riyadh from 16 to 18 October 1976, on the initiative of His Majesty King Khalad bin Abdel Aziz Al Saud of the Kingdom of Saudi Arabia and His Highness Sheikh Sabah Al Salem Al Sabah, Ruler of the State of Kuwait,

Having reviewed the resolutions adopted by the Council of the League of Arab States at its extraordinary sessions on 8 - 10 June 1976, 23 June 1976 and 1 July 1976, and at its session on 4 September 1976,

Recognizing the national commitment to preserve the unity, security and sovereignty of Lebanon, to ensure the continuation of Palestinian resistance, as represented by the Palestine Liberation Organization, recognized by the Rabat resolutions to be the sole legitimate representative of the Palestine people and to increase the capacity of the Palestine Liberation Organization to resist threats to the existence of the Palestinian people, their right to self-determination and their right to return to their national soil,

Having faith in the unity of objective and destiny binding the two fraternal Lebanese and Palestine peoples and in the impossibility of any contradiction of interests between these two peoples,

Determined to transcend the attitudes and negativism of the past, to face the future in a spirit of reconciliation, dialogue and cooperation, to accelerate the establishment of conditions and guarantees necessary to ensure stability and normalcy in Lebanon, to consolidate the political, economic and other institutions of Lebanon, and to enable the Palestine Liberation Organization to attain its national goals,

Recognizing the positive and constructive spirit demonstrated by the leaders attending this Conference, as well as their sincere desire irrevocably and decisively to end the crisis in Lebanon and to overcome any disputes that might arise in the future,

Decides the following:

1   That all parties should definitively cease fire and terminate fighting in all Lebanese territories as from 6.00 a.m. on 21 October 1976, and that they shall all be fully committed thereto;

2   That existing Arab security forces should be expanded to 30,000 men so that they might become a deterrent force operating inside Lebanon under the personal command of the President of the Lebanese Republic with, *inter alia,* the following principal tasks:

(a) Ensuring observance of the ceasefire and termination of hostilities, disengaging belligerent troops and deterring any violation of the agreement;

(b) Implementing the Cairo Agreement and its annexes;

(c) Maintaining internal security;

(d) Supervising the withdrawal of armed troops to positions they held prior to 13 April 1975 and removing all military installations in accordance with the schedule set out in the enclosed annex;

(e) Supervising the collection of heavy weaponry such as artillery, mortars, rocket-launchers, armoured vehicles, etc., by the parties concerned;

(f) Assisting the Lebanese authorities when necessary with respect to taking over public utilities and institutions prior to their re-opening as well as guarding public military and civilian establishments;

3   That, as a first stage, the normal situation in Lebanon, as it existed prior to the incidents (i.e. prior to 13 April 1975) will be restored in accordance with the schedule set out in the annex;

4   That the implementation of the Cairo Agreement and its annexes and the observation of the letter and spirit of their contents shall be guaranteed by the Arab States participating in the Conference; a committee is to be established, comprising representatives of the Kingdom of Saudi Arabia, the Arab Republic of Egypt, the Syrian Arab Republic and the State of Kuwait to ensure co-ordination with the President of Lebanon in respect of the implementation of the Cairo Agreement and its annexes; the mandate of the said committee will cover a period of 90 days, beginning on the date of the announcement of the cease-fire;

5   That the Palestine Liberation Organization shall affirm its respect of the sovereignty and security of Lebanon, as well as its non-interference in Lebanese internal affairs, recognizing in this respect its full commitment to the national objectives of the Palestinian cause. For their part, the legitimate authorities in Lebanon shall, in accordance with the Cairo Agreement and its annexes, guarantee security to the Palestine Liberation Organization with respect to its presence and activities in Lebanese territory;

6   That the Arab States participating in the Conference pledge their respect for the sovereignty, security, and territorial integrity of Lebanon, as well as the unity of its people;

7   That the Arab States participating in the Conference reaffirm their commitment to the decisions taken at the Summit Conferences held in Algiers and Rabat to support and uphold Palestinian resistance, as represented by the Palestine Liberation Organization, and to respect the right of the Palestinian people to use all means at their disposal in their struggle to recover their national rights;

8 That, with respect to information:
(a) All publicity campaigns and psychological warfare by all parties should be stopped;
(b) Information activities should be directed towards consolidating the termination of hostilities, establishing peace and promoting a spirit of cooperation and brotherhood on all sides;
(c) Action should be taken to unify official information activities;
9 That the attached Schedule concerning the implementation of these resolutions is to be considered an integral part of the resolutions.

Signed:

Ruler of the State of Kuwait
President of the Syrian Arab Republic
Chairman of the Palestine Liberation Organization
President of the Lebanese Republic
President of the Arab Republic of Egypt
King of the Kingdom of Saudi Arabia

Annex

Schedule Regarding the Implementation of the Resolutions of the Six-Party Summit Conference Held in Riyadh from 16 to 18 October 1976

1. Declaration of final cease-fire and termination of fighting in all Lebanese territories by all parties as from 6.00 a.m. on 21 October 1976 (D-Day).
2. Establishment of check-points by the deterrent security force after the creation of buffer zones in areas of tension in order to consolidate the cease-fire and the termination of fighting.
3. Withdrawal of all armed troops, collection of heavy weaponry and removal of military installations in accordance with the following schedule:
(a) Mount Lebanon: within five days (D-Day + 5).
(b) Southern Lebanon: within five days (D-Day + 5).
(c) Beirut and outskirts: within seven days (D-Day + 7).
(d) Northern Lebanon: within ten days (D-Day + 10).
4. Reopening of international highways:
(a) The following international highways shall be reopened within five days (D-Day + 5):
—Beirut/Al Masnaa
—Beirut/Tripoli/The Borders
—Beirut/Tyre
—Beirut/Sidon/Marjoyoun/Al Masnaa

(b) Checkpoints and patrols shall be established along unsafe routes, and shall consist of units from the deterrent security force as agreed by the parties concerned and the commander of the said force.

5. The legitimate Lebanese authorities shall take over public, military and civilian utilities and establishments:

(a) after the removal of armed troops and non-employees, the Arab security force shall be assigned to guarding such utilities and establishments and facilitating their operation by employees who shall begin work within 10 days (D-Day + 10);

(b) the utilities and establishments shall be handed over to an official central Lebanese commission which shall, in turn, be responsible for forming a sub-committee in each utility or establishment to make an inventory of its contents and to take over.

6. The forces required to strengthen the Arab security force shall be formed in agreement with the President of the Lebanese Republic, and these forces shall arrive in Lebanon within two weeks (D-Day + 15).

7. As a second stage, the Cairo Agreement and its annexes shall be implemented, particularly those provisions concerning the existence of weapons and ammunitions in refugee camps and the exit of those armed Palestinian forces that entered the country after the beginning of the incidents. The implementation of the agreement is to be completed within 45 days, beginning on the date of the formation of the Arab deterrent security force.

Communiqué concerning the first extraordinary session of the Arab summit conference.

Cairo, 25–26 October 1976

The Kings and Heads of State of the League of Arab States met in Cairo in order to examine the crisis in Lebanon, to consider ways of solving it, to protect the security, sovereignty and unity of Lebanon, to safeguard Palestinian resistance as represented by the Palestine Liberation Organization and to enhance Arab solidarity.

They recognize the national and historical commitment to enhancing the collective Arab role in such a way as to ensure the settlement of the situation in Lebanon and to prevent any further outbreak of hostilities, to provide the guarantees necessary to ensure stability and normalcy, to preserve the political, economic and other institutions of Lebanon, to preserve the country's sovereignty and to ensure the continuation of Palestinian determination.

They are convinced that the liberation of the Arab territories occupied by Israel and the recovery of the national rights of the Palestinian people, notably the right to return to their national soil and establish their own independent state, require the further strengthening of Arab solidarity, and the mobilization of Arab efforts and potential in the service of this great cause.

They are aware of the need to help Lebanon overcome its crisis and reconstruct its economy, institutions and utilities in order to restore normal life and the country's effective role in the Arab economic domain.

They have examined the present situation in Lebanon in the context of preserving Lebanese sovereignty and independence and ensuring the solidarity of the Lebanese and Palestinian peoples.

They welcome the outcome of the Six-Party Arab Summit Conference in Riyadh, and express their appreciation for its achievements with respect to promoting the settlement of the Lebanese crisis, the continuation of Palestinian resistance and the further strengthening of Arab solidarity. The Conference decides to approve the resolutions of the Six-Party Arab Summit Conference published on 18 October 1976.

The Arab Kings and Heads of State reaffirm their commitment to providing the necessary guarantees with respect to the consolidation of the ceasefire announced at 6.00 a.m. on 21 October 1976, the aim being to put an end to all forms of fighting in Lebanon, and to restore normal life there. They further reaffirm that the Arab security force will be strengthened so that it might become a deterrent force operating inside Lebanon under the personal command of the President of Lebanon.

They unanimously reject the partition of Lebanon in any form, whether legally or in practice, expressly or implicitly; they are also unanimous in their commitment to maintain Lebanon's national unity and territorial integrity, and to refrain from prejudicing the unity of its land or interfering in its internal affairs in any way.

They have also examined with great attention the situation in southern Lebanon, and are extremely concerned over the growing number of Israeli acts of aggression against Lebanese territory, particularly in the south, as well as over Israel's persistence in its aggressive expansionist policy in Arab territories.

They further stress the importance of implementing the Cairo Agreement and its annexes, to which the Chairman of the Palestine Liberation Organization has declared his full commitment. They have agreed on the formation of a committee comprising representatives of the Kingdom of Saudi Arabia, the Arab Republic of Egypt, the Syrian Arab Republic, and the State of Kuwait in order to ensure co-ordination with the President of Lebanon in respect of the implementation of the Cairo Agreement; the committee's mandate will cover a period of 90 days beginning on the date of the announcement of the ceasefire.

The Arab Kings and Heads of State reaffirm their commitment to the decisions of the Seventh Arab Summit Conference held at Rabat, decisions whereby the Palestinian Liberation Organization was declared to be the sole legitimate representative of the people of Palestine, all Arab States belonging to the League of Arab States pledged their support for the Palestine Liberation Organization and undertook not to interfere in its affairs, and the Palestine Liberation Organization affirmed its policy of non-interference in the internal affairs of any Arab State.

The Arab Kings and Heads of State have agreed that Arab countries should contribute to the reconstruction of Lebanon, to the removal of the traces of the armed conflict and to the making good of damage affecting the Lebanese and Palestinian peoples, and for that purpose have agreed to extend urgent assistance to them.

The Arab Kings and Heads of State have paid particular attention to the consolidation of Arab solidarity, this being the essential basis for the success of joint Arab action and for the realization of the Arab nation's objectives concerning liberation and development. In this respect, they also reaffirm their full commitment to implementing the decisions of the Arab summit conferences and the Council of the League of Arab States, particularly the Charter of Arab Solidarity issued by the Casablanca Summit Conference on 15 September 1965.

They have studied with great concern the explosive situation in the occupied Arab territories, a situation caused by continued Israeli occupation, the increasing incidence of oppression, intimidation and expulsion, as well as the confiscation of land and the desecration of religious places, particularly the Al Ibrahimi Mosque; all of these measures are being applied by the occupying authorities in flagrant violation of the provision of international law and the Charter of the United Nations.

They hail the steadfast Arab people in the occupied territories and their legitimate national struggle, and reaffirm the support of all Arab States.

They call on all countries and peoples of the world to condemn and stand up against continuing Israeli aggression and to discontinue any dealings with Israel that might consolidate the Israeli occupation of Arab territories, or allow the continuation of oppressive Israeli measures directed against the population of these territories.

Resolutions adopted at the first extraordinary session of the Arab summit conference.

Cairo, 26 October 1976

The Kings and Heads of State of the League of Arab States meeting from 25 to 26 October 1976 at the quarters of the League of Arab States in Cairo,

Having examined the present situation in Lebanon and the outcome of the Six-Party Arab summit conference held in Riyadh, as announced on 18 October 1976, and having examined also the importance of further strengthening Arab solidarity

Decide the following:

I.   The situation in Lebanon:

1. To approve the statement, resolutions and annexes, issued on 18 October 1976, by the Six-Party Arab Summit Conference held at Riyadh, attached hereto;

(The Delegation of Iraq did not agree to this paragraph.)

2. That Arab States should, according to their individual capabilities, contribute to the reconstruction of Lebanon, and help meet the related material requirements in order to remove the traces of the armed conflict and make good damage affecting the Lebanese and Palestinian peoples; Arab States should also extend urgent assistance to the Lebanese Government and to the Palestine Liberation Organization.

II   Further strengthening of Arab solidarity:

To reaffirm the commitment of the Arab Kings and Heads of State to the relevant provisions of the resolutions adopted by Arab summit conferences and the Council of the League of Arab States, particularly the Charter of Arab Solidarity published in Casablanca on 15 September 1965, and to take steps towards their immediate and full implementation.

III   Financing of Arab Security Forces:

The Arab Summit Conference: With a view to providing the financial resources required to maintain the Arab security forces in Lebanon, forces established in accordance with the second resolution adopted at the Riyadh Summit Conference,

Having reviewed the relevant report of the Military Secretariat of the League of Arab States,

Decides the following:

1. A special fund shall be set up to meet the requirements of the Arab security forces in Lebanon;

2. Each member state of the League of Arab States shall contribute a certain percentage to the fund, to be determined by each State according to its capabilities;

3. The President of the Republic of Lebanon shall supervise the fund, and, in consultation with the General-Secretariat of the League of Arab States and those States contributing at least 10 per cent, shall work out general rules governing payments from the fund and its liquidation when its term expires; the present regulations for the Arab security force shall remain in effect until new regulations are drawn up;

4. The fund shall be set up for a six-month period, renewable by a decision of the Council of the League of Arab States; the Council shall meet for this purpose at the request of the President of the Republic of Lebanon.

IV   Renewal of the appointment of the Secretary-General of the League of Arab States:

The Arab Summit Conference decides to renew the appointment of Mr Mahmoud Riad as Secretary-General of the League of Arab States for another term beginning at the end of his present term.

V   Special resolution:

The Arab Summit Conference, holding its first extraordinary session in Cairo, having met in an atmosphere of brotherhood and concern with respect to the further strengthening of Arab solidarity, and having successfully concluded its work, is pleased to express its deep gratitude to the President, Government and people of the Arab Republic of Egypt, for hosting and welcoming the Conference and providing for its success. The Conference is also pleased to express its deep appreciation for the sincere efforts of President Mohamed Anwar El Sadat during preparations for the Conference, for his wise chairmanship, which enabled the Conference to attain its objectives, and for his efforts towards the further strengthening of Arab solidarity.

Appendix IV
The Cairo and Melkart Agreements*

The Cairo Agreement, 3 November 1969

On Monday, 3 November 1969 the Lebanese delegation headed by Army Commander Emile Bustani and the PLO delegation headed by Yasser Arafat met in Cairo. . . . It was agreed to re-establish the Palestinian presence in Lebanon on the basis of:

1 The right of Palestinians presently living in Lebanon to work, reside and move freely;

2 The establishment of local committees from Palestinians living in the camps to look after the interests of the Palestinians there, in cooperation with the local authorities and within the context of Lebanese sovereignty;

3 The presence of command centres for the Palestine Armed Struggle Command inside the camps to cooperate with the local authorities and guarantee good relations. These centres will handle arrangements for the carrying and regulation of arms within the camps, taking into account both Lebanese security and the interests of the Palestinian revolution;

4 Permission for Palestinian residents in Lebanon to join the Palestinian revolution through armed struggle within the limits imposed by Lebanese security and sovereignty.

*Yehuda Lukacs (ed.), *Documents on the Israeli-Palestinian Conflict 1967-1983* (1984), p.215.

Commando Operations

It was agreed to facilitate operations by (Palestinian) commandos through:

1) Assisting commando access to the border and the specification of access points and observations posts in the border region;

2) Ensuring the use of the main road to the Arqub region;

3) Control by the Palestine Armed Struggle Command of the actions of all members of its organisations and to prevention of any interference in Lebanese affairs;

4) The pursuit of mutual cooperation between the Palestine Armed Struggle Command and the Lebanese army;

5) An end to media campaigns by both sides;

6) A census of the complement of the Palestine Armed Struggle Command through its leadership;

7) The appointment of representatives of the Palestine Armed Struggle Command to the Lebanese High Command;

8) Study of the distribution of suitable concentration points in the border regions to the Lebanese High Command;

9) Organization of the entry, exit and movement of Palestine Armed Struggle elements;

10) Abolition of the Jainoun base;

11) Assistance by the Lebanese army in the work of medical centres, and evacuation and supply for commando operations;

12) Release of all internees and confiscated arms;

13) Acceptance that the civil and military Lebanese authorities will continue to exercise effective responsibility to the full in all regions of Lebanon and under all circumstances;

14) Confirmation that the Palestine Armed Struggle acts for the benefit of Lebanon as well as for the Palestinian revolution and for all Arabs.

The Melkart Agreement, 17 May 1973

Both parties eagerly agree to serve the Palestinian cause and to continue its struggle, and to preserve the independence of Lebanon and its sovereignty and stability, and in the light of contracted agreements and Arab decisions, comprising: the Cairo agreement and all its annexes; agreements concluded between Lebanon and the leadership of the resistance forces; and decisions taken at the Joint Arab Defence Council; it was agreed on all points as follows:

Presence in the Camps of Personnel

1) No commando presence;

2) Formation of permanent Palestine Armed Struggle Command units;

3) Confirmation of militia presence for the guarding and internal protection of the camps. By militia is understood Palestinians residing in the camps who are not members of the resistance force and who practise normal civilian duties;

4) Establishment of a guardpost for Lebanese internal security forces at a location to be agreed upon close to each camp.

Presence in the Camps of Arms

1) The militia will be permitted to carry light arms individually;

2) No medium or heavy weapons will be permitted within the camps (e.g. mortars, rocket-launchers, artillery, anti-tank weapons, etc.).

Presence in the Border Regions

1) Western sector: presence and concentration outside the camps is forbidden. . .

2) Central sector: According to agreements made at the meeting between the Lebanese High Command and the resistance forces leadership on 8 October 1972: Presence will be permitted outside Lebanese villages in certain areas by agreement with the local Lebanese sector commander. Resistance forces are not permitted east and south of the line running Al-Kusair/Al-Ghandouriya/Deir Kifa/ Al-Shihabia/ Al-Salasel/ Al-Saltania/ Tabnin/Haris/Kafra/Sadikin/Qana. This prohibition applies to all these points inclusively. Concentration of resistance forces at a guardpost south of Hadatha is permitted. The number allowed is between five and ten men in civilian clothes, with all military appearance to be avoided. They will be supplied by animal transport. At all these places the total number permitted must not exceed 250.

3) Eastern sector: According to decisions taken by the Lebanese High Command and the resistance forces leadership, three bases will be permitted in the southern Arqub at Abu-Kamha Al Kharbiya (Al-Shahid Salah base) and Rashaya al-Fakhar (Jabal al-Shahr). Each base will contain no more than 30 to 35 men each. Supply for these bases will be by motor-transport. Elements at these bases will be forbidden to proceed in the direction of Marjayoun unless they have a permit. The carrying of arms in Marjayoun is forbidden. . . . In the northern Arqub and at Rashaya al-Wadi, presence is permitted at a distance from the villages, but not west of the Masnaa-Hasbaya road. . . . At Baalbeck no commando presence is permitted except at the Nabi Sbat training base.

Note: Medium and light arms are permitted in these sectors; commando presence inside Lebanese villages is not allowed; all units which have been reinforced in Lebanon from abroad will be adjusted.

Movement [in the camps]

Movement will be allowed without arms and in civilian dress.

Movement in the [frontier] areas

Movement will be allowed by arrangement with local Lebanese commanders and according to agreement.

Movement of Civilian and Military Leaders

Military leaders will be allowed to move freely provided they are above the rank of lieutenant, carrying no more than a personal weapon and are accompanied by a driver only. Civilian leaders will be supplied with numbered permits signed by the responsible joint liaison committee. The number of permits issued to area leaderships will be determined by the Lebanese liaison centre and supplied under the request of the Palestinian Political Committee in Lebanon.

Military Training

[Military] training is forbidden in the camps, but allowed at the training base at Nabi Sbat. Technical military training is permitted at points to be agreed upon by arrangement with the Lebanese High Command liaison centre. Practising with arms is forbidden outside the training base.

Operations

All [commando] operations from Lebanese territory are suspended according to the decisions of the Joint Arab Defence Council. Departure from Lebanon for the purpose of commando operations is forbidden.

Command

The Palestinian side reaffirms that the chief command base is Damascus, and that the Damascus office has representatives in other countries including Lebanon. The Palestinian side pledged to reduce the number of offices [in Lebanon].

Information

The Palestinian side affirmed that the resistance in Lebanon only produces:

a) *Filastin al-Thawra*; b) Wafa news agency, in addition to certain cultural and educational publications issued by Palestinian organizations publicly or for their own use; c) The Palestinian side pledged that these publications would not touch upon the interests and sovereignty of Lebanon; d) the Palestinian side adheres to the abstention from broadcasting in Lebanon; e) the Palestinian side pledges not to involve Lebanon in any of its publications or broadcast news items or announcements emanating from resistance sources in Lebanon.

Controlling Contraventions and Offences

Lebanese laws will be implemented on the basis of Lebanese sovereignty and offenders will be referred to the responsible courts.

1)   Contraventions in military sectors will be submitted to local liaison committees. In cases where no result is achieved, they will be referred to the Higher Coordination Committee which will give an immediate decision.

2)   Contraventions inside the camps will be the charge of the internal security forces in cooperation with the Palestine Armed Struggle Command, regarding the pursuit of all crimes, civil or criminal, which occur within the camps whoever the offender. They will also be responsible for delivering all legal notices and orders pronounced against persons residing in the camps. Incidents occurring in the camps between the commandos which have a bearing on the security and safety of the Palestinian revolution will be excluded from this procedure and be the responsibility of the Palestine Armed Struggle Command.

3)   Contraventions outside the camps shall be subject to Lebanese law. The Palestine Armed Struggle Command will be informed of detentions and the procedures taken against offenders. In the case of commandos being apprehended in an offence and where the Lebanese authorities deem necessary the cooperation of the Palestine Armed Struggle Command, contact will be made through the liaison committee and the decision on the offender will be left to the Lebanese authority.

The Palestinian side condemned detention of any Lebanese or foreigners and the conduct of any investigation by resistance forces and pledged no repetition of such matters.

Regarding traffic offences, it has been agreed previously that a census would be taken of cars with Lebanese number plates under the auspices of the Internal Security Forces, and cars entering Lebanese territory under temporary licensing regulations of the customs authorities. Therefore any commando vehicle on Lebanese territory will be prohibited unless it carries a legal license according to Lebanese traffic regulations.

Foreigners

By the term foreigners it meant not Arab commandos.

The Palestinian side pledges to deport all foreigners with the exception of those engaged in non-combatant work of a civilian or humane nature (including doctors, nurses, translators and interpreters).

Co-ordination

Implementation will be supervised by the Liaison Committee and its branches in co-ordination with the Palestinian side.

Highly Confidential
Aspirations of the Palestinian side after the joint meetings
— Re-establishment of the atmosphere to its state before the incidents of 9 May 1973;
— Gradual easing of armed tension;
— Reduction of barriers of suspicion;
— Aspirations towards the cancellation of the emergency situation;
— Dealing with the matter of fugitives from the law, particularly those persons pursued as a result of the incidents of 23 April 1969;
— Freeing of those persons detained as a result of the incidents of 2 April 1973;
— Return of arms confiscated since 1970;
— Facilitation of employment for Palestinians resident in Lebanon.

For the Palestinian side
Lt-Col. Abal Zaim
Abu Adnan
Al Sayyid Salah Salah

For the Lebanese Side
Lt-Col. Ahmad al-Hajj
Col. Nazih Rashid (Col. Salim Moghabghab)
Col. Dib Kamal

Index

Abbasid Caliphate 25
Abdul-Hamid, Sultan 30
Adbul-Majid, Sultan 28
Abdullah, Emir 2
Abu Bakr 25
Acre 26, 36
Adana 27
Aggression, UN definition of 170, 172, 176n, 177n
Ahdab, Brigadier Aziz 73
Ahmad, Ahmed Iskandar 75
Ahmed, S Habib 62n
Ain el-Roumaneh 67, 127, 130, 131, 139
Akkar 68
Alami, Musa 3
Alawite 26, 27, 40
Albania 49
Aleppo 27, 35, 40
Alexandretta 35, 41
Alexandria Protocol 3, 4, 5, 17n
Aley 122, 134
Algeria 74, 75, 129, 133
    and participation in Arab League Force 108, 109, 121
Ali 25

Amal 142
American University of Beirut 30
Anatolia 36
Antioch, siege of 26
Aqaba 26
Arab Deterrent Force 83–92, 98, 160
    and Beiteddine Conference 89
    and Chtaura Agreement 88
    composition of 109
    endorsement by League of Arab States 87-8, 193–7
    establishment of 120–21
    functions and powers 83–7, 120, 121
    legal basis of 95–6
    performance of 122–48
    termination of 145–7
    See also Arab League Force in the Lebanon, Symbolic Arab Security Force
Arab League see League of Arab States
Arab League Force in the Lebanon
    composition of 108–10
    financing of 112–15
    and intervention in civil war 97–8

legal assessment of 162–4
legal basis of 93–107
nature of 93–8, 99, 106n
and ONUC 102
organisation and control of 110-12
and peacekeeping 95, 96
performance of 119–58
political assessment of 159–62
termination of 145–7
and UN Charter 100–103
Arab National Congress 31
Arab Nationalism 1–2, 16n, 30, 31, 41
Arab Tribunal of Arbitration 7
Arafat, Yassir, 55, 71, 87
Arbitration 11–13
    See also Council of League of Arab
    States
Armed attack, concept of 48, 49,
    151n, 156n 168
    See also Self-defence 169, 170-72,
    173, 174
Arqoub 54, 55
Ashrafiyeh 125, 126, 131, 133
Aslam, Gerneral Ali 112
Assad, Ahmad 43, 77n
Assad, Kamal 55
Assad, President Hafez 26, 72, 119,
    129, 132, 135, 137, 138, 145,
    158n, 164
Assad, Rifaat 142
Assyrians 24
Athens 54
Austria 27, 29
Axis powers 1, 2
Azkoul, Ambassador 45, 50
Azzam, Abdel Rahman 9

Baabda 73
Ba'ath 138, 140
Baghdad 36
Bahrein 114
Balfour Declaration 36–7
Begin, Menachem 131, 138, 145
Beirut 23, 26, 27, 29, 38, 39, 54, 55,
    56, 67, 68, 69, 70, 71, 108, 110,
    112, 119, 121, 122, 125, 126, 127,
    130, 131, 133, 134,, 136, 137, 138,
    141, 143, 144, 146, 160, 162

and Arab Deterrent Force 84, 89
Beirut-Damascus highway 119, 143
Beiteddine Conference 89, 114, 132,
    133, 134
    See also Arab Deterrent Force 136,
    141
Bekaa 23, 29, 36, 38, 40, 68, 74, 136,
    138, 140, 143, 144
Belgian troops in Congo 96
    See also ONUC
Bertoli, Cardinal 71
Beyoglu Protocol 29
Bowett, Professor D.W. 51
Brieh 125
Britain, *see* Great Britain
Brownlie, Professor I. 48, 49, 63n,
    171, 173
Bulgaria 49
Bustani, Emile 55

Caesarea 26
Cairo 2, 8, 55, 61n, 87, 90n, 109, 133
    removal of League's headquarters
    from 7
Cairo Agreement 55, 65n-66n, 73,
    111, 128, 133, 136, 159, 161,
    198-9
    Annexes to 86, 111, 128
    and Beiteddine Conference 89
    and Chtaura Agreement 88, 124
    implementation by Arab Deterrent
    Force 83, 121
    See also Melkart Understanding
Cairo Summit Conference 83, 86, 88,
    93, 94, 110, 111, 113, 120, 121,
    129, 133, 149n, 160, 161, 162,
    193-7
Camp David 131
Canada 45
Caroline incident 165n
Catroux, General 41
Certain Expenses Case 95, 98-9, 100,
    101, 102, 162n, 165n
El Chaer, General Ali 111
Chamoun, Camille 42, 43, 53, 55,
    60n, 68, 71, 72, 126, 128, 132,
    141, 160
Chamoun, Dany 139

Chapultepec, Treaty of 51
Chatila Camp 146
Chiah 127, 130
China 45
Chouf region 26, 71, 124
Christian militias 69, 77n, 123-4, 125,
    139, 140, 146, 150n
    See also Lebanese Forces militia,
    Phalange
Chtaura Agreement 88, 124, 125, 128,
    150n, 160
    See also Arab Deterrent Force
Civil Conflicts and International Law
    97-8, 105n, 174-5
Committee of National Dialogue 69
Committee of Union and Progress
    (CUP) 30-31
Congo 95, 96, 97, 162
    See also ONUC
Contras 173, 175, 176
Corfu Channel Case 176n
Costa Rica 168, 170, 172
Council of League of Arab States
    and collective security 13
    and dispute-settlement 11-13
    functions and powers 7
    membership of 7
    meetings of 7
    and revised Pact 8
    and voting 7-8
    See also League of Arab States
Couve de Murville, M. 71
Crane, Charles B. 37
Crimean War 28
Crusades 26

Damascus 27, 28, 35, 37, 38, 40, 120,
    127, 132, 134, 137, 138, 141, 143,
    164
Damour 71, 72
al-Darazi 26
Dbayyeh 72
Dekwaneh 137
Dhour Shuwair region 119
Djibouti 149
Druze 23, 27, 28, 29, 39, 40, 68, 160
    and fighting in Chouf 71, 124

Eddé, Raymond 55
Edessa 26
Egypt 2, 6, 9, 12, 28, 35, 43, 118, 148n
    participation in Arab League Force
    109, 121, 122, 133
    participation in General Arab
    Congress 3-4, 5
    participation in Riyadh Summit
    Conference 85, 120
    and peace treaty with Israel 7, 9
    and San Francisco Conference 103
    suspension from League 7
    and UN Emergency Force 82
Ehden 131
Eisenhower doctrine 43
El Salvador 168, 170, 172
Enforcement Action, concept of
    101-2

Al Fatah 55, 67, 72, 142
Fatimid Caliphate 26
Fayadiyah 126
Fedayeen 85, 86, 128
Feisal, King 37, 38, 44
Fez, Arab Summit Conference 114,
    148, 158n
First World War 35-9
France 28, 29, 30, 34n, 45
    interests in Syria 36
    intervention in Syria 28-9, 33n-34n
    and King-Crane Commission 37-38
    mandate over Syria and Lebanon
    39-42, 59n
    and Multinational Force 144, 146
    negotiations with Britain 35
    proclamation of Lebanon's
    independence 23
    and Sykes-Picot Agreement 37
    withdrawal from Lebanon 42
Franco-Lebanese Treaty 41
Frangieh, Tony 130, 131
Frangieth, Suleiman 55, 66n, 68, 71,
    72, 73, 108, 118, 119, 130, 138
    and Syrian troops in Lebanon 75-6

Galilee 143
Garib, Lieutenant-Colonel 111
Gaza 54

General Arab Congress 2
    Preparatory Committee 2-3, 4
    See Alexandria Protocol 3, 4, 5, 17n
Gemayel, Amin 115, 146, 147, 158n
Gemayel, Bashir 128, 131, 138, 139,
    140, 141, 144, 160, 175
Gemayel, Pierre 55, 56, 67, 132
Geographical Syria 2, 23-4
Georges-Picot 35
Germany 30, 35
Ghoneim, Major-General 111, 118,
    121
Golan 54
Gouraud, General 38, 39
Great Britain 29, 30, 39, 45
    attitude to US intervention in
        Lebanon 53
    involvement in Syria and Lebanon
        41, 42
    and King-Crane Commission 37-8
    and Mandate over Palestine 23, 42,
        43
    participation in Multinational
        Force 146
    plans for post-war settlement 35
    support for Arab independence 1,
        16n, 35
    See also Balfour Declaration,
        Sykes-Picot Agreement
Greater Lebanon 40
Greece 49
Greek Orthodox community 29
Gulhane Decree 28

Habib, Philip 142
Haddad, Major 127, 136, 139, 140
Haifa 26, 36, 127
al-Hakim 26
al-Hajj, Colonel 87, 94, 111, 112, 121,
    122, 124, 165n
Hama 35, 114
Hammarskjold, Secretary-General
    95, 96
Hasbaya 38
Hassan 25
Hassouna, Abdel Khalek 9
Hassouna, H.A. 61n, 94
Hejaz 39

Helou, Charles 54
Higgins, Professor 14, 53
Hitti, Professor 23
Homs 35
Honduras 168, 170, 172
Hoss, Salim 132, 135
Humanitarian Intervention 73n,
    175-6
Hussein 25
Hussein, Sherif 35, 36, 39

Inter-American Treaty of Reciprocal
    Assistance (1947) 52
International Court of Justice 95-6,
    102, 116n-17n, 165n, 167-76
    *See also Certain Expenses Case,
        Corfu Channel Case, Nicaragua
        Case*
Iraq 1, 2, 12, 14, 43, 44, 102, 129, 133,
    140, 149n
    opposition to Arab Deterrent
        Force 121
    participation in General
        Arab Congress Preparatory
        Committee 3-4, 5
    threat to annex Kuwait 14-16
    See also Feisal, King
Islam 30
Isma'ilis 26
Israel 37, 48, 85, 122, 124, 138, 140,
    142, 148, 150n, 151n-52n,
    155n-56n, 160
    assault on Beirut airport 54, 65n
    assault on PLO camps 139, 143
    attack on Israel's Ambassador in
        London 143
    clashes with Syria in Bekaa 144, 145
    establishment of 13, 43, 60n
    and Melkart Understanding 86
    and PLO attacks 127, 135, 136
    and siege of West Beirut 145, 146
    and Six Day War 54
    support for Christian militias 123,
        124
    Treaty of Peace with Egypt 7, 9
    and withdrawal from Lebanon 127
Israel-Lebanon General Armistice
    Agreement 60n

Israel-Lebanon Troop Withdrawal
    Agreement 148, 158n
Italy
    participation in Multinational
        Force 144, 146

al-Jabiri, Sa'dallah 41
Jamil, General 111
Jarring, Ambassador 46
ad-Jazzar, Ahmad 27
Jebel Druze 27, 40, 41
Jerusalem, siege of 26, 36, 42
Jesuits 30
Jews 27, 31
    community in Palestine 31
    Muslim discrimination against 25
Jezzine 143
Jisr al-Pasha 72, 119, 137
Joint Defence and Economic
    Cooperation Treaty, 11, 13, 14,
    15
Jordan 15, 37, 54, 55
    See also Transjordan
Jordan river 26, 49
Jubayl 68
Jumblatt, Kamal 43, 61n, 67, 124

Karami, Rashid 53, 61n, 68, 71, 109,
    118
Karbala, battle of 25
Kassem, General 15, 16
Kataeb militia *See* Phalange
Katyusha rockets 25
Kelsen, Hans 173
Kemal, Mustafa 38
Khaddam, Halim 69
Khalidi, Walid 126, 150n
Khatib, Lieutenant Ahmed 73
al-Khatib, Lieutenant-Colonel Sami
    112, 124, 135, 147, 150n
Khoury, Bishara 41, 42, 43
Khoury, General 137
King, Henry C. 37
King-Crane Commission 37, 38, 39
Klibi, Chedli 9
Kuwait 14, 69, 132
    Arab League Force in 14-16, 21n
    and Beiteddine Conference 89

and funding of Arab Deterrent
    Force 113-14, 134, 135
and Riyadh Summit Conference
    85, 120

League of Arab States
    and collective security 13-14
    Council 7-8, 10, 11, 44
    Council resolution on Lebanese
        crisis 186-7
    See also Council of the League
        of Arab States
    functions and powers 5, 17n, 99
    and Israel 13
    membership 6-7
    and non-member Arab states 6
    organs 7-10
    Pact of the League 4, 5, 9, 11, 12,
        13, 70, 93, 99, 116n, 157n-58n,
        163, 164, 179-83
    and peaceful settlement of disputes
        11-13, 70
    and peacekeeping 14-16, 98-100
    permanent committees 9-10, 19n
    permanent secretariat 8-9, 19n
    Political Committee 9-10
    referral of Lebanese crisis 69-74
    revisions to Pact 8, 19n
    Secretary-General, functions of
        8-9, 15, 94
    Summit Conferences 8
    and the UN Charter 10-11
    See also Joint Defence and
        Economic Cooperation Treaty,
        Arab League Force in the
        Lebanon
League of Nations 40, 57
    and mandated territories 1, 16n,
        39, 57n
Lebanese Forces militia 139
Lebanese Organic Statute 29
Lebanon 1, 2, 24, 27, 35, 36, 37, 39
    Arab Army of 73, 74
    and Arab Deterrent Force 83-92
    and Beiteddine Conference 89
    and Cairo Agreement 85, 86
    Chamber of Deputies 72
    and Chtaura Agreement 88, 124

Consent to Arab League Force 97
and General Arab Congress
Preparatory Committee 3-4, 5
and Higher Coordination
Committee 71
and Higher Military Committee 72
Leftist factions 73
and National Covenant 41-2, 72,
73, 78n
Palestinian minority in 54
and Riyadh Summit Conference
120
under French mandate 39-42
and Symbolic Arab Security Force
74-6, 83-92
US intervention in 44-53
See also Syria
Libya 69, 149n
participation in Arab Deterrent
Force 118, 121, 122, 129, 133
participation in Symbolic Arab
Security Force 75, 108, 109, 118
withdrawal from Arab Deterrent
Force 110
Litani river 122, 127, 128, 136, 139
Lodge, Ambassador 44
London 143
Loutfi, Ambassador 45, 52

Macedonians 24
Mamluk dynasty 26-27, 28
Mandates, *See* League of Nations
Mandate over Syria and Lebanon 40
Marjayoun 84, 139
Maronites 23, 25, 26, 27, 29, 39, 41,
43, 55, 56, 68, 94, 123, 126, 131,
134, 139, 140, 141, 150n, 160,
161, 162
attacks on Palestinian camps 72,
119
clashes with Syrian troops 110, 111,
120
fighting in Chouf 71
relations with Muslims 43, 60n
See also Lebanese Forces militia,
Phalange
Maroun, John 25
Maslakh 72

Al Masnaa 84
al-Matni, Nasib 44
McMahon, Sir Henry 35, 36
Melkart Understanding 56, 86, 88,
124, 128, 150n, 199-203
See also Cairo Agreement
Meouchi, Paul 43
Mersina 35
Mesopotamia 38
Millet system 27
Morocco 109
Mount Lebanon 23, 27, 39, 84, 132
Movement of the Disinherited 56
Mu'awiya 24
Muhammad 24, 25
Muhsin, Zuhair 72
Multinational Forces 144, 146, 148,
157n
Mutasarrif 29

Naba'a 72
Nahas Pasha 2
Napoleon 28
Nasser, President 8, 43
National Movement 56, 67, 120, 126,
133, 142
National Pact 42-3
Naulilaa Case 166n
Necessity 49, 156n
Nicaragua 167, 169, 171, 173, 174, 175
Nicaragua Case 167-76, 177n
Nidal, Abu 143
North Atlantic Treaty 51
North Yemen 109, 110, 115n, 121
ibn-Nusair, Muhammad 25
Nusairi, *See* Alawite

Oman 114
ONUC 95, 96, 102, 104n, 105n, 162,
165n
and intervention in civil conflicts
97
similarities to Arab Deterrent
Force 102
Operation 'Peace for Galilee' 48
Organization of American States 168
Ottoman Empire 26, 27-31, 32n, 35

Pact of the League of Arab States

See League of Arab States
Palestine 1, 2, 23, 24, 31, 36, 38
   British mandate for 23, 42
   as homeland for Jewish people 36-7
   participation in General Arab
      Congress Preparatory
      Committee 3
   participation in League of Arab
      States 6, 18n
   See also Alexandria Protocol,
      Balfour Declaration, PLO
Palestinian guerrillas, *See* PLO
Palestinian-Leftist forces 23, 24, 25
Paris 31
Parsons, Sir Anthony 63n
Peacekeeping, concept of 14, 93, 94,
   95, 96, 98, 102, 104n, 105n, 161,
   162, 163, 164n
   under Pact of the League of Arab
      States 98-100
Permanent Mandates Commission 40
Persian empire 24
Phalange 55, 56, 67, 68, 131, 133, 138,
   140, 141, 142, 144, 146
PLA 72, 77n-78n, 86, 110, 123, 134,
   159
PLO 55, 56, 69, 71, 85, 97-8, 111, 118,
   120, 124, 125, 135, 136, 139, 143,
   144, 146, 149n, 160, 171
   attack at Athens airport 54
   and Cairo Agreement 85, 86
   and Chtaura Agreement 88, 124
   and Melkart Understanding 86
   participation in Arab Deterrent
      Force 120, 121, 122, 126
   participation in Riyadh and Cairo
      Summit Conferences 97, 106n
   participation in Symbolic Arab
      Security Force 75, 108, 109
   raids into Israel 117, 135, 139
   and Resolutions of Riyadh Summit
      Conference 128
   withdrawal from Beirut 144
   See also Al Fatah
Porte 29
Prussia 29

Qarantina 72, 133

Qatar 89, 113-14, 134
al-Quwatli, Shukri 41

Rabat, Arab Summit Conference 6
Ras Beirut 71
Rashaya 38
Red Cross 132
Regional action, concept of 102-3,
   162-3
   See also UN Charter, Art. 52
Riad, Mahmoud 9, 76, 87, 109, 111
Rifai, Brig.-Gen. Nureddin 68
Rihane 139
Riyadh Summit Conference 86, 87,
   88, 89, 91n, 93, 94, 97, 109, 110,
   111, 112, 120, 121, 129, 133, 135,
   136, 149n, 160, 161, 162
   Resolutions of 83, 85, 122, 128,
      188-93
Roman Empire 25
Rothschild, Lord 36
Russia 27, 29
   claims to Anatolia 35-6
   Jewish community in 36
   See also Soviet Union

Saad, Marouf 56
Sabra camp 146
Sadat, President 129
Sadr, Musa 56
al-Said, Nuri 2
Saiqa 72, 73
Salam, Saeb 43, 55, 61n, 66n
San Francisco discussions 51
San Remo 38
Sarkis, Elias 74, 109, 111, 112, 119,
   120, 121, 122, 126, 129, 131, 132,
   134, 135, 145, 162
Saudi Arabia 2, 12, 15, 39, 75, 120,
   132, 134, 148n-49n, 162
   funding of Arab Deterrent Force
      113-14, 135
   membership of League 6
   participation in Arab Deterrent
      Force 109, 110, 121, 122, 130,
      152n-53n
   participation in General Arab
      Congress 3, 5

participation in Riyadh Summit
  Conference 85
participation in Symbolic Arab
  Security Force 108, 118
Schachter, Oscar 96
Schwebel, Judge 168-9, 171, 172, 174
Seleucids 24
Self-defence 13, 14, 22n, 48, 49, 50,
  51, 151n-52n, 162, 165n, 168,
  169, 170, 174, 177n
  and anticipatory self-defence 156n,
    168-69, 176n
  and 'armed attack' concept 48-9,
    151n, 156n, 168, 169, 170-72,
    173, 174
  collective self-defence 44, 46, 50,
    51, 52, 97, 105n, 168, 169, 170,
    172-3
  and intervention 170, 171, 173, 174,
    177n
  and necessity 168, 169, 170
  and *Nicaragua Case* 168-73
  and ONUC 102
  and peacekeeping 94, 95, 96, 104n,
    105n
  and proportionality 64n, 163-64,
    166n, 168, 169, 170
  and UN Members 63n
  and US intervention in Lebanon
    47-8, 50, 53, 64n, 173, 177n
  and 'use of force' concept 170, 171,
    173, 174
  See also UN Charter, Arts. 2(4), 51
Sèvres 38
Sharon, Ariel 144, 145
Shia 25, 27, 39, 54, 56, 68, 140, 160
Shihab, General 44, 53, 54, 66n, 69,
  74
Shihabi, Bashir 27
Sidon 23, 26, 29, 38, 39, 56, 84, 122,
  143
Sin el-Fil 133, 137
Sinai 54
Sobolev, Ambassador 45, 50, 52, 62n
Sofar 74
Solh, Rashid 67
Solh, Riad 41, 42, 121

South Yemen 109, 110, 115n, 121,
  122, 129, 130, 133
Soviet Union 144
  and Syrian intervention in Lebanon
    74
  and US intervention in Lebanon
    45, 46, 48
Stone, Julius 173
Sudan 15
  and Beiteddine Conference 89
  participation in Arab Deterrent
    Force 109, 121, 130, 134, 162
  participation in Symbolic Arab
    Security Force 75, 108, 118
Suez, Anglo-French intervention in
  43
Sunni 25, 39, 41, 43, 68, 160
Supranationality 3
Supreme Allied Council 38
Sweden 46
Sykes-Picot Agreement 36
Symbolic Arab Security Force 94, 98,
  102, 122, 159
  command of 110-11
  composition of 108
  effectiveness of 119
  establishment of 74-76
  functions and powers of 82, 120
  funding of 112
  legal basis of 98-100
  performance of 119-122
  termination of 121
  See also Arab Deterrent Force,
    Arab League Force in the
    Lebanon
Syria 1, 2, 12, 27, 28, 29, 37, 38, 43,
  46, 54, 68, 69, 160, 162, 163, 164
  Arab conquest of 24-6
  attitude to UNIFIL 127-8
  Ba'ath Party 26
  and Beiteddine Conference 89
  and Chtaura Agreement 88, 124
  and clashes with Israeli forces 136,
    139, 140, 141, 143-4
  and establishment of Arab League
    Force 97
  French mandate over 39-41

French occupation of 38
and General Syrian Congress 23-4, 37, 38
and intervention in Lebanon 73, 74, 75, 79n-80n, 94, 119, 120, 147-8, 149n
and King-Crane Commission 37
and Lebanese civil war 71-3
membership of League of Arab States 6
participation in Arab Deterrent Force 109, 110, 111, 114, 115, 121, 122, 125, 126, 129, 130, 131, 132, 133, 134, 135, 136, 137, 139, 140, 141, 142, 143
participation in General Arab Congress Preparatory Committee 3, 4, 5
participation in Symbolic Arab Security Force 108, 118, 119, 120
and revolt of 1925 41, 59n
and Riyadh Summit Conference 85
and withdrawal from Beirut 137, 145-6, 147, 148, 158n
Syrian National Party 41
Syrian Social Nationalist Party 44

Tal Zaatar 72, 119, 133, 137
Tarsus 27
Tibawi, Professor 30
Tiger militiamen 139
Transjordan 1, 2, 23, 43
membership of League of Arab States 6
participation in General Arab Congress Preparatory Committee 3-4, 5
See also Jordan
Treaty of Friendship and Alliance 59n
Treaty of Peace between Egypt and Israel 7, 9
Tripoli 23, 26, 38, 43, 67, 68, 69, 71, 72, 84, 122, 140, 142
Tunis 7
Tunisia 9, 109, 121
Turkey 38, 41
Turkish Ottoman Empire 1

Tyre 23, 38, 84

ulama 25
Umayyad Caliphate 24-5
UNEF 83
Uniate Christian Communities 29
UNIFIL 127, 128, 140
United Arab Emirates 110, 162
funding of Arab Deterrent Force 113-14
participation in Arab Deterrent Force 121, 122, 130, 132, 134
United Arab Republic 6, 15, 43, 44, 45, 47, 49, 103
support for Lebanese rebels 47, 49, 170
and US intervention in Lebanon 46, 48
United National Front 44, 61n
United Nations
and Arab League 10-11
and establishment of Arab League Force in the Lebanon 93, 103, 104n
General Assembly 42, 49
Palestine partition resolution 42, 60n
and peacekeeping 94, 104n, 98, 113, 116n-17n
Security Council 11, 42, 44, 47, 49, 50, 61n, 103, 128, 146
See also ONUC, UNEF, UNIFIL, UNOGIL
United Nations Charter:
Art. 2(4) 49, 171, 172
Art. 11 102
Art. 34 11
Art. 35 11
Art. 39 95-6
Art. 42 96, 102
Art. 51 10, 44, 45, 46, 47, 50, 52, 62n, 63n
Art. 52 11, 100-101, 102, 107n, 163, 164
Art. 53 101, 102, 162, 165n
Chapter VIII 13

United States 30, 124, 147, 148, 167, 168, 169, 170, 171, 172, 173, 174, 175, 176
  and Balfour Declaration 36-7
  and Eisenhower doctrine 43
  and 'enforcement action' 107n
  intervention in Lebanon 44-53, 62n, 64n, 105n-106n, 173, 175
  and King-Crane Commission 37
  and MNF 146, 147, 148
United States-Nicaragua Treaty of Friendship, Commerce and Navigation 168
Université Saint-Joseph 30
UNOGIL 44, 46, 47, 53
Urban II, Pope 26
Uthman 25

Wadi al-Taym 40
Waldock, Sir Humphrey 169, 176n

Webster, Secretary of State 165n
West Bank 54
Wilson, President 37
World Zionist Congress 34

Yahya, Imam 3
Yazid 25
Yemen 2
  membership of League 6
  participation in General Arab Congress Preparatory Committee 3
  See also North and South Yemen
Yugoslavia 49

Zahlé 68, 71, 140, 141, 142
Zahrani 122
Zghorta 55, 68, 69, 71, 72
Zippori, Mordechai 139